S0-BDI-189

FATHER-DAUGHTER INCEST

Judith Lewis Herman
With Lisa Hirschman

With a new Afterword

Harvard University Press
Cambridge, Massachusetts
and London, England

Copyright © 1981, 2000 by the President and Fellows
of Harvard College
All rights reserved
Printed in the United States of America
Second printing, 2003

Library of Congress Cataloging in Publication Data

Herman, Judith Lewis, 1942–
    Father-daughter incest / Judith Lewis Herman with Lisa Hirschman.
       p.   cm.
    Originally published: Cambridge, Mass. : Harvard University Press, 1981.
    With a new afterword.
    Includes bibliographical references and index.
    ISBN 0-674-00270-9
    1. Incest—United States.   2. Fathers and daughters.   I. Hirschman, Lisa.
    II. Title.
    [DNLM: 1. Incest.]
    HQ71 .H46 2000
    306.877—dc21

                                                                99-059169

Contents

Preface   vii

Author's Note, 2000: In Memory of Lisa Hirschman   xiii

Introduction: Cinderella or Saint Dympna   1

One The Incest Secret

1 A Common Occurrence   7

2 The Question of Harm   22

3 The Question of Blame   36

4 The Rule of the Father   50

Two Daughters' Lives

5 Incestuous Fathers and Their Families   67

6 The Daughter's Inheritance   96

7 Seductive Fathers and Their Families   109

Three Breaking Secrecy

8 The Crisis of Disclosure   129

9 Restoring Families   144

10 Criminal Justice   162

11 Remedies for Victims   177

12 Preventing Sexual Abuse   202

Afterword, 2000: Understanding Incest
   Twenty Years Later   219
Appendix: The Incest Statutes, by Leigh Bienen   253
Notes   293
Index   309

Preface

This book began with two women talking to each other. Lisa Hirschman and I were both starting our clinical practice. We met to give each other supervision and support. In the course of these meetings, we discovered that both of us had seen what seemed like an alarming number of women with a history of incest. We were disturbed both by our patients' complaints and by the way these complaints had been ignored by more experienced clinicians. What little literature we could find on the subject of overt incest was so contaminated by sexist bias as to be essentially useless. Since nothing satisfactory seemed to have been written about father-daughter incest, we were finally driven to write about it ourselves.

That was in 1975. If anyone had told us at the time that we were embarking upon a five-year collaboration that would ultimately result in a book, we would have been appalled. Incest is not a topic that one embraces; one backs into it, fighting every step of the way. What kept us going was the response of the women we reached through our research and our writing. Women we had never met wrote to us to encourage us and to tell their stories. They convinced us that any secret so long and so vigorously suppressed must be worth pursuing.

Since we began our collaboration, incest has been rediscovered as a major social problem. In the past two or three years, feature articles on the topic have appeared in leading publications and special documentary reports have been aired on national network television. Confessional accounts of incest have begun to appear, and more speakouts can be expected. This growing awareness is largely a result of the women's liberation movement. In the past decade, women have directed public attention to the problems of rape, wife-beating, and child abuse, all previously forbidden subjects. Incest, the most extreme form of sexual abuse, has until recently remained within the domain of pornography and scandal, but we believe the time has finally arrived for serious discussion.

Our book is written, first, for those women, estimated by us to be in the millions, who have personally experienced incestuous abuse. Most incest victims still bear the burden of their secret alone, considering it too disgraceful to reveal to anyone. We hope that this book will find its way into their hands, and that it will help to alleviate feelings of isolation and shame. The book is also written for professionals in the areas of mental health, child protective services, law, and law enforcement, who regularly encounter cases of father-daughter incest.

The book is divided into three parts. Part One develops an analysis of the phenomenon, based upon survey data, clinical material, anthropological literature, popular literature, and pornography. For our scholarly sources we naturally relied on libraries; but for much of the popular literature we relied on the help of friends, acquaintances, and strangers who clipped newspaper or magazine articles and called our attention to publications that we would not ordinarily have seen. We are particularly indebted to Rick Snowdon, who shared his collection of "kiddie porn" with us and thereby spared us the dreary task of wading through the material ourselves.

Part Two describes a clinical study of our own, based upon interviews with patients in therapy or their therapists. Forty incest victims and twenty women whose fathers had been seductive but not overtly incestuous participated in our research. Their contribution was of the most disinterested kind. Since anonymity was a condition of their participation, they can never be credited publicly for their courage and generosity. The results reported here incorporate an earlier study, first published in *Signs: Journal of Women in Culture and Society* in 1977, as well as much additional data. This phase of our work was supported in part by a grant from the Center for the Prevention and Control of Rape, part of the National Institute of Mental Health.

Part Three reviews the social responses to discovered incest, including crisis intervention, family treatment, and prosecution. It also deals with the possibilities of healing and prevention. Our discussion is based upon interviews with professionals in the mental health system, child protective services, and law enforcement, and upon site visits to programs that have developed innovative approaches to the problem. The programs we visited are the Child Sexual Abuse Treatment Program in the Juvenile Probation Department of Santa Clara County, San Jose, California; the Child Protective Services, Tacoma, Washington; Rape Relief, Tacoma,

Washington; the Sexual Assault Center at Harborview General Hospital, Seattle, Washington; the Presentence Diagnostic Program in the Adult Probation Department, Seattle, Washington; Christopher Street, Inc., Minneapolis, Minnesota; the Hennepin County District Attorney's Office, Minneapolis, Minnesota; the Center for Rape Concern (now called the Joseph J. Peters Institute), Philadelphia, Pennsylvania; and the Sexual Trauma Treatment Program in the Department of Children's and Youth Services, Hartford, Connecticut.

The similarities among these centers impressed us at least as much as their differences. They were created by people who cared deeply about their work, and they could not be reproduced by legislative fiat or the infusion of federal grants. The workers recognized the extraordinary demands of becoming involved with incestuous families or with adult victims. All had evolved methods of nurturing each other and of dealing with the painful feelings continally aroused by their work. Recognizing the difficulty of the task, they were respectful even in their criticism of one another. For sharing their experiences with us, we want particularly to thank Henry Giarretto, Bob Carroll, and Dorothy Ross of the San Jose Child Sexual Abuse Treatment Program, Peter Coleman of the Tacoma Child Protective Service, Connie Murphy of Tacoma Rape Relief, Chuck Wright of the Seattle Presentence Diagnostic Unit, Deborah Anderson of the Hennepin County District Attorney's Office, Elaine Bencivengo and Maddi Jane Stern of the Philadelphia Center for Rape Concern, and Suzanne Sgroi and Norma Totah of the Hartford Sexual Trauma Treatment Program. Twice in our travels we were welcomed not only as colleagues but as sisters. For this generosity we are indebted to Barbara Myers and the staff of Christopher Street, and to Shirley Anderson, Lucy Berliner, Caren Monastersky, Doris Stevens, and the staff of the Haborview Sexual Assault Center.

Many people gave us encouragement in the early stages of this project when it was most needed. Karen Al-Aidroos, Ellen Bassuk, Phyllis Chesler, William A. Christian, Jr., Elaine Hilberman, Mary Howell, Charles Magraw, Lynn Meyer, Jean Baker Miller, Carl Oglesby, Michelle Zimbalist Rosaldo, Kathie Sarachild, and Roland Summit read our first tentative writings and gave help and criticism. Pauline Bart was an enthusiastic supporter who showed more confidence in us than we had in ourselves. Larry Constantine, David Finkelhor, Florence Rush, and Hollis Wheeler allowed us to see unpublished manuscripts and shared their data and observations with us. In later stages, parts of the manuscript were reviewed by Joyce Backman, Lucy Berliner, Leigh Bienen,

Sandra Butler, Linda Gordon, and A. Nicholas Groth. Their criticism consistently elevated our level of understanding. William Bennett and Virginia LaPlante, our editors at Harvard University Press, were everything an author could wish for. Finally, Anne Smith somehow got the manuscript into presentable form.

Lisa Hirschman participated in every stage of this project except the writing of the book. She and I collaborated fully on the clinical research, the visits to treatment programs, and the development of an outline. Originally, we had also planned to write the book together. A three-thousand mile separation, work, and child-care commitments ultimately made this impossible. Because I had the greater flexibility in my working life, the job of completing the project we had begun together fell to me. It is not a task I would ever have undertaken alone, or could have done without her partnership.

The Women's Mental Health Collective of Somerville, Massachusetts, supported me in every aspect of this work. The Collective patiently tolerated my reduced presence through the birth both of my daughter and of this book. Michele Clark, Virginia Donovan, Noel Jette, and Ronnie Littenberg, members of the Collective, discussed cases with me, helped me clarify ideas, and contributed their own insights. One member of the Collective in particular, Emily Schatzow, shared deeply in this project. She and I collaborated in the treatment of several families and in the development of therapy groups for incest victims. We also traveled together to treatment programs and worked to develop more appropriate services in our own community.

My parents, Naphtali and Helen Block Lewis, contributed in many ways, not the least by their own example of scholarship and respect for ideas. My brother, John Block Lewis, taught himself elementary statistics in order to teach me how to analyze the data. Jerry Berndt, who endured daily life with me while the book was being written, was my best friend and most reliable critic. He also postponed many of his own aspirations in order to share equally in child care. Our daughter, Emma Lewis Berndt, took me away from my writing and brought me back to it. She was a constant reminder of the incredible attractiveness and vulnerability of children.

                                                                        JLH

Collaborator's Note

During the research phase of this project certain people were very helpful to me in the formulation of ideas and in turning parts of the research into written form. I especially want to thank Gene Bocknek, Leslie Goodwoman, Eileen Nickerson, and Abigail Stewart. My husband, Peter Gourevitch, helped through many stages of this project. He did more than his share of both housework and child care; without this time the research for the book could not have been done. My son Alexander provided me with moments of pleasure and amusement, reminding me of the joy of childhood as I wrote about its sad and painful side.

LH

Author's Note, 2000: In Memory of Lisa Hirschman

Lisa died last year at the age of fifty-two, torn away much too soon from a family and a community that treasured her. Her absence is felt all the more keenly because in life she had such extraordinary presence. When we worked together, I was struck by her capacity to pay close attention to others and to stay engaged no matter how emotionally demanding the situation. She listened, she understood, and she resonated to the truth of each encounter fearlessly, with laughter, tears, or righteous anger. She brought this observant quality into every aspect of her life: marriage, parenthood, and the quiet work of the psychologist. Lisa kept her work close to the experience of life lived daily. I think this is what enabled her, twenty years ago, to notice what others did not. More recently, in a paper entitled "Restoring Complexity to the Subjective Worlds of Profound Abuse Survivors,"[*] she described her work with incest survivors as "detailing." I give this paper now to my students, who are learning the craft of psychotherapy, and sometimes, as they share with me the moments of insight and liberation that are the reward of this patient discipline, I am reminded of Lisa, the master craftswoman, and the many privileged moments that we shared in our collaboration.

[*] In *Conversations in Self Psychology: Progress in Self Psychology*, vol. 13, ed. Arnold Goldberg (Hillsdale, N.J.: The Analytic Press, 1997), pp. 307–323.

Father-Daughter Incest

Introduction
Cinderella or Saint Dympna

Deep water has no ford.
The broad field has no end.
Small stones have no number.
A pretty girl has no kinsmen.
   —Slovenian folk song

Every little girl knows the story of Cinderella, who was persecuted by her wicked stepmother and stepsisters, and who was rescued at last by her prince. The fairy tale most commonly repeated in Western culture warns girls to expect nothing but abuse from women, and teaches them to look to men for salvation. But the currently popular Cinderella story is only one variant of an old tale which has been preserved in folklore for many centuries. In other versions, the tale is about the sorrows of a girl who has lost her mother, and her persecution by an incestuous father.

Many variations of the story begin with a description of the good and beautiful mother who dies while her daughter is still young. The tales recount the daughter's grief, her longing for her absent mother, and her devotion to her mother's memory. In one version, the little girl plants a twig on her mother's grave and waters it each day with her tears. The twig grows into a sheltering tree, which later, in times of adversity, becomes her refuge and the source of her gifts.[1]

The Cinderella story warns little girls that it is dangerous to be left alone with a widowed father, for a widowed father must remarry, and the daughter's fate depends upon his choice of a wife. In some variants of the tale, the daughter suffers because the father replaces her mother with a cruel stepmother. In others, the daughter suffers because the father wishes to marry her himself.

Thus in the tale of Many-Furs, a widowed king sends his messengers to search the kingdom for a woman who exactly resembles his lost wife. No one meets the test but his beautiful daughter. The king then resolves to marry her. To discourage him, the daughter asks for gifts of ever finer dresses. Each time, the father meets her request. Finally, when she can put him off no longer, the daughter flees, disguised in a coat made of many furs. In a foreign land she works as a scullery maid while awaiting rescue by her prince. Like Cinderella, she is discovered when she attends a dance, wearing one of the fine dresses given to her by her father.[2]

This same folk tale has been preserved in Christian martyrology as the legend of Saint Dympna. The secular tale ends happily, with the daughter's successful escape and marriage; the Christian tale ends tragically, with her murder. According to popular belief, Dympna was the daughter of an Irish heathen king and a Christian princess, who died while Dympna was still a child. After her death, the bereaved king was inconsolable, until he noticed Dympna's extraordinary resemblance to her mother. He thereupon resolved to marry her. Unable to dissuade him, Dympna, like Many-Furs, fled across the ocean in disguise. She was accompanied by her priest and confessor, Gereberus. The two settled in a forest at Gheel, near Antwerp, and for a short time lived a simple and peaceful life. But the king, infuriated by his daughter's escape, pursued her relentlessly until he found her. When she once again refused to submit to him, he ordered his men to kill her and her companion. The king's men struck off Gereberus' head without hesitation, but no one dared to touch Dympna. Thereupon the king drew his own sword and beheaded his daughter, leaving her body for the animals to devour. She was said to be fifteen years old.[3]

Beginning in the thirteenth century, a popular cult grew up around the bones of Saint Dympna. Many miraculous cures of insanity and demonic possession were attributed to her intercession, and she came to be regarded as the patroness of the mentally ill. By the end of the thirteenth century, a hospital for the insane had been founded in her name at Gheel. This institution still exists and is even now widely regarded as one of the best of its kind. A notable feature of the sanatorium is the boarding of patients in the homes of townspeople, where they assist with household duties and share in family life. This humane policy has only been recently rediscovered in the American mental health system.

Like many martyrs, Dympna was canonized first by the people, and only belatedly and grudgingly by the church hierarchy. The biographies of the saints, in which her story is recorded, all register their protest at the contamination of hagiography by folklore. Dympna's story is not "authenticated." No written record documents her life. Perhaps she never existed at all. No matter. Dympna was sanctified by the people because she represents the real experience of numberless women. Like so many female martyrs, she resisted rape, forced marriage, or incest, even at the cost of her life. Women who have endured centuries of sexual victimization honor Dympna for her heroism and recognize her authenticity, whether or not it is documented to the satisfaction of the authorities.

It is appropriate that the patron saint of the mentally afflicted should be an incest victim. No one could understand better than she what it means to undergo emotional torment. No one knows better what it means to be an orphan, to be driven too soon from one's home, to live as an outsider, to feel like an exile in normal society. To those who feel themselves burdened with unspeakable secrets, and who have despaired of human understanding, Saint Dympna represents the folk wisdom that it has all happened many times before. This book is dedicated to all the heroines who cannot be honored in their own names, the modern-day Cinderellas and Saint Dympnas, who have been victims of incest.

It is not possible to write dispassionately about incest. The subject is entirely enmeshed not only in myth and folklore, but also in ideology. We have found that a frankly feminist perspective offers the best explanation of the existing data. Without an understanding of male supremacy and female oppression, it is impossible to explain why the vast majority of incest perpetrators (uncles, older brothers, stepfathers, and fathers) are male, and why the majority of victims (nieces, younger sisters, and daughters) are female. Without a feminist analysis, one is at a loss to explain why the reality of incest was for so long suppressed by supposedly responsible professional investigators, why public discussion of the subject awaited the women's liberation movement, or why the recent apologists for incest have been popular men's magazines and the closely allied, all-male Institute for Sex Research.

An understanding of incest also rests on certain basic assumptions about the power of parents and the needs of children. It is regarded as axiomatic that parents have more power than children. This is an inescapable biological fact; young children are completely dependent on their parents or other caring adults for survival. It is further assumed that children need the unconditional protection and nurturance of their parents for healthy development; they cannot provide care in return. Parents may find many rewards in the raising of children, but they cannot expect their own needs for food, clothing, shelter, or sex to be fulfilled by their children. When a parent compels a child to work to support the family, that is the exploitation of child labor. When a parent compels a child to fulfill his sexual needs, that is incest.

For this reason, incest must be considered a crime, one for which the adult is fully responsible. The terms "offender" and "victim" describe the situation accurately, even though many people find this language objectionable. Use of these terms is not meant to reduce complex human beings to simple categories. A man who sexually abuses his daughter is more than just an offender; a woman who has had a sexual relationship with her father does not derive her complete identity from her status as a victim. But these terms should be used in relation to the incest offense in order to make it clear where the responsibility lies.

Father-daughter incest is not only the type of incest most frequently reported but also represents a paradigm of female sexual victimization. The relationship between father and daughter, adult male and female child, is one of the most unequal relationships imaginable. It is no accident that incest occurs most often precisely in the relationship where the female is most powerless. The actual sexual encounter may be brutal or tender, painful or pleasurable; but it is always, inevitably, destructive to the child. The father, in effect, forces the daughter to pay with her body for affection and care which should be freely given. In so doing, he destroys the protective bond between parent and child and initiates his daughter into prostitution. This is the reality of incest from the point of view of the victim. Measures can and must be taken to change that reality.

Outside the scope of this discussion are those rare cases of sexual relations between consenting adults. These instances are frequently cited by pornographers and others who would liberate us all from the incest taboo. The vast majority of incest begins years before the earliest conceivable age of consent. For the same reason, the discussion does not dwell on those spontaneous instances of exploratory sex play between siblings close in age. The horror of incest is not in the sexual act, but in the exploitation of children and the corruption of parental love.

One
THE INCEST SECRET

1
A Common Occurrence

Almost all of my women patients told me that they had been seduced by their father. I was driven to recognize in the end that these reports were untrue and so came to understand that the hysterical symptoms are derived from phantasies and not from real occurrences . . . It was only later that I was able to recognize in this phantasy of being seduced by the father the expression of the typical Oedipus complex in women.
—*Sigmund Freud,* Introductory Lectures of Psychoanalysis, *1933*

Female children are regularly subjected to sexual assaults by adult males who are part of their intimate social world. The aggressors are not outcasts and strangers; they are neighbors, family friends, uncles, cousins, stepfathers, and fathers. To be sexually exploited by a known and trusted adult is a central and formative experience in the lives of countless women.

This disturbing fact, embarrassing to men in general and to fathers in particular, has been repeatedly unearthed in the past hundred years, and just as repeatedly buried. Any serious investigation of the emotional and sexual lives of women leads eventually to the discovery of the incest secret. But until recently, each investigator who has made this discovery has ended by suppressing it. The information was simply too threatening to be maintained in public consciousness.

Our own discovery of the incest secret took place when, as beginning clinicians, we encountered many incest victims among our first patients. Consider these cases, all of which were seen during the course of an ordinary psychiatric residency:

A forty-year-old mother of six children was admitted to the hospital after ingesting an overdose of sleeping pills. Suicide appeared to her to be the only means of escape from a twenty-year marriage to a brutally abusive husband. In psychotherapy she confided that as a child she had been repeatedly molested by her stepfather. Her husband was the only person who knew her secret. She found it impossible to leave her husband because she feared that he would expose her incest history. He had often threatened to use the incest history to prove her an unfit mother and obtain custody of the children, should she attempt to divorce him.

A fifteen-year-old girl appeared in the outpatient clinic asking for tranquilizers. She had a history of addiction to alcohol and barbiturates, had been hospitalized several times for detoxification, and had had a number of unsuccessful placements in various residential treatment programs for adolescents. She revealed that from the age of eight she had been involved in a sexual relationship with her father which included fellatio and mutual masturbation. She ran away from home at age twelve, when her father attempted intercourse, and had essentially lived on the street since then. She expressed the hope, which seemed quite unrealistic, that her mother would divorce her father and allow her to come home.

A twenty-five-year-old office worker was seen in the emergency room with an acute anxiety attack. She was pacing, agitated, unable to eat or sleep, and had a feeling of impending doom. She related a vivid fantasy of being pursued by a man with a knife. The previous day she had been cornered in the office by her boss, who aggressively propositioned her. She needed the job badly and did not want to lose it, but she dreaded the thought of returning to work. It later emerged in psychotherapy that this episode of sexual harassment had reawakened previously repressed memories of sexual assaults by her father. From the age of six until mid-adolescence, her father had repeatedly exhibited himself to her and insisted that she masturbate him. The experience of being entrapped at work had recalled her childhood feelings of helplessness and fear.

The histories that these women reported had all the vividness, the accuracy of detail, and the internal coherence characteristic of real memories. Moreover, in each case, the incest trauma was directly implicated in the patient's presenting problem. Nevertheless, in every case the veracity of the patient's history was officially questioned. We were reminded by our supervisors, as if this were something everyone knew, that women often fantasize or lie about childhood sexual encounters with adults, especially their fathers.

Increasingly troubled by the number of incest cases we had seen, we decided to go to the literature. We wanted to find out what was known about incest and to learn the source of the received opinion that women lie about it. What we discovered was a vastly elaborated intellectual tradition which served the purpose of suppressing the truth about incest, a tradition which, like so many others, originates in the works of Freud.

The patriarch of modern psychology stumbled across the incest secret in the early and formative years of his career. It was Freud's ambition to discover the cause of hysteria, the archetypal female neurosis of his time. In his early investigations, he gained the trust and confidence of many women, who revealed their troubles to him. Time after time, Freud's patients, women from prosperous, conventional families, unburdened painful memories of childhood sexual encounters with men they had trusted: family friends, relatives, and fathers. Freud initially believed his patients and recognized the significance of their confessions. In 1896, with the publication of two works, *The Aetiology of Hysteria* and *Studies on Hysteria*, he announced that he had solved the mystery of the female neurosis. At the origin of every case of hysteria, Freud asserted, was a childhood sexual trauma.[1]

But Freud was never comfortable with this discovery, because of what it implied about the behavior of respectable family men. If his patients' reports were true, incest was not a rare abuse, confined to the poor and the mentally defective, but was endemic to the patriarchal family. Recognizing the implicit challenge to patriarchal values, Freud refused to identify fathers publicly as sexual aggressors. Though in his private correspondence he cited "seduction by the father" as the "essential point" in hysteria, he was never able to bring himself to make this statement in public.[2] Scrupulously honest and courageous in other respects, Freud falsified his incest cases. In *The Aetiology of Hysteria*, Freud implausibly identified governesses, nurses, maids, and children of both sexes as the offenders. In *Studies on Hysteria*, he managed to name an uncle as the seducer in two cases. Many years later, Freud acknowledged that the "uncles" who had molested Rosalia and Katharina were in fact their fathers. Though he had shown little reluctance to shock prudish sensibilities in other matters, Freud claimed that "discretion" had led him to suppress this essential information.[3]

Even though Freud had gone to such lengths to avoid publicly inculpating fathers, he remained so distressed by his seduction theory that within a year he repudiated it entirely. He concluded that his patients' numerous reports of sexual abuse were untrue. This conclusion was based not on any new evidence from patients, but rather on Freud's own growing unwillingness to believe that licentious behavior on the part of fathers could be so widespread. His correspondence of the period reveals that he was particularly troubled by awareness of his own incestuous wishes toward his daughter, and by suspicions of his father, who had recently died.[4]

In 1897, Freud wrote to his confidant, Wilhelm Fliess, explaining why he had finally rejected his seduction theory: "Then there was the astonishing thing that in every case blame was laid on perverse acts by the father, and realization of the unexpected frequency of hysteria, in every case of which the same thing applied, though it was hardly credible that perverted acts against children were so general." Freud concluded that his patients' reports of sexual abuse were fantasies, based upon their own incestuous wishes. To incriminate daughters rather than fathers was an immense relief to him, even though it entailed a public admission that he had been mistaken. As he continued in the letter to Fliess: "It is curious that I feel not in the least disgraced, though the occasion might seem to require it. Certainly I shall not tell it . . . in the land of the Philistines— but between ourselves, I have a feeling more of triumph than of defeat."[5]

At the moment that Freud turned his back on his female patients and denied the truth of their experience, he forfeited his ambition to understand the female neurosis. Freud went on to elaborate the dominant psychology of modern times. It is a psychology of men. The incestuous wishes of the male child, his hostile rivalry with his father, and the struggle to master these feelings and enter into the world of men became the central focus of psychoanalytic inquiry. The incestuous wishes of parents, and their capacity for action, were all but forgotten. This does not matter very much in the case of boys, for, as it turns out, boys are rarely molested by their parents. It matters a great deal in the case of girls, who are the chief victims. Since much of psychoanalytic theory originated in the refusal to validate a common and central female experience, it is not surprising that Freud and his followers were never able to develop a satisfactory psychology of women.

For years after Freud disavowed the seduction theory, clinicians maintained a dignified silence on the subject of incest. Helene Deutsch's massive *Psychology of Women*, published in 1944, makes no mention of it whatsoever.[6] As recently as 1975, a basic American psychiatry text-book estimated the frequency of all forms of incest as one case per million.[7]

The legacy of Freud's inquiry into the subject of incest was a tenacious prejudice, still shared by professionals and laymen alike, that children lie about sexual abuse. This belief is by now so deeply ingrained in the culture that children who dare to report sexual assaults are more than likely to have their complaints dismissed as fantasy. Within the medical profession, denial persists even in the presence of incontrovertible physical evidence, such as venereal disease in children. Rather than acknowledge the possibility of sexual abuse, physicians have been known to assert that children can contract venereal disease from clothing, towels, or toilet seats, an idea that transcends the limits of biological possibility and which would be considered laughable if applied to adults.[8]

Prejudice against the child victim within the medical profession bolsters a similar prejudice within the legal profession. The most famous legal text ever published in this country, John Henry Wigmore's *Treatise on Evidence* (1934), set forth a doctrine impeaching the credibility of any female, especially a child, who complained of a sex offense.[9] Wigmore warned that women and girls were predisposed to bring false accusations against men of good character, and that these accusations might convince unsuspecting judges and juries. He therefore recommended that any female complainant, but especially a girl who accused her father of incest, should be examined by a psychiatrist to determine her credibility. To support his opinion, Wigmore drew upon the pronouncements of eminent psychiatric authorities. Where their published case reports suggested the possibility of real sexual abuse, Wigmore, like Freud, falsified or omitted the evidence. For example, in his discussion of incest, Wigmore cited case reports of two girls, ages seven and nine, who accused their fathers of sexual assault. In both cases, the original clinical reports documented the fact that the children had vaginal infections. The seven-year-old had gonorrhea, and the nine-year-old's vagina was so inflamed and swollen that the doctor could not make a physical examination.[10] This and other corroborating evidence was systematically omitted in Wigmore's presentation, and the cases were discussed as examples of pathological lying in children.[11] Wigmore's assertions, supposedly based upon medical expertise, remained unchallenged for decades in the legal literature, and still retain great prestige and influence in the courtroom.[12]

A half-century after Freud repudiated his seduction theory, incest was "discovered" for a second time. New information was unearthed not by clinicians, who had willfully blinded themselves to the reality, but by social scientists, who were relatively uninfluenced by psychoanalytic tradition. As the survey and the questionnaire came into widespread use, investigators once again conceived of the daring idea of asking women about their sexual lives and listening to their replies. Between 1940 and the present, five surveys, including the famous Kinsey report, addressed the subject of sexual encounters between female children and adults. Although incest was not a specific subject of inquiry, it was included in the more general survey data. Cumulatively, these studies recorded information from over 5000 women, from many different geographic areas, and primarily from the privileged strata of American society.

The largest of the studies, by Alfred Kinsey and his associates in 1953, was based on over 4000 personal interviews with young, white, predominantly middle-class, urban, educated women.[13] A second study, by John Gagnon in 1965, was based on more extensive data gathered from 1200 women in Kinsey's group.[14] Two other surveys, by Judson Landis 1956 and David Finkelhor in 1978, recorded information from questionnaires given to approximately 2000 college students.[15] These four studies were restricted to women in good health. The fifth study, by Carney Landis in 1940, surveyed 142 psychiatric patients and 153 "normal controls." No significant differences were recorded in the early sexual experiences of these two groups of women.[16] In general, the poor, blacks and other minorities, rural people, and the mentally ill—those groups that are stereotypically suspected of deviant sexual activities—were conspicuous by their absence from these studies.

The results of these five surveys were remarkably consistent. One fifth to one third of all women reported that they had had some sort of childhood sexual encounter with an adult male. Between four and twelve percent of all women reported a sexual experience with a relative, and one woman in one hundred reported a sexual experience with her father or stepfather (see Table 1.1).

The data from these five studies are even more consistent than might be apparent at first glance. Much of the variation that does exist can be accounted for by differences in the types of sexual encounters reported. In Judson Landis' study, for example, over half (54.8 percent) of the incidents reported by women were single encounters with exhibitionists, in which no physical contact occurred. In these cases, the offenders were almost always strangers (87 percent) rather than trusted familiar figures, and the episodes generally left no lasting impression. By contrast, only 20

Table 1.1. Sexual abuse of female children

Study	Date	No. of female subjects	Population	Sexually abused by adult (%)	Abused before puberty (%)	Mean age of child	Abused by family member (%)	Abused by father or stepfather (%)	Sex of adult aggressor Male (%)	Sex of adult aggressor Female (%)
C. Landis	1940	295	Middle-class hospital patients and controls	—	23.7	—	12.5	—	—	—
Kinsey	1953	4441	White middle class	—	24	9.5	5.5	1.0	100	0
J. Landis	1956	1028	College students	35	24	11.7	—	—	100	0
Gagnon	1965	1200	White middle class	—	28	9.9	4.0	0.6	98.5	1.5
Finkelhor	1978	530	College students	19.2	17.0	10.2	8.4	1.3	94	6

percent of the incidents reported by women in Finkelhor's study were encounters of this type, whereas 75 percent were episodes that involved physical contact, 55 percent involved force, and 40 percent were repeated more than once. The differences in the types of events reported to these two investigators are probably attributable to differences in the questionnaires used. If contacts with exhibitionists are excluded, the data from these two surveys are congruent: 15.8 percent of the women in Landis' survey and 14.4 percent of the women in Finkelhor's study reported a childhood sexual encounter involving physical contact with an adult.

There is some reason to suspect that these estimates may actually be low when applied to the entire population, because they are based almost entirely on reports from white middle-class women. Since poor and minority women are subjected to all types of violence and abuse more frequently than the population at large, it is reasonable to suppose that these groups also suffer a higher incidence of sexual assault in childhood. There are no valid data, however, to confirm or disprove these speculations.

Applying the figures obtained from these five surveys to the general population, Finkelhor surmised that somewhere in the neighborhood of one million American women have been involved in incestuous relations with their fathers, and that some 16,000 new cases occur each year.[17] These are conservative estimates, and the real incidence of father-daughter incest may well be considerably higher than the figure he suggested.

Less information is available on the early sexual experience of boys. Those studies that have been done make it clear, however, that boys are abused far less often than girls. Kinsey and his associates, in their exhaustive survey of over 5000 men, considered sexual contacts between boys and adults so unusual that they did not even bother to report numerical data on this type of activity. They did indicate, however, that most contacts between boys and adults were homosexual.[18] Finkelhor, in a survey of 266 college men in 1978, found that 8.6 percent had had a childhood sexual experience with an adult. Again, most were homosexual encounters. Family members were implicated in only four cases.[19] Only one study, carried out by Judson Landis in 1956, records an incidence of sexual abuse of boys comparable to that of girls.[20] Thirty percent of the 467 young men in this series reported that they had had a sexual encounter, usually involving physical contact, with an adult; in this study too, however, the overwhelming majority of the aggressors (84 percent) were men (see Table 1.2).

Table 1.2. Sexual abuse of male children

Study	Date	No. of male subjects	Population	Sexually abused by adult (%)	Mean age of child	Abused by family member (%)	Abused by father or stepfather (%)	Sex of adult aggressor	
								Male (%)	Female (%)
J. Landis	1956	467	College students	30	14.4	—	—	83.8	16.2
Finkelhor	1978	266	College students	8.6	11.2	1.5	0	84	16

The Kinsey studies became a household word in America and brought their authors international fame. Many of their findings on previously taboo subjects, such as masturbation, extramarital sex, and homosexual contacts among men, received an enormous amount of attention and became part of common knowledge and folklore. By contrast, the finding that grown men frequently permit themselves sexual liberties with children, while grown women do not, made virtually no impact upon the public consciousness, even though this finding was repeatedly confirmed by other investigators.

Kinsey himself, though he never denied the reality of child sexual abuse, did as much as he could to minimize its importance. Some 80 percent of the women who had experienced a childhood sexual approach by an adult reported to Kinsey's investigative team that they had been frightened and upset by the incident. Kinsey cavalierly belittled these reports. He hastened to assure the public that children *should not* be upset by these experiences. If they were, this was the fault not of the sexual aggressor, but of prudish parents and teachers who caused the child to become "hysterical": "It is difficult to understand why a child, except for cultural conditioning, should be disturbed at having its genitalia touched, or disturbed at seeing the genitalia of other persons, or disturbed at even more specific sexual contacts . . . Some of the more experienced students of juvenile problems have come to believe that the emotional reactions of the parents, police officers, and other adults who discover that the child has had such a contact, may disturb the child more seriously than the sexual contacts themselves."[21]

Kinsey and his colleagues might have found it less difficult to understand why a child would be disturbed by the imposition of adult sexual demands if they had had greater respect for the personal integrity of the child. If the Kinsey researchers felt any sensitivity toward the child's need for autonomy or recognized any concept of the child's right to privacy, it was not apparent in their writings. By contrast, this group demonstrated a keen sensitivity toward the adult offender. As scientists and leaders in the struggle for enlightened sexual attitudes, they felt it incumbent upon themselves to plead the offender's case. They pointed out, quite correctly, that existing laws regarding sex were so restrictive, and so out of touch with the realities of human behavior, that a large portion of the population lived their lives in technical violation of the law. In their plea for greater tolerance, however, they failed to distinguish between essentially harmless acts committed by consenting adults, "nuisance" acts such as exhibitionism, and frankly exploitative acts such as the prostitution of women and the molesting of children. Ignoring issues of dominance and power, they took a position that amounted to little more than advocacy of greater sexual license for men.[22] Kinsey in fact saw the unfortunate male in need of defense against the persecution of malicious females, old and young:

> In many instances the law, in the course of punishing the offender, does more damage to more persons than was ever done by the individual in his illicit sexual activity. The histories which we have accumulated contain many such instances. The intoxicated male who accidentally exposes his genitalia before a child may receive a prison sentence which leaves his family destitute for some period of years, breaks up his marriage, and leaves three or four children wards of the state and without the sort of guidance which the parents might well have supplied. The older, unmarried women who prosecute the male whom they find swimming nude may ruin his business or professional career, bring his marriage to divorce, and do such damage to his children as the observation of his nudity could never have done to the woman who prosecuted him. The child who has been raised in fear of all strangers and all physical manifestations of affection may ruin the lives of the married couple who had lived as useful and honorable citizens through half or more of a century, by giving her parents and the police a distorted version of the old man's attempt to bestow grandfatherly affection upon her.[23]

While Kinsey and his associates dared to describe a vast range of sexual behaviors in exhaustive detail, they declined to specify what might be involved in the "bestowing" of grandfatherly—or fatherly—affection upon little girls. On the subject of incest, apparently, they felt the less said the better. This, in spite of the fact that they had accumulated the largest body of data on overt incest that had ever appeared in the scientific literature. Extrapolating as best we can from Kinsey's statistics, we estimate that these researchers interviewed over forty women who reported incestuous relations with their fathers, and an additional two hundred women who had had sexual experiences with older brothers, uncles, or grandfathers. To date, this remains the largest number of incest cases ever collected from the population at large, rather than from advertisements, clinic files, or court records. The wealth of information contained in these interviews remained buried in the files of the Institute for Sex Research. The public, in the judgment of these men, was not ready to hear about incest.

Perhaps they were right. In 1955, two years after the publication of *Sexual Behavior in the Human Female*, S. Kirson Weinberg, a sociologist, published a thorough and scholarly study, *Incest Behavior*, based on 203 cases reported by the courts and social agencies in the area of Chicago, Illinois.[24] No sensation, in fact no public response of any kind, attended its publication. Weinberg went on to study other, more acceptable subjects, and *Incest Behavior* quietly went out of print. Wider public discussion of the subject would have to wait another twenty years.

Incest was rediscovered for a third time in the 1970s by the women's liberation movement. As feminists brought the reality of sexual oppression to public consciousness, many previously forbidden or ignored subjects, such as rape, wife-beating, and sexual abuse of children, became legitimate topics for serious research. And this time, the information could not be suppressed once it was uncovered, for it began to reach the awareness of those who stood in the greatest need of knowledge, namely, the victims themselves.

Between 1970 and the present, four large surveys of over fifty incest cases and many smaller studies appeared in the professional literature.[25] Popular, confessional accounts by incest victims also began to proliferate.[26] These works confirmed many of the observations that Weinberg had made twenty years earlier. In particular, they confirmed the fact that incest follows the general pattern of child sexual abuse, in which the majority of victims are female and the majority of offenders are male. In Weinberg's series of 203 cases, 164 were instances of father-daughter incest; only two were cases involving a mother and son. Subsequent studies in this country and in France, Germany, Japan, and Ireland conformed to the same general pattern. A review of the five largest studies of parent-child incest, documenting a total of 424 cases, indicates that the father was the offender in 97 percent of the cases, while the mother was the offender in only three percent (see Table 1.3).

Incest between mother and son is so extraordinary that a single case is considered worthy of publication, and we have been able to find a grand total of only twenty-two documented cases in the entire literature. Another eight cases reported as mother-son incest might more accurately be described as rape, since they involve situations in which an adolescent or adult son subjected his mother to forced intercourse. In most of these

Table 1.3. Parent-child incest

Study	Date	Population	No. of incest cases	Parent-child	Father-daughter	Father-son	Mother-son	Mother-daughter
Weinberg	1955	Court cases (Illinois)	203	166	164	0	2	0
Lukianowicz	1972	Clinic records (Ireland)	55	38	35	0	3	0
Maisch	1972	Court cases (Germany)	78	74	66	4	3	1
Meiselman	1978	Clinic records (California)	58	43	38	2	2	1
Justice & Justice	1979	Clinic records (Texas)	112	103	96	5	2	0
Totals			506	424	399	11	12	2
%				100	94.1	2.6	2.8	0.5

cases, the son was psychotic, mentally retarded, or otherwise severely disturbed. Where incest was initiated by the mother, a nonsexual motive was sometimes involved, as in this case report from Japan:

> He suffered meningitis when three years old and has an advanced degree of feeble-mindedness which is more or less equivalent to imbecility.
>
> He developed sexual desires when in the fifth grade of primary school and made sexual advances towards dogs, cats, pigs, and other domestic animals and chased after girls in the neighborhood. Finally, he began threatening women with a knife. His mother could not bear to allow him to carry on and offered her body so that he would not perform such acts outside. These incestuous acts between mother and son continued until her death when he was age 14.

In this case, one might surmise that the mother's sacrifice was motivated in part by a desire to protect her brain-damaged child and fear that his uncontrolled aggressions against others would eventually lead to his incarceration. She need not have troubled herself on that score. After her death, the son remained at liberty, and a new victim was found for him:

> After his mother's death, his abnormal sex drive returned and he had intercourse with anything possible. He assaulted women on several occasions, masturbated in public, and committed sodomy; and therefore he was married to a feeble-minded woman, but there was no stop to the above-mentioned acts. He was seen fondling his daughter's private parts."[27]

The feelings of the woman to whom this man was married and the child he fathered were not recorded.

This pitiable story is by no means the most grotesque among recorded instances of mother-son incest. Almost all the cases involve marked social deviance and severe psychopathology in either the son, the mother, or both. Many cases involve violence. The most extreme instance, recorded by Wenzel Brown, culminated in the son's murder of his mother.[28] Apparently the taboo against mother-son incest is breached only in bizarre circumstances.

When a boy is molested by a parent, the aggressor is as likely to be a father as a mother. Altogether, we were able to discover thirty-two cases of father-son incest in the literature. In one recent clinical report, ten cases of father-son incest were identified within the population of a single child-guidance clinic in Ohio. The authors were not looking for incest and were astonished by the large number of cases they encountered. The cases lacked the bizarre features of most documented cases of mother-son incest and resembled the much more common cases of father-daughter incest. The authors were led to the conclusion that father-son incest may be significantly under-reported.[29]

The enormous difference in the behavior of mothers and fathers toward their children, by now amply documented, would seem to call for some commentary. Very few investigators, however, have made any attempt to explain why fathers quite commonly molest their children while mothers hardly ever do so. Most authors simply accept this as part of the natural order of things. Others attempt to deny the discrepancy. For instance, Blair and Rita Justice, a team of psychologists who have treated many incestuous families, attribute their overwhelming preponderance of cases of father-daughter incest to differential reporting.[30] Why reports of sexual aggressions by fathers should exceed those of mothers by thirtyfold or more is a puzzle these authorities leave unsolved.

Perhaps the most ingenious denial of the realities of incestuous child abuse was suggested by a psychiatrist of our acquaintance who advanced the theory that mother-son incest is rampant before the son reaches the age of five and is thereafter repressed in the child's memory. This explanation supposes an almost preternatural cleverness on the part of mothers, who must somehow manage to desist just in time to escape detection. Even if this should prove to be the case, which is doubtful, it would still fail to explain why fathers do not exhibit any comparable restraint, since they are often reported to continue their sexual approaches well into their daughters' adolescence.

The concept of repression might be more aptly invoked to describe the social response to the reality of incest. Until the resurgence of the women's liberation movement, even the most courageous explorers of sexual mores simply refused to deal with the fact that many men, including fathers, feel entitled to use children for their sexual enjoyment. Nevertheless, this fact is established by now beyond any reasonable doubt.

2

The Question of Harm

In my own mind back then, I thought I was doing her a favor. I made myself feel that I was not doing anything wrong, that I was actually sexually educating her. We never did have complete intercourse. I thought . . . just touching and playing and fondling and all that, that wasn't harmful. —a father, television interview, 1979

Denial has always been the incestuous father's first line of defense. For a long time it has served him well. The belief that incest is extremely uncommon, and the tendency to discredit children's reports of sexual encounters with adults, have until recently remained entrenched in the public consciousness. With the collusion of the larger society, the incestuous father has thus been largely successful in preserving his secret.

In the last decade, as increasing evidence of the wide prevalence of father-daughter incest has been amassed, and as the victims themselves have become emboldened to speak out, it has grown more difficult to suppress the truth about incest. But the exposure of so large-scale an abuse of power on the part of fathers represents a serious challenge to the ideology of male dominance, and inevitably provokes a defensive reaction. Hence the marshaling of new arguments that tend to exonerate the incestuous father. As the public debate over incest intensifies, one can expect to hear these arguments reiterated with increasing frequency. Boiled down to their essentials, the excuses of the father are these: first, he did no harm, and second, he is not to blame. With monotonous regularity, these arguments appear in every sort of literature on the subject, from the scholarly to the pornographic, showing how widespread is the tendency to defend male sexual prerogatives.

The argument that incest is harmless has been promoted aggressively in recent years by the publishers of men's sex magazines. It is also advanced by a certain school of sociologists and sex researchers, mainly those associated with the Institute for Sex Research, who still carry with them the prestige, the resources, and the male bias of the Kinsey era. Even among clinicians, it is possible to find professionals willing to assert that sexual contacts with adults are at worst harmless to children, and at best may be good for them.

The new apologists for incest are found in positions of influence both in the popular culture and in academia. They have become sufficiently noticeable to generate commentary and social analysis in their own right. Culture critic Benjamin DeMott has dubbed this group "the pro-incest lobby."[1] Members of the lobby tend to cast themselves in the role of crusaders for sexual liberation. They often portray themselves as an embattled minority, gamely challenging obsolete social and religious conventions. Their opposition is depicted as a benighted army of prudes. Because their ideas are widely encountered, their arguments cannot be ignored or dismissed, but must be understood.

The current manifesto of the pro-incest school of thought was written by the sociologist James Ramey and published in the widely distributed newsletter of SIECUS, a respected national sex-education organization.[2] Ramey equates the prohibition on incest with other sexual taboos that have not withstood scientific scrutiny. "We are roughly in the same position today regarding incest as we were a hundred years ago with respect to our fear of masturbation." On the question of harm, he argues, people are simply afraid to face the possibility that many, perhaps most, participants in incest suffer no dire consequences. Alluding to suppressed data that would purportedly support his point of view, Ramey conjures up a vision of incest as a positive and consensual experience: "When speaking of family pressure on the child not to testify in court we often ignore those instances in which incest victims flatly refuse to cooperate against a love partner. In such cases these individuals and their families often appear happy and well adjusted despite the incest—which was usually brought to the attention of the authorities by a third party."

Ramey considers the point already proven that whatever damage occurs as the result of incest is mainly attributable to social intervention: "Over the years it has been shown again and again that the harmful effects on the family brought about by official recognition and punishment of incest were more serious than the effects of the incest itself." In support of this assertion, Ramey cites three sources in German, two dating from before 1930. A large body of more recent American literature, including the testimony of victims, is rejected as "unrepresentative" of the general population.

Instead of expressing concern for the effects of sexual exploitation on child victims, Ramey voices worry over the harmful effects of exposure and public discussion:

> We may be doing considerable damage to those who have been or are currently involved in incest. The blatant sensationalism of television, added to congressional hearings which equate incest with rape, child abuse, violence, child slavery, and child pornography, combine to scapegoat many people. After a recent front-page incest story in one North Carolina newspaper, the sex "hot-line" was deluged with calls from women and girls with stories just like the one in the paper. It is easy to blame one's problems on the latest scapegoat. It is also easy to set up guilt reflexes where no guilt existed before.

Most incest victims, by implication, would be untroubled by their experiences if they were not manipulated by the media. Women's courage in daring for the first time to complain about sexual abuse is thus dismissed as an artifact of female suggestibility.

The only criterion of harm that Ramey is willing to recognize is physical damage. Even here, only extreme forms of abuse are condemned: "Those individuals who use extreme coercion, violence, or rape in the commission of incest should be summarily punished." A little bit of coercion, apparently, is nothing to get upset about.

Finally, Ramey explores the harm caused by the observance, rather than the breach, of the incest taboo. Negative attitudes toward incest are blamed for inhibiting healthy family life:

> There is a huge group of individuals who are being damaged by our drum beating—those who have *not* been involved in incest. American families have been so imbued with prohibitions against incest that they bend over backward to avoid any possibility of incestuous involvement or the possible accusation that they might become involved. This results in complete and total abandonment of parent-child contact at puberty, just when the child needs its reassurance most . . . This is a peculiarly American problem—the withdrawl of all touching contact—and children, especially girls,

feel the lack very keenly. Who knows how much psychic damage we cause our children with such well-meant but inhuman attitudes?

In the past few years, the same arguments have been encountered with increasing frequency in the pages of popular men's magazines. This is not a coincidence, for researchers of the pro-incest school have made use of direct connections with the popular sex media to promulgate their point of view. For example, in 1976 Wardell Pomeroy, a Kinsey associate, called for a "new look" at the incest taboo in the pages of *Forum*.[3] The following year Warren Farrell, a sociologist who had been given access to the suppressed Kinsey data, was interviewed by Philip Nobile for an article on incest that appeared in *Penthouse*. Farrell's as yet unpublished findings were cited enthusiastically to lend dignity to the thesis that "few things are as powerful as a deviation whose time has come. Homosexuality, wife swapping, open marriage, bisexuality, S & M, and kiddie porn have already had their seasons. Just as we seemed to be running low on marketable taboos, the unspeakable predictably popped up ... After centuries of restraint, incest is finally a hit."

These opening lines might lead the reader to suspect that the current interest in incest is a product of an increasingly jaded and predatory male appetite. Not so, Nobile assures him; what is really at stake is the sexual liberation of children. Here he quotes Farrell on his mission of enlightenment: "Millions of people who are now refraining from touching, holding, and genitally caressing their children, when that is really part of a caring, loving expression, are repressing the sexuality of a lot of children and themselves. Maybe this needs repressing and maybe it doesn't."[4] The same argument appeared a year later in the pages of *Hustler*, in an article by Dr. Edwin J. Haeberle, who argues that children are being denied their 'right to sexual satisfaction." Eager to take up the cause of this deprived group who cannot speak for themselves, Haeberle proposes a number of reforms, among them the abolition of the laws against incest: "It would be a crime to force our children and adolescents into blind acceptance of a morality long overdue for reform."[5]

Such statements of concern for the well-being of children seem a bit out of place, appearing as they do in publications whose main purpose is to supply masturbatory fantasy material to men, and which generally display an attitude toward children ranging from utter indifference to the most violent hostility. The panderer's interest in the sexual "rights" of children must be considered on a par with the mill-owner's interest in the "right" of children to work in factories. Thus, when pleas for the expression of "caring and loving" feelings toward children or for "children's rights" suddenly appear in the pages of the men's magazines, they must be greeted with a certain amount of skepticism.

But the same general arguments can also be found in recent professional literature. As in the popular literature, recommendations of greater sexual access for adults are couched in the rhetoric of children's rights. It is repeatedly stressed that children are sexual beings, and that their range of sexual expression has long been severely curtailed. From these unimpeachable premises, advocates of incest abruptly conclude that sexual relations with adults are among the "rights" which children should no longer be denied. The available data on the effects of such relations on children are selectively interpreted in support of the notion that children suffer no lasting harm and may even benefit from their sexual encounters with adults. The concept of harm is often limited to a simplistic notion of physical damage, acknowledged only if the encounter is violent or if intercourse is involved. In the case of intercourse, the only damage recognized is the loss of the child's virginity, which does decrease her market value. Psychological harm, if acknowledged at all, is generally attributed to social intervention rather than the sexual relationship itself.

Consider, for example, the conclusions of Larry Constantine, a professor of psychiatry, after reviewing thirty studies on the effects of early childhood sexual experiences in approximately 2500 subjects. Although all but one of the studies report at least some negative outcomes, Constantine stresses the six studies that claim to show some positive or at least neutral effects, and these mostly in cases of sibling rather than parent-child incest. This distorted emphasis is rationalized, once again, with an attack upon prudery and a defense of the sexual rights of children: "While some of us are prepared to admit that children *are* sexual beings, we do not want them to *behave* as sexual beings, and certainly not to have a good time at it."[6]

Constantine does not go so far as to assert that all sexual contacts between adults and children are harmless. He points out that virtually every study correlates positive outcome of a sexual experience with the child's perception of freely chosen participation. He therefore advances the concept of "healthy" sexual encounters between adults and children based on the principle of informed consent: "Legitimate sexual experiences are . . . ones in which the child is sexually knowledgeable and fully comprehends the activity, to which he or she freely consents on the basis of that comprehension, which take place in a family or social setting which affirms such sexual experiences as appropriate, and which (therefore) do not result in symptoms of dysfunction in the child or the family."

This argument ignores the question of power. It avoids coming to grips with the reality that, in relations with adults, there is no way that a child can be in control or exercise free choice. Power, according to Constantine, is "a subtle element of interpersonal relations." On the contrary, there is nothing subtle about the power relations between adults and children. Adults have more power than children. This is an immutable biological fact. Children are essentially a captive population, totally dependent upon their parents or other adults for their basic needs. Thus they will do whatever they perceive to be necessary to preserve a relationship with their caretakers. If an adult insists upon a sexual relationship with a dependent child, the child will comply.

Given this reality, it makes no sense to invoke the idea of consent. Consent and choice are concepts that apply to the relationships of peers. They have no meaning in the relations of adults and children, any more than in the relations of freemen and slaves. Instances in which an unusually assertive child was able to discourage an adult's sexual advances do exist. Similarly, in the days of slavery, some exceptional slaves were doubtless able to talk their masters out of beating them, or selling their children, or copulating with their wives, or doing whatever it was that they intended. But just as, in those cases, the final decision rested with the master, the final choice in the matter of sexual relations between adults and children rests with the adult.

Because a child is powerless in relation to an adult, she is not free to refuse a sexual advance. Therefore, any sexual relationship between the two must necessarily take on some of the coercive characteristics of a rape, even if, as is usually the case, the adult uses positive enticements rather than force to establish the relationship. This is particularly true of incest between parent and child: it is a rape in the sense that it is a coerced sexual relationship. The question of whether force is involved is largely irrelevant, since force is rarely necessary to obtain compliance. The parent's authority over the child is usually sufficient to compel obedience. Similarly, the question of the child's "consent" is irrelevant. Because the child does not have the power to withhold consent, she does not have the power to grant it.

It is probably for these reasons that most people who have had childhood sexual encounters with adults, especially parents, remember them as unpleasant. The data on this point are substantial. Thus, 76 percent of the women in Judson Landis' survey reported that they were frightened, shocked, or emotionally upset by their sexual encounters with adults. Only 2.1 percent said that they found the experiences "interesting."[7] In John Gagnon's review of the Kinsey data, 84 percent of the women reported negative reactions to sexual contacts with adult men, 13 percent had mixed reactions, and only 3 percent of the informants felt positive about the episode. "The most common reaction," according to Gagnon, "was one of simple fright, but there were also more extreme reactions of vomiting and severe hysteria."[8] In Carney Landis' study, 56 percent of the women who had had prepubertal sexual contacts with adults found the experience "unpleasant" or "extremely unpleasant." Only 5 percent reported that they liked the experience or were surprised but not upset.[9] In David Finkelhor's survey, 58 percent of the women reported reacting with fear, and 26 percent with shock; only 8 percent responded with pleasure. Finkelhor's survey is particularly noteworthy, because he interviewed both men and women and was able to identify a number of factors that contributed to the victim's overall evaluation of the experience. For both sexes, the greater the age difference between the child and older partner, the more negatively the experience was perceived. The greater the degree of force used by the older partner, the more unpleasant the experience. And for both sexes, experiences with adult men were much more unpleasant than experiences with adult women. Finally, of all the types of experience reported, incestuous contacts with fathers and stepfathers received the most negative possible evaluations.[10]

These findings on the unpleasantness of the experience for children are confirmed even by researchers committed to a positive view of incest who have specifically solicited testimony to support their point of view. Thus, both Warren Farrell and the psychologist Joan Nelson, who advertised for informants with positive incest experiences, found many fathers but very few daughters willing to express any enthusiasm for incest. In Farrell's survey, 85 percent of the women who had been sexually involved with their fathers felt negative about the experience.[11] And Nelson, in her study of one hundred incest cases, was able to find only three daughters who remembered their incestuous relationships in a positive light.[12]

Although the great majority of children find sexual contacts with adults disagreeable, many do not perceive themselves to be permanently harmed by the experience. This is particularly true of incidental, nonviolent encounters with strangers. Thus, for example, in Judson Landis' survey, two thirds of the victims did not know the offenders, and over half of the offenses involved no physical contact. In this group, 66 percent of the women and 81 percent of the men felt that they had suffered no lasting emotional damage.[13] In Gagnon's study, over three quarters of the episodes were single encounters, and half involved no physical contact. Here, too, no apparent ill effects were observed in the majority, or 75 percent, of these cases.[14]

Thus, it would be an exaggeration to state that victims of sexual abuse inevitably sustain permanent damage. There is nevertheless considerable evidence to suggest that child victims, as a group, are more vulnerable to the number of pathological developments in later life, and that a considerable number of victims suffer lasting harm. This seems to be particularly true where the sexual relationship involved the use of force, was of long duration, or where the offender was a relative or family member.

In Gagnon's study, for example, while most victims were not judged to be permanently harmed, the group who had endured what Gagnon called "coerced" relationships with relatives suffered very severe disturbances. Eighty percent of these women were judged to be in serious difficulty, as evidenced by a history of three or more divorces, institutionalization, or prostitution. Gagnon concluded that, "even with the very small number of cases at hand, it is evident that the victims who report coerced sexual contact over a long period of time have a very high incidence of damage."[15]

Using a different criterion of long-term outcome, Finkelhor found that men and women who had been victimized in childhood showed impairment in "sexual self-esteem," as compared to their peers and classmates who had not been abused. Again, this study confirmed the observation that relationships involving force or lasting for a long time are particularly noxious.[16]

Carney Landis also found that women with a childhood history of sexual abuse complained of sexual difficulties in adult life. Women reporting sexual agressions in childhood were "more apt to say that they were disgusted by all sexual subjects." The strongest emotional reactions were reported by women who had been molested by relatives, namely uncles, brothers, or fathers.[17]

Incestuous abuse has also been frequently associated with a tendency toward repeated victimization in adult life. For example, a team of workers at a hospital rape crisis center in Albuquerque, New Mexico, reported that 18 percent of the women who had been raped more than once had a history of incest.[18] Another rape relief group, based in Tacoma, Washington, estimated that 35 percent of the rape victims in their series had been incestuously abused.[19] Both groups tentatively concluded that a history of incest is associated with some impairment of the normal adult mechanisms of self-protection, and hence with a higher than average rate for rape. Childhood sexual abuse has also been implicated in the histories of battered women, adolescent runaways, and prostitutes. In one study of 118 girls who had left home before age sixteen, over half (52 percent) had a history of incest.[20] And in a survey of 136 street prostitutes, 25 percent reported having been molested by fathers or "father figures" (stepfathers or foster fathers). The authors of this study speculated that incest and other forms of sexual abuse foster the development of a deviant and debased self-image which in turn predisposes the victims toward adopting a career of prostitution.[21]

Thus a review of the evidence available from surveys and studies of special populations indicates that sexually abused children run a higher than usual risk of coming to grief in their adult sexual lives. Clinical literature provides further confirmation of the destructive effects of child sexual abuse. Most clinical studies lack a control group; therefore, it is often unclear whether their findings are applicable to a broader population. However, the insights of a skilled clinician cannot be matched by any questionnaire or survey instrument presently available. Subtle forms of emotional damage, which may not be detected in broader sociological studies, are apparent in clinical reports.

Clinicians who have evaluated children soon after the disclosure of sexual abuse generally find significant evidence of distress. Vincent De Francis, reporting on 250 sexually abused children seen at a New York child protective agency, found that the majority (66 percent) of victims showed emotional disturbance as a consequence of the assault. Fourteen percent were judged to be severely disturbed. As in other studies, the children were least likely to show significant disturbances when the offender was a stranger, and most likely to show obvious distress when the offender was a relative. Symptoms included guilt, shame, feelings of inferiority and low self-esteem, anxiety, imitative ritualized sexual behavior, hostile or aggressive behavior, and school problems.[22] Irving Kaufman and his associates, who studied eleven incest victims referred to a private child guidance clinic in Boston, reported that "depression and guilt were universal clinical findings." Other symptoms ranged from learning disabilities and somatic complaints to "promiscuous" behavior and a "masochistic search for punishment." In every case the child appeared to be motivated by an intense fear of parental abandonment: "These girls had long felt abandoned by the mother as a protective adult. This was their main anxiety. Though the original sexual experience with the father was at a genital level . . . the sexual act . . . seemed to have the purpose of receiving some sort of parental interest. The underlying craving for an adequate parent . . . dominated the lives of these girls."[23]

Similarly, Noel Lustig, in a study of father-daughter incest, remarked that the daughters felt emotionally abandoned by both parents and had complied with their father's sexual demands out of a dread of actual desertion. Lacking parental nurturance, they developed highly negative images of both their mothers and themselves: "All of these girls viewed women's role as depreciated and self-sacrificing, requiring much with very little in return. They perceived their assignment as substitute mothers as due to their sex and viewed boys as freer to be children." Lustig described these daughters as "pseudomature." Though they appeared unusually precocious in sexual and nurturant functioning, this behavior was understood to be a facade, covering intense unmet dependency needs.[24]

Paul Sloane and Eva Karpinski, who studied adolescent girls seen at a family service organization in rural Pennsylvania, reported that "the most outstanding finding was the degree of guilt feeling which each of the girls experienced." They concluded that "indulgence in incest in the post-adolescent period leads to serious repercussions in the girl."[25]

The noxious effects of incest observed by clinicians at the time of disclosure cannot be presumed to disappear with time. In many cases, residual psychological damage can be observed lasting into adult life. For example, Mavis Tsai and Nathaniel Wagner, a team of psychologists at the University of Washington, studied fifty women who had been sexually molested as children, mostly by their fathers or other close relatives. All of the women, whose mean age was thirty years, had been out of their homes for a number of years, and many had married and had children of their own. The women were predominantly white and middle class. All were participants in therapy groups for victims of sexual abuse who had referred themselves for treatment after hearing advertisements of the group in the media. The victims' most common complaints were feelings of shame and guilt, depression, and low self-esteem. They frequently reported problems in interpersonal relations, including feelings of isolation, mistrust of men, and what the authors called a "repetition compulsion" with respect to abusive relationships. As one woman in the group put it: "I have a pattern of getting attached to assholes. My current lover is a xerox copy of my stepfather." Victims also complained of various kinds of sexual dysfunction.[26]

It might be objected that these are merely the complaints of any population seeking therapy and tell nothing specific about the long-term effects of sexual abuse. This objection is put to rest by the research of another psychologist, Karin Meiselman, working in an outpatient clinic in Los Angeles. Meiselman compared a group of therapy patients who were incest victims with another matched group of patients who had no known history of sexual abuse. None of the victims was still involved in an ongoing incestuous relationship; a minimum of three years had elapsed since the end of the sexual contact. The majority of the victims had never told anyone about the sexual relationship before seeking therapy, and often the incest history did not figure prominently in their initial complaints. Nevertheless, as a group, the incest victims appeared significantly more disturbed than other patients in therapy. They had more difficulty in interpersonal relationships, more marital conflicts, more physical problems, and more complaints in general than the comparison group. Sexual problems were particularly prominent. Meiselman also noted a tendency toward "masochistic" behavior and repeated victimization among the incest victims which was not apparent in the comparison group. The incest victims seemed to lack a normal degree of self-regard and a normal capacity for self-protection. As Meiselman drily observed, "None of the patients or therapists thought that incest had improved the daughter's adjustment."[27]

Occasionally there do arise in the clinical literature what appear to be exaggerated claims of harm. In these instances, the authors are usually concerned about the effects of mother-son incest. During the 1950s, when it was fashionable to blame "schizophrenogenic" mothers for inducing psychosis in their children, a few authors went so far as to imply that mother-son incest might be responsible for the development of schizophrenia in adolescents. Thus, for example, Charles Wahl, describing a psychotic son who raped his mother, allowed himself this flight of fancy:

> The unconscious fear is not just of the powerful, retributive, castrating father, but also of the all-encompassing mother who gives not only the breast but takes, as the female spider takes—leaving the hollow husk of her mate as a memento of their ecstasy ... It should not be surprising therefore to find that the [incest] case

described here is associated with the most seriously disorganizing and ego-shattering illness which we know . . . It would be most instructive to know how often this forbidden, tabooed wish is a stressor and precursor in the genesis of schizophrenia.[28]

In response to this gothic sort of speculation, some clinicians have reported cases, especially of boys, with a relatively benign outcome. For example, Atalay Yorukoglu and John Kemph, reporting on two adolescents, a boy and a girl, noted that they were "not severely damaged" by their sexual involvement with a parent. By this, they apparently meant that neither child had developed a major mental illness.[29] Lauretta Bender and Alvin Grugett, in a follow-up study of two girls and two boys with an incest history, found that one girl became psychotic, whereas the others, a girl and a boy who had been molested by their fathers and a boy who had attempted to have intercourse with his mother, responded well to psychotherapy. These outcomes were cited as evidence only that incest was not as malignant as might be supposed, not that it was harmless to the children.[30]

One recent clinical study is of particular interest, because it indicates that the victim herself may be the most reliable judge of the long-term effects of her experience. Mavis Tsai and her associates compared two groups of women who had been sexually molested in childhood. The first group considered themselves permanently injured and sought therapy for problems they associated with their childhood victimization. The second group considered themselves "well-adjusted" and did not request therapy. Using a standard personality profile and a questionnaire on sexual functioning, Tsai found that the first group indeed seemed quite disturbed, while the second group appeared indistinguishable from a control group of women who had never been molested. Many of the women who had escaped without permanent harm remembered particular people who had helped them to integrate and overcome their sexual trauma. Most frequently cited were supportive friends and family members, who assured these women that they were not at fault, and patient lovers, who helped them rediscover and reclaim their sexuality.[31]

To summarize the question of harm: the preponderance of evidence suggests that for any child, sexual contact with an adult, especially a trusted relative, is a significant trauma which may have long-lasting deleterious effects. The sexual trauma does not necessarily lead to the development of a major mental illness; in fact, it does not necessarily lead to any permanent emotional damage. Many circumstances determine the course of a child's development, and the effect of a single trauma such as sexual abuse may be exacerbated or offset by other aspects of the child's environment. Nevertheless, sexual abuse does increase the risk that the victim will experience a variety of difficulties in later life. Most victims recall their experiences as upsetting and unpleasant, and a significant number feel themselves to be permanently scarred. Women who have been initiated into sex prematurely by an act of exploitation appear particularly vulnerable to a wide range of traditional female misfortunes. They have more than their share of difficulty developing a positive, self-respecting sexual identity and a rewarding sexual life. For too many, childhood sexual abuse is an introduction to a life of repeated victimization, an early and indelible lesson in woman's degraded condition.

The final word on the question of harm belongs, of course, to those who have the greatest expertise on the subject, the women who have had personal experiences of incest. We defer, therefore, to Louise Armstrong, a woman who has had the courage to speak out publicly. Armstrong rejects pity. She does not like to be considered a victim, but rather a survivor. She is interested more in getting on with her present business than in dwelling on past hurts. Nevertheless, her testimony, in the form of a conversation with herself, makes it clear that her incestuous involvement with her father has had a formative and destructive effect on her life, and that she is still struggling with the consequences:

> I didn't seem to be easily discouraged. I seemed to be sure there was somebody out there one could turn into a serviceable daddy.
> Was there?
> No.
> Flashbacks?
> Oh yes. I'd wake up feeling I was being gagged. A funny pressure on my jaws. But I didn't make the connection at the time. Not for years. See for a long time I could say, "My father chased me around a hotel room." But without remembering exactly how he caught me. It was too blinding to look at. I was in my twenties, and married, before one night I got up and wrote it all out, all of it—tersely though. To conceal, rather than reveal. Then I filed it away. Forgot I'd done it. Like I planted a second land mine for myself. It was a real jolt when I found it later.
> And?
> Kept moving. Kept working. Tried crying. Didn't suit me.

Tried laughing. Liked it better . . . Grew up a little. Lucked out a little. Got married. Had kids. Kept working. Chose the cheerful.

How do you feel about it now?

Talking about it? Sad. Very sad.

So it doesn't go away?

It recedes.

I don't like that.

You don't have to like it. You just have to live with it. Like a small, nasty pet you've had for years.[32]

3
The Question of Blame

Frigid gentlewomen of the jury! I had thought that months, perhaps years, would elapse before I dared to reveal myself to Dolores Haze, but by six she was wide awake, and by six fifteen we were technically lovers. I am going to tell you something very strange; it was she who seduced me.
—Vladimir Nabokov, Lolita, 1955

If it must be conceded, first, that father-daughter incest occurs commonly, and second, that it is not a harmless pastime, then apologists for the incestuous father are thrown back upon their third and final excuse: he is not responsible for his actions. Most commonly, they blame his daughter, his wife, or both. Thus we make the acquaintance of the two major culprits in the incest romance, the Seductive Daughter and the Collusive Mother. Ensnared by the charms of a small temptress, or driven to her arms by a frigid, unloving wife, Poor Father can hardly help himself, or so his defenders would have us believe. Often he believes it himself.

The image of the Seductive Daughter is part of the literary and religious tradition. It is found in the biblical story of Lot, a man who managed to impregnate both his daughters while apparently maintaining complete innocence of the matter. Initiative for the sexual encounters is ascribed entirely to the daughters, and Lot is spared even the responsibility of conscious memory through the merciful effects of alcohol:

> And Lot went up out of Zoar, and dwelt in the mountain, and his two daughters with him; for he feared to dwell in Zoar: and he dwelt in a cave, he and his two daughters.
> And the first born said unto the younger, Our father is old, and

there is not a man in the earth to come in unto us after the manner of all the earth.

Come, let us make our father drink wine, and we will lie with him, that we may preserve the seed of our father.

And they made their father drink wine that night: and the first-born went in, and lay with her father; and he perceived not when she lay down, nor when she arose.

And it came to pass on the morrow, that the first born said unto the younger, Behold, I lay yesternight with my father: let us make him drink wine this night also, and go thou in, and lie with him, that we may preserve the seed of our father.

And they made their father drink wine that night also: and the younger arose, and lay with him; and he perceived not when she lay down, nor when she arose.

Thus were both the daughters of Lot with child by their father.[1]

Lot's nameless daughters at least have the dignity of a serious motive. In extraordinary circumstances, the Bible story makes clear, the higher good of preserving the father's seed takes precedence over the incest taboo. Thus, even though the daughters are portrayed as entirely responsible for the incest, their actions are to some extent excused. No such charity applies to the Seductive Daughters in secular literature. Their motives are assumed to be entirely perverse.

The modern American version of the Seductive Daughter is familiar to everyone. She has been immortalized in the popular literature as Lolita. Vladimir Nabokov's immensely successful novel has been understood on many levels, but on perhaps the simplest level, *Lolita* is a brilliant apologia for an incestuous father. Humbert Humbert is charming, intelligent, and maddeningly witty in defense of his passion. Since he has expiated his sin by transforming it into art, the reader is permitted to enjoy it, indeed, to revel in it, as he does. And this in no small measure may account for the novel's enormous popular appeal.

Humbert's account of his seduction by twelve-year-old Lolita reads like a fairy tale in reverse: he, the stepfather and cultured man of the world, is portrayed as Sleeping Beauty, awakened by a kiss. Lolita, described as a "sportive lassie," takes the initiative and makes the proposition: "All at once, with a burst of rough glee (the sign of the nymphet!), she put her mouth to my ear—but for quite a while my mind could not separate into words the hot thunder of her whisper, and she laughed, and

brushed the hair off her face, and tried again, and gradually the odd sense
of living in a brand new, mad new dream world, where everything was
permissible, came over me as I realized what she was suggesting." As
Humbert, still unbelieving, hesitates, Lolita climbs astride him and says,
"Okay, this is where we start." Even the uncomfortable thought of the
difference in size between a grown man and a half-grown girl is banished
by Humbert's assurance that Lolita is on top and thoroughly in control:
"However, I shall not bore my learned readers with a detailed account of
Lolita's presumption. Suffice it to say that not a trace of modesty did I
perceive in this beautiful hardly formed young girl whom modern co-
education, juvenile mores, the campfire racket and so forth had utterly
and hopelessly depraved."[2] At twelve, Lolita is already a hard case: not
even a virgin. Hence, by implication, any concerns about her childhood
vulnerability would be misplaced.

Lolita has become the model for countless nymphets who appear,
unredeemed by Nabokov's elegant prose, in the literature of male sexual
fantasy. Here is the same seduction scene, rendered with less art but still
recognizable, as it appears in the pages of one men's magazine. The
anonymous author of this allegedly true story responded to a questionnaire on incest published by the magazine:

> Our sexual encounter began innocently enough. I was explaining
> the facts of life to her.
>
> If you could have seen her at 13—her young body in the first
> bloom of womanhood, her soft blond hair cascading in ringlet
> curls down to her shoulders, her face as sweet and pretty as could
> be—you would understand how it happened. I couldn't help but
> get aroused as I explained sexual intercourse to her, and I sud-
> denly realized that a visible erection was bulging inside my pants.
>
> As I was explaining to her how a man's penis enters a woman's
> vagina, she glanced at my pants and said teasingly, "Why don't
> you show me, Daddy?"

This particular episode proceeds to intercourse and ends with "an or-
gasm that made all my other climaxes seem like empty rituals."[3] The
same romance, indistinguishable but for minor variations, has appeared
in virtually every men's magazine in the past few years. The daughter
may be a redhead or a brunette instead of a blonde. She may be fourteen
or fifteen instead of thirteen. For special effects, she may invite a girlfriend to join in. Otherwise, she is the same sorry, debauched Lolita.

Thus the Seductive Daughter lives on, an active inhabitant of the fantasy life of the millions of ordinary citizens who constitute the readership of *Chic, Hustler, Playboy, Penthouse,* and the like.

What is more surprising to learn is that the Seductive Daughter also appears regularly in the professional clinical literature. Though most clinicians until recently tended to ignore the issue of child sexual abuse altogether, a few authors were apparently troubled by a need to account for those cases in which sexual relations between children and adults had undeniably occurred. In general, these investigators tended to focus on qualities in the child victims which might have fostered the development of an incestuous relationship. They, too, conjured up the image of the magical child, the nymphet, who has the power to entrap men.

Consider, for example, this description of sixteen children, ranging in age from five to twelve, all of whom had been sexually abused, and all of whom were sufficiently disturbed to be admitted to the children's ward of a psychiatric hospital. The senior author of the report is Lauretta Bender, an eminent child psychiatrist and psychoanalyst. The date is 1937:

> These children undoubtedly do not deserve completely the cloak of innocence with which they have been endowed by moralists, social reformers, and legislators. The history of the relationship in our cases usually suggested at least some cooperation of the child in the activity, and in some cases the child assumed an active role in initiating the relationship . . . It is true that the child often rationalized with excuses of fear of physical harm or the enticement of gifts, but these were obviously secondary reasons . . . Finally, a most striking feature was that these children were distinguished as unusually charming and attractive in their outward personalities. Thus it is not remarkable that frequently we considered the possibility that the child might have been the actual seducer rather than the one innocently seduced.

Bender considered the child the instigator of the sexual relationship even in cases where, as she delicately put it, "physical force may have been applied by the adult."[4] The child's failure to report the abuse was interpreted as willing acquiescence.

Subsequent psychiatric publications have returned again and again to the theme of the seductive child. As late as 1975, the Seductive Daughter was still appearing in the professional literature. Here is her portrait as drawn by D. James Henderson, an authority on incest, in a major psychiatry textbook:

> The daughters collude in the incestuous liaison and play an active and even initiating role in establishing the pattern. The girls may be frightened and lonely and welcome their fathers' advances as expression of parental love. The incestuous activity often continues until it is discovered, and the girls do not act as though they were injured ... Like her mother, the incestuous daughter is unlikely to report the liaison at first or to protest about it. If she eventually does, it is as much precipitated by anger at her father for something else or jealousy of his relationship with another woman, as a real objection to his incestuous behavior.[5]

Here the daughter is judged to be a willing participant in the incestuous "liaison," whether or not she objects to it. If she does not protest, her silence is adduced as evidence of her complicity. If she does, her complaints are attributed to "jealousy" or "something else," anything but the incest itself. Thus the incestuous father who seeks to put the blame on his wanton daughter finds corroboration and support throughout the literature on the subject, in the pronouncements of medical authorities no less than in the pages of a skin magazine.

The daughter, when she dares to express her point of view, remembers the encounter quite differently. Here is the testimony of Maya Angelou in her personal account of sexual abuse. With great honesty, Angelou describes her childhood longing for affection which led her to seek the attention of Mr. Freeman, her mother's boyfriend. She clearly portrays the immense gulf in intention and understanding between adult and child. At one point in her narrative, when she is eight years old, she has already had one sexual encounter with Mr. Freeman, which she found bewildering but not altogether unpleasant, and which she has been warned to keep a secret:

> I began to feel lonely for Mr. Freeman and the encasement of his big arms. Before, my world had been Bailey, food, Momma, the Store, reading books and Uncle Willie. Now, for the first time, it included physical contact.
>
> I began to wait for Mr. Freeman to come in from the yards, but when he did, he never noticed me, although I put a lot of feeling into "Good evening, Mr. Freeman."

One evening, when I couldn't concentrate on anything, I went over to him and sat quickly on his lap. At first Mr. Freeman sat still, not holding me or anything, then I felt a soft lump under my thigh begin to move. It twitched against me and started to harden. Then he pulled me to his chest. He smelled of coal dust and grease and he was so close I buried my face in his shirt and listened to his heart, it was beating just for me. Only I could hear the thud, only I could feel the jumping on my face. He said, "Sit still, stop squirming." But all the time, he pushed me around on his lap, then suddenly he stood up and I slipped down to the floor. He ran to the bathroom.

For months he stopped speaking to me again. I was hurt and for a time felt lonelier than ever. But then I forgot about him, and even the memory of his holding me precious melted into the general darkness just beyond the great blinkers of childhood.[6]

Angelou does not deny that she initiated this encounter. She longed for affection and physical contact and she wanted to be held. She wanted the romance of hearing a man's heart "beating just for me." But she was unprepared for the adult's sexual response, which she describes without any of the coy sentimentality found in men's magazines. While she acknowledges her part in the episode, she clearly depicts the utter incongruity between her childish longings and adult sexuality.

The same incongruity is described by Katherine Brady, pseudonym for another incest victim who has written about her experience. Brady's involvement with her father was far more protracted than Angelou's relationship with Mr. Freeman. Starting at age eight, when she crawled into bed with her father to seek comfort during a thunderstorm, Brady maintained an incestuous relationship with her father for ten years. She is frank about the fact that she not only solicited the encounters, but often felt sexual pleasure in them. But she also makes clear that her primary motivation was a desperate need for attention and affection. She acquiesced in a sexual relationship, which she felt was wrong, because she understood very well that this was the price she had to pay for her father's care. She even understood that her father wished to be exonerated from responsibility, and in compliance with his wishes, she played the role of the aggressor:

I now welcomed summer visits to relatives; they were reprieves from his relentless attention. Still, when I was home, I sought out that attention as avidly as ever. My need to please him and to receive the emotional reassurance he was willing to give me in return was so much greater than the uneasiness I felt. When his strange, cooing voice bothered me, the tenderness of his words erased my misgivings. When he touched my breasts, comparing them favorably to Mother's, my qualms were quieted by the comfort his gentleness gave me. *This* man, the one beside me in bed, was so much nicer than the exacting, austere authority who stalked about in the other rooms of the house, or the torpid figure who sat rocking for hours at a time, staring into space. Who wouldn't want to make *this* man appear as often as possible?[7]

Children do have sexual feelings, and children do seek out affection and attention from adults. Out of these undeniable realities, the male fantasy of the Seductive Daughter is created. But as the testimony of these women makes clear, it is the adult, not the child, who determines the sexual nature of the encounter, and who bears the responsibility for it.

On the subject of the mother's responsibility or complicity, there is a similar concordance of opinion among authors who might ordinarily shun each other's company. The doctor, the man of letters, and the pornographer, each in his accustomed language, render similar judgments of the incestuous father's mate. By and large, they suggest, she drove him to it. The indictment of the mother includes three counts: first, she failed to perform her marital duties; second, she, not the father, forced the daughter to take her rightful place; and third, she knew about, tolerated, or in some cases actively enjoyed the incest.

Consider first the portrait of the mother which appears in popular men's magazines. The authors of these romances do not mince words about what is wrong with the mother: she is worthless for sex. She is over the hill, or frigid, or temporarily out of service because of some illness or accident. Knowing that her husband has to have an uninterrputed sex supply, she compliantly offers her daughter in order to keep her man from roaming too far afield. Here is one version of the story of the Collusive Mother which appeared in *Penthouse:* "When [father and daughter] were six months into the incest, the wife unexpectedly returned to the apartment from shopping and caught the pair in the act. Despite some initial hysteria, the wife okayed the whole thing. Apparently, she was relieved that her husband's strong sexual demands could be met at home rather than with hookers, and she hinted that she'd like to watch the two of them in bed."[8]

The mother's portrait in the psychiatric literature is only slightly more refined. Professional authors do not say that the mother is "no good in bed," but the language of many of them barely disguises the same judgment. Bruno Cormier, a psychiatrist, characterizes mothers in incestuous families as "frigid, hostile, unloving women."[9] David Walters, an authority on child abuse, sees fit to remark that many of the mothers in incestuous families are "very unattractive."[10] Another authority describes the mothers as "cold" and "rejecting" women who "cause" their husbands to "seek sexual satisfaction elsewhere."[11] Blair and Rita Justice echo the same refrain in their description of the mother: "She keeps herself tired and worn out . . . She is frigid and wants no sex with her husband. This is another way of bowing out of her role as a wife and giving reason to the husband to look elsewhere for sex."[12] These authorities implicitly blame the mother for whatever sexual problems might be encountered in the parental couple. They apparently assume without question that a wife is required to service her husband on demand, and that if she fails to provide complete satisfaction, the husband is entitled to whatever replacement might be most convenient.

Many studies of incestuous families do report a high incidence of marital discord and sexual estrangement between the parents. Herbert Maisch, for example, in his study of 72 cases reported to the German courts, indicated that 88 percent of the couples had a "disturbed or disorganized marriage" prior to the onset of incest, and 41 percent had a disturbed sexual relationship. The fathers universally described their wives as "frigid" or "cold" and blamed their wives for destroying the marital relationship and driving them to commit incest. The investigator, however, indicated that in most cases the "negative influence of the husband" was the major disruptive factor in the parental relationship.[13]

Careful interviewing of incest offenders, moreover, reveals that even in very disturbed marriages, the father is usually able to command sex from his wife. No father is driven to incest for lack of sexual access to his spouse. For example, Nicholas Groth, a psychologist with extensive experience treating sex offenders, reports on a series of incestuous fathers: "The men were having sexual relations with their daughters or sons in addition to, rather than instead of, their wives. Those offenders who confined their sexual activity to children did so through choice. There was no one for whom no other opportunity for sexual gratification existed."[14]

The issue of the mother's sexual availability to the father is, in the final analysis, a trivial one. But the question of her role in the genesis of incest is not. If the father's sexual complaint is reinterpreted as a statement about the mother's emotional distance from the family, then it does reveal something about the dynamics of incest. For the theme of maternal absence, in one form or another, is always found in the background of the incest romance.

In the archetypal incest stories, the mother's absence is literal and final. Lot's wife is dead, punished by God who turned her into a pillar of salt. In the many variants of the Cinderella story, the mother's death is the beginning of the daughter's misfortunes. Women's literature on incest generally treats the theme of maternal absence tragically. Men's literature trivializes it or treats it comically. And clinical literature tends to treat it judgmentally.

The personal accounts of incest victims are replete with descriptions of distant, unavailable mothers and with expressions of longing for maternal nurturance. In Maya Angelou's autobiography, her mother is portrayed as a goddess, worshipped from a great distance. The daughter's craving for everyday affection and closeness makes her susceptible to the advances of her mother's boyfriend. Charlotte Vale Allen, another incest victim who has told her story publicly, describes her relationship with her mother in these terms:

> I lived for my mother's embraces, and tried to inveigle my way into her rounded arms, up against the softness of her breasts in order to close my eyes and breathe in the scent and familiarity of this woman, my mother; this person who'd surely display love and liking for me if I came back again and again seeking her out.
>
> Sometimes her embraces were gentle, unhurried, immensely comforting and reassuring. At those times, I believed she might love me. But the majority of the time they were quick, too hard, too brief. She was busy getting a meal, or on her way out; she was in a bad mood and still upset from something that, perhaps, had gone on the night before. Yet even these too hasty hugs were acceptable. I was too often in disgrace, however: for having, yet again, talked back; for having dirtied my clothing or lost my hair ribbons; for having spilt the milk or sworn within her hearing; for having come home late from playing. All sorts of things. She'd become enraged. Then, I felt as if I hated her: I'd back out of the kitchen hissing under my breath, I hate you, hate you. It didn't

deter me from hoping that the next time I'd be able to go away whispering, I love you love you love you.[15]

Although Allen certainly does not deny her anger at her mother's unavailability, she struggles throughout her narrative to understand her mother rather than simply to blame her for being a cold or negligent parent: "With the advantage of time, motherhood, and some definite perspectives, I can readily sympathize with my mother. She had a lot to contend with. And while I'm able—just—to cope with my one child, when I mentally multiply times three, and then throw in my father for good measure, I can understand her exasperation. I know now I was loved by her. It simply wasn't in the demonstrative way I needed."[16]

Whereas the women's descriptions of their mothers are filled with sorrow, the men's literature generally depicts maternal absence as a convenience or a joke. Lolita's mother, scorned as a loathsome specimen of the mature female, is dispatched offstage in a ludicrous accident, just as she threatens to become a serious obstacle to Humbert's designs. That is the last anyone hears about her. In the men's magazines, the mother's absence is reduced to a trivial circumstance: she is "out shopping," "visiting relatives," or perhaps recuperating from a minor illness. No emotional reaction to the mother's absence is registered.

In the clinical literature, by contrast, the theme of maternal absence is emphasized almost to the exclusion of anything else. The mother in the incestuous family is judged and found deficient in maternal love. Because she does not live up to traditional, idealized expectations of what a mother should be, she is implicitly blamed for causing the incestuous relationship to develop.

It has frequently been observed that the mother in incestuous families is ill, incapacitated, or for some reason emotionally unavailable to her husband and children. The families adapt to this stressful situation by reassigning many of the mother's traditional obligations to the oldest daughter. The family may come to rely on this daughter for a large part of the housework and child care and for emotional support and comfort. For the daughter, the duty to fulfill her father's sexual demands may evolve almost as an extension of her role as "little mother" in the family.

This situation, often described in the clinical literature as a "role reversal" between mother and daughter, is generally recognized to be destructive to the daughter, since it forces her to fulfill obligations which are inappropriate for her age and interferes with the normal course of her maturation. But even though this distortion of ordinary family roles involves all family members, the clinical literature generally holds the mother alone accountable for it. Regardless of the circumstances, the mother is blamed for abdicating her responsibilities. Here is the judgment of Blair and Rita Justice: "She seeks a role reversal with the daughter. The mother wants to become the child and wants the child to become the mother. This basic symbiotic quality is reflected in nearly all . . . the mothers whose husbands and daughters engage in incest. It expresses the mother's struggling attempt to get the care and nurturing that she missed in her own childhood. In inviting the daughter to take over her role, she is suggesting that the daughter also become her mate's sex partner."[17] Or in the words of Lora Heims and Irving Kaufman: "Mothers in these families were infantile persons pushing their daughters prematurely into the mothering role, including the incestuous relationship with the fathers."[18]

Such descriptions abound in the psychiatric literature. Implicit in these descriptions is a set of normative assumptions regarding the father's prerogatives and the mother's obligations within the family. The father, like the children, is presumed to be entitled to the mother's love, nurturance, and care. In fact, his dependent needs actually supersede those of the children, for if the mother fails to provide the accustomed attentions, it is taken for granted that some other female must be found to take her place. The oldest daughter is a frequent choice. The idea that the father might be expected to take on the mother's caretaking role is never entertained. The father's wish, indeed his right, to continue to receive female nurturance, whatever the circumstances, is accepted without question.

The third count in the indictment of the mother concerns her knowledge of and acquiescence in the affair. Some clinicians have gone so far as to assert that in every case, the mother is aware of the incestuous relationship.[19] In the pornographic literature, one finds a similar assertion, sometimes with the added filip that the mother gets her kicks by watching.[20]

The argument that all mothers are complicit in father-daughter incest is refuted by numerous examples of mothers who, upon discovering the incest, react with shock, outrage, and prompt action in defense of their daughters. In Narcyz Lukianowicz' study, for example, 16 out of 26 mothers were found to be unaware of the incest until their daughters came forward to reveal the secret, and two mothers filed criminal charges against their husbands immediately upon being informed.[21] S. Kirson Weinberg offers this statement from a mother who reported her husband to the police: "Disgrace! Shame . . . He don't think of anyone but himself. If he gets out [of jail] and I get my hands on him, I'll have to go to the electric chair. He has misused us enough."[22]

On the other hand, it is clear that not all mothers are entirely ignorant of the situation, and some mothers do knowingly tolerate incest. Consider, for example, these case reports, from a New York child protective agency:

> The daughter, when she was eight years old, told the mother that she was being molested by the father. The mother slapped her face and called her a bad girl. The case was reported by the mother seven years later, when the victim attempted to commit suicide. (Father returned to the home one month after the initial complaint was filed.)

> The mother was informed by a younger sister that the father locked them (the children) in a room while he stayed out with the oldest daughter. A younger brother mentioned that once he had looked in through a window and had seen them together in bed. The case was reported after six years of regular sexual activity, by the mother's brother. Girl was pregnant.

> All four daughters complained to the mother that the father was manipulating (or attempted to manipulate) their breasts and vaginas. The mother told them that they misunderstood their father, he was merely trying to show affection. The case was reported by a relative, when the oldest girl became pregnant by the father.[23]

These cases represent an extreme failure of maternal protectiveness. How is one to account for them? The answer lies in an analysis of the mother's position in the family. Mothers who are strong, healthy, and competent do not tolerate incest. But mothers who have been rendered unusually powerless within their families, for whatever reason, often tolerate many forms of abuse, including sexual abuse of their children.

Numerous studies support the contention that daughters run a high risk of sexual victimization when their mothers are absent or in any way disabled. David Finkelhor, for example, in his study of 795 college students, found that girls whose mothers were often ill were almost twice as likely as the average girl to be sexually abused in childhood. While 19 percent of the general female student population reported a childhood sexual encounter with an adult, 35 percent of the women whose mothers were chronically ill had had such an experience. Girls who had lived for any period of time without their mothers were three times as likely to be victimized. Fifty-eight percent of these girls had been abused. Emotional alienation between mother and daughter also seemed to increase the risk to the child. It appears from these data that only a strong alliance with a healthy mother offers a girl a modicum of protection from sexual abuse.[24]

The nature of the mother's disability in the incestuous family has been variously described. In Maisch's study, a significant proportion (33 percent) of the mothers suffered from serious physical illnesses.[25] Diane Browning and Bonny Boatman, in a clinical study of eight families, characterized the mothers as suffering from previously undiagnosed depressions. These mothers reportedly responded well to treatment, once their problems were recognized.[26] Several clinicians categorize the mothers as passive-dependent personalties. Richard Sarles, for example, observes of incestuous families: "Wives tend to be immature and infantile individuals who are passive and strongly attached to and dependent upon their own mothers. They tend to marry earlier than normal to a male who fulfills a patriarchal role and who deprives them of any self-fulfillment even within the family."[27]

Some mothers in incestuous families may indeed have personality disorders. However, the social factors which may account for the mother's relative helplessness must also be considered. Finkelhor, for example, noted that daughters of mothers who were poorly educated were twice as likely as the average girl to be sexually abused.[28] Child protective worker Yvonne Tormes also noted a wide disparity in educational level between husbands and wives in families where daughters are sexually victimized. Tormes further observed that mothers in incestuous families marry younger, more commonly have histories of premarital pregnancy, bear more children, and have less work experience outside the home, compared to a control group of mothers of similar socioeconomic status:

> The mother in the incest group, like other mothers, tends to obtain her basic life satisfaction only within the home and the family. What distinguishes her from others is that she seems to have been deprived of self-fulfillment even within the family. By brutality and by superior initiative, her husband has nullified her roles of wife and mother. Even prior to tolerating incest, she seems to have tolerated an increasing amount of deviant behavior, violent and/or non-violent, from him, and her forbearance seems to have encouraged his progress to the incest offense.[29]

In short, even by patriarchal standards, the mother in the incestuous family is unusually oppressed. More than the average wife and mother, she is extremely dependent upon and subservient to her husband. She may have a physical or emotional disability which makes the prospect of independent survival quite impractical. Rather than provoke her husband's anger or risk his desertion, she will capitulate. If the price of maintaining the marriage includes the sexual sacrifice of her daughter, she will raise no effective objections. Her first loyalty is to her husband, regardless of his behavior. She sees no other choice. Maternal collusion in incest, when it occurs, is a measure of maternal powerlessness.

As for the question of the mother's responsibility, maternal absence, literal or psychological, does seem to be a reality in many families where incest develops. The lack of a strong, competent, and protective mother does seem to render girls more vulnerable to sexual abuse. Maternal disability of any sort represents a significant family stress and is perceived by all family members as a deprivation.

But no degree of maternal absence or neglect constitutes an excuse for paternal incest, unless one accepts the idea that fathers are entitled to female services within their families, no matter what the circumstances. Implicitly the incestuous father assumes that it is his prerogative to be waited upon at home, and that if his wife fails to provide satisfaction, he is entitled to use his daughter as a substitute. It is this attitude of entitlement—to love, to service, and to sex—that finally characterizes the incestuous father and his apologists. In a patriarchal society, the concept of the father's right to use female members of his family—especially his daughters—as he sees fit is implicit even in the structure of the incest taboo.

4
The Rule of the Father

The prohibition of incest is less a rule prohibiting marriage with the mother, sister, or daughter, than a rule obliging the mother, sister, or daughter to be given to others. It is the supreme rule of the gift, and it is clearly this aspect, too often unrecognized, which allows its nature to be understood.

—*Claude Levi-Strauss*, The Elementary Structures of Kinship, 1949

The incest taboo is universal in human culture. Though no single definition of the taboo applies among all peoples, no known culture permits unrestricted sexual union among kin. Almost all cultures prohibit intercourse and marriage within what is known as the nuclear family, that is, between parents and children, brothers and sisters.[1] The particular forms of the incest taboo, the types of behavior forbidden, the range of persons to whom the prohibition applies, and the punishments that attend its violation vary endlessly from one society to another. What is common to most cultures, however, is the seriousness with which the taboo is regarded. It is commonly understood as a fundamental rule of social order. It is the primordial law, which defines the special place of human society within the natural and the supernatural world. It is the mark of humanity. In many cultures, violations of the taboo are associated with a desecration of the basic social contract: with bestiality, with cannibalism, with witchcraft.[2] These beliefs are common to the Western cultural tradition, as they are to the science of anthropology, which is one of that tradition's more recent products. In the words of Claude Levi-Strauss, the great theorist in anthropology: "If social organization had a beginning, this could only have consisted in the incest prohibition, since . . . the incest prohibition is, in fact, a kind of remodeling of the biological conditions of mating and procreation (which know no rule, as can be seen from observing animal life) compelling them to be perpetuated only in an artificial framework of taboos and obligations. It is there, and only there, that we find a passage from nature to culture, from animal to human life."[3]

Explaining the incest taboo has been a central preoccupation of anthropology for the past hundred years. The origin of the taboo and the reasons for its perpetuation have been consuming subjects of debate. But curiously, the question of sex differences in the observance of the incest taboo has received relatively little attention. None of the three major theories of the incest taboo—the biological, the psychological, or the social—fully explains the puzzling discrepancy in the behavior of mothers and fathers toward their children.

The biological theory explains the fundamental purpose of the incest taboo as the prevention of inbreeding. It is therefore conceived as a prohibition on sexual intercourse between fertile blood relatives. Its function is to regulate reproduction. According to this theory, the selective advantages of human inbreeding are slight, while the disadvantages are considerable.[4] These arguments are substantiated by the data showing a high incidence of stillbirths, early infant deaths, congenital anomalies, and mental retardation in children born of incestuous unions within the nuclear family, and a lower but still discernible incidence of the same problems in the offspring of cousin marriages.[5]

The biological theory maintains that the incest prohibition is not uniquely human; that even without the intervention of language and culture, many animal species have evolved some mechanism to discourage inbreeding. This is apparently particularly true of larger, longer-lived, slower-maturing, more intelligent animals, and of animals living in family groups.[6] The "incest barrier" is therefore conceived as a product of natural selection. Those animal species and human cultures which have evolved a mechanism for discouraging nuclear family inbreeding have prevailed over the millennia because of the selective advantage that such a mechanism confers. The operation of human consciousness is considered incidental to the workings of what is, in effect, a biological law.

This theory, like all other explanations of the incest taboo, has strengths and weaknesses. Its obvious attractions are in the linkages of human and animal behavior that make it possible to imagine antecedents from which human incest taboos might have originated. The theory accords with genetic data, and with much of human mythology that associates incestuous matings with the birth of monstrosities.[7] Its major weakness is its failure to explain the prohibition of sexual expression other

than intercourse and the elaboration of the incest taboo outside the nuclear family. In many cultures, distinctions are made in the operation of
the incest rules which have no correspondence whatsoever to the biological degree of relatedness. For example, in many societies, marriage with
one set of cousins is forbidden, while marriage with another set of cousins
is allowed. Such rules defy any explanation based on genetic principles
or natural selection.

The biological theory also fails to explain why the barrier to father-
daughter matings might be weaker than the barrier against the mating of
mother and son. The genetic disadvantages of both types of matings are
presumably the same. If anything, father-daughter matings might be expected to produce more unfavorable results, since a high incidence of
abortion, stillbirth, and complications of all sorts attends the pregnancies
of immature females.[8] Yet nowhere in the animal kingdom is the barrier
against father-daughter mating observed to be stronger than that against
mother and son. In fact, in many animal species, as in humans, the barrier against father-daughter matings appears to be relatively weak. This
is the case particularly in species that establish a strong rank order, with
a presiding dominant male, and in species that observe a marked distinction in the socialization of young males and females. In species where
male dominance is pronounced, as in the gibbon or the rhesus monkey,
sexual access to all the females in the family group is a prerogative of the
dominant male. Young males are often driven out of the family group by
the older males as they approach sexual maturity. In animals which fol-
low a strongly sex-segregated pattern in their division of labor, young
males often go through an "emancipatory change," leaving the family
group as they approach maturity, while young females are kept within
the family group and taught to nurture infants. In both instances, the
isolation of young males from the family group effectively prevents
mother-son and brother-sister matings, while the retention of young females within the group increases the likelihood that father-daughter
matings will occur.[9] Indeed, in some species, father-daughter matings are
prevented only by "raids" on the family group conducted by young
males, in which young females are captured.[10] The females themselves
have no power to determine their sexual fate. The analogies between the
social world of male-dominant primates and the incestuous human family will turn out to be uncomfortably close.

If the incest taboo is understood, then, as a biological law, there is
nothing in the operation of the law itself to explain the asymmetries in its
observance by males and females. Natural selection shows no special

lenience toward father-daughter incest. Rather, it is the operation of the incest barrier through the institutions of male dominance and the sexual division of labor, institutions that are widespread in the animal kingdom, as in human society, which determines the relative weakness of the barrier against father-daughter matings.

The second major school of thought in anthropology explains the incest taboo primarily in terms of its psychological functions. The taboo is conceived as a rule governing all forms of sexual expression, not merely sexual intercourse, within the family. The purpose of the taboo is to establish the necessary conditions for family life: to regulate sexual conflicts and rivalries, to secure an appropriate environment for the socialization of children, and ultimately to ensure the dissolution of the nuclear family and the formation of new families.

An early proponent of this theory was Sigmund Freud. On the basis of very weak anthropological evidence, Freud speculated that the taboo was created after the murder of an original patriarch by his sons, the "band of brothers," in order to prevent their ungoverned sexual rivalries from degenerating into perpetual warfare.[11] Nearly seventy years after the publication of Freud's view, more sophisticated anthropologists have rejected his data but embraced his theory that the taboo exists primarily to control male sexual rivalry and promote peace within the family.[12]

Others, most notably the sociologist Talcott Parsons, have emphasized the function of the incest taboo in creating the proper climate for the socialization of children.[13] This view stresses the need both for the formation of primary erotic attachments and for the frustration of genital sexuality between parents and children. The erotic bond is a precondition for the child's ability to form relationships and a sense of self, and for the development of a basic sense of well-being that will survive the inevitable frustrations and disappointments of life. Genital frustration is essential to the child's ultimate ability to separate from parents and to subordinate sexual needs to social regulation. The struggle to accept and master the disappointment engendered by the incest taboo is a requisite step in the child's maturation; without it, the child fails to develop the separate identity and the internalized sense of social morality which are essential characteristics of well-adapted adults. The taboo is thus necessary to each individual, to ensure the successful passage from childhood to maturity. It is equally necessary to society, to ensure that enough children grow up to carry out adult functions, including the dissolution of old families and the creation of new ones.[14]

The attractions of the psychological theory are numerous. Unlike the biological theory, it explains the taboo on all forms of sexual activity within the family, and on sexual contact between family members who are related by adoption or marriage, not by blood. It explains the preservation of the taboo in advanced industrialized societies where kinship structures are relatively unimportant and where the possibility of birth control renders any genetic argument obsolete. It explains the dual nature of the taboo, as a convention which both fulfills and frustrates deep psychological needs. The major weakness of this theory, as of the biological theory, is its inability to account for the extensive development of incest taboos outside the nuclear family.

The psychological theory is also incapable, in the abstract, of explaining sex differences in the observance of the taboo. From the point of view of family harmony, there is no reason to suppose that father-daughter incest would be any less disruptive than any other kind. From the point of view of child development, there is no reason to suppose that the maturation of girls would be any less impaired by overt incest than that of boys. From the point of view of the wider society, there is no reason to suppose any lesser requirement for healthy adult women than for healthy adult men. Thus it is hard to understand why father-daughter incest should be viewed with any special tolerance.

The asymmetry in the observation of the incest taboo makes sense psychologically only in one particular kind of family: a father-dominated family, with a rigid sexual division of labor, in which mothers care for children of both sexes, and fathers do not. A patriarchal family structure secures to fathers immense powers over their wives and children. Traditionally, these powers include an unrestricted right of physical control, unrestricted sexual rights to wives (hence rape has no legal meaning within marriage), and extensive sexual rights in children. Fathers have the right to limit the sexual activity of their children, and to determine their choice of sexual and marriage partners (hence fathers "give away" daughters in marriage). In modern Western society, these rights are legally abrogated when children reach majority. In many other societies, fathers' rights, particularly in their daughters, are terminated only by marriage, and sometimes, as in ancient Greece, not even then.[15] The only sexual right in their children that fathers do not have in any society is that of personal use. But given all his other powers, a father may easily choose to extend his prerogatives to include the sexual initiation of his children.

Even within a patriarchal family structure, however, mothers as well as fathers have considerable power over children. Moreover, as the primary caretakers of children, they have ample opportunity to act upon their own incestuous wishes, should they choose to do so. Thus the power relations in the family do not suffice to explain why fathers frequently take advantage of their superior position to make sexual use of their children while mothers do not. It is the sexual division of labor, with its resultant profound differences in male and female socialization, which determines in mothers a greater capacity for self-restraint, and in fathers a greater propensity for sexually exploitative behavior.

Recent feminist revisions of psychoanalytic theory, especially the works of Juliet Mitchell, Helen Block Lewis, and Nancy Chodorow, have focused upon the psychological consequences of the sexual division of labor in child care.[16] These authors have repeatedly called attention to the profound sex differences created by the fact that mothers, not fathers, nurture children. The rearing of children by subordinate females ensures that boys and girls will differ in almost every aspect of personality development, including the formation of gender identity, the acquisition of conscience, the growth of the capacity to nurture, and the internalization of the incest taboo. The result is the reproduction of a male psychology of domination and a female psychology of victimization.

Because mothers, not fathers, nurture children, mothers are the primary love object for children of both sexes. Initially, the child's attachment to the mother knows nothing of time, place, sex, or any other social reality. The child's discovery of the meaning of gender, the incest taboo, and the relative position of men and women in the world therefore initiates a profound crisis, which Freud called in both sexes the Oedipus complex. Boys and girls alike must come to terms with the fact that the object of their first love is socially regarded as an inferior being, as the possession of a powerful father. The resolution of this crisis constitutes the child's initiation into the adult social order.

Consider the case of the boy. When he learns the place of women in the social world, he discovers that his first love is both an inferior and unlike himself. The price of his initiation into the privileged masculine world is the ruthless suppression of all things feminine in himself. His capacity for nurturance and for affectionate identification with women is therefore systematically suppressed. Development of a contemptuous attitude toward women becomes a normal, even necessary part of this masculine identity.[17]

The boy also discovers that in his love for his mother he challenges a formidable rival, for his mother belongs to his father, and his father rules the family. To violate the incest taboo is to call down upon himself the most terrible and feared punishment, for the father has the power to deny the little boy admission into the fraternity of adult men. It is fear of this punishment which Freud named the castration complex. Renunciation of love for the mother is the sacrifice by means of which the boy submits to his father's authority and gains entry into the privileged male order. In the words of Freud, the boy's infantile love for his mother is not merely transcended in the resolution of the Oedipal crisis; it is "smashed to pieces."[18] In compensation, the boy learns that as an adult, he will inherit many privileges, including sexual rights in women who are younger and weaker than himself.

The common product of this developmental process is an adult male whose capacity to nurture is severely impaired, whose ability to form affectionate relationships is restricted, and whose masculine identity, since it rests upon a repudiation of his identification with the person who first cared for him, is forever in doubt.[19] Sexual contact with a woman of inferior status affords to this psychologically rather fragile and constricted person the only permissible outlet for expression of a wide range of emotional needs: the need for intimacy, for comfort, for reassurance. The right to initiate and consummate sexual relations with subordinate women becomes, therefore, a jealously guarded male prerogative, guaranteed by the explicit or tacit consent of all men.

The tendency in men toward sexually exploitative behavior of all sorts, including rape, child molestation, and incest, thus becomes comprehensible as a consequence of male socialization within the patriarchal family.[20] The adult male's diminished capacity for affectionate relating prevents him from empathizing or identifying with his victim; without empathy, he lacks a major internal barrier to abusive action. At the same time, because other types of relationships are restricted, the need for a sexual relationship with a compliant and submissive female is exacerbated. Hence it is that adult men so frequently seek out sexual relationships not only with adult women who are younger and weaker than themselves, but also with girl children.

The path to adulthood is very different for girls. At the point of initiation into the adult order, a girl learns that her first love, her mother, is both an inferior and like herself. Like the boy, the girl first reacts to this discovery with a rejection of her mother and an attempt to separate from her. But unlike the boy, she cannot entirely repudiate her identification with her mother, since they are of the same gender. Hence, the primary bond between mother and daughter is more fully preserved into adult life, and on this basis are developed the girl's capacity for nurturance, for intimacy, and for affectionate identification with children.[21]

The girl's eroticized interest in her father does not develop out of an earlier bond with the father as caretaker. Rather, it is a reaction to the girl's discovery that males are everywhere preferred to females, and that even her mother, the object of her first love, chooses men above women, her father and brother above herself. She turns to her father in the hope that he will make her into an honorary boy. In her imagination, her father has the power to confer the emblem of maleness (penis or phallus) upon her. It is for this reason that she wishes to seduce or be seduced by him. By establishing a special and privileged relationship with her father, she seeks to be elevated into the superior company of men.[22]

No threat comparable to the punishment feared by boys attends the expression of the girl's incestuous wishes. If she fears her mother's rivalry, it is because she does not want to lose her mother's love, not because her mother has the power to deprive her of manhood. She has already been made a female; nothing worse can befall her.

In boys, the suppression of incestuous wishes is rewarded by initiation into male privilege. The girl's renunciation of her incestuous wishes finds no comparable reward. It is rather through the consummation of incest that the girl seeks to gain those privileges which otherwise must forever be denied to her. Thus the girl has little inducement to overcome her infantile attachment to her father: she can be neither rewarded for submitting to the incest taboo nor punished for failing to do so.[23] If the girl does renounce her hopes of acquiring male status through a special, incestuous relationship, it is only because these hopes are ultimately disappointed. The father's behavior toward his daughter thus assumes immense importance. If the father chooses to eroticize the relationship with his daughter, he will encounter little or no resistance.

Even when the girl does give up her erotic attachment to her father, she is encouraged to persist in the fantasy that some other man, like her father, will some day take possession of her, raising her above the common lot of womankind. The successful attainment of conventional adult heterosexuality in fact requires an incomplete resolution of the female Oedipus complex and a channeling of female sexuality into submissive relationships with older, stronger, richer, more powerful men. Feminist psychologist Phyllis Chesler states the same point more bluntly: "Women are encouraged to commit incest as a way of life . . . As opposed to marrying our fathers, we marry men like our fathers . . . men who are older than us, have more money than us, more power than us, are taller than us . . . our fathers."[24] Not surprisingly, many women do not succeed in traversing this tortuous and narrow path toward "mature" femininity and remain erotically undeveloped.

Traditional psychoanaytic authorities have even suggested that normal feminine development will not occur without a certain degree of paternal seductiveness. Helene Deutsch, for example, implicates an eroticized relationship with the father in the genesis of "feminine masochism," a vague term which seems to describe the woman's acceptance of her inferior status and her willingness to make others rather than herself the center of her moral universe. Deutsch associates the "turn toward masochism" in feminine development with the renunciation of active and aggressive strivings in response to social demands enforced by the father: "The bribe offered to the little girl by the father, as a representative of the environment, is love and tenderness. For its sake she renounces any further intensification of her activity, particularly of her aggressions." Without a degree of paternal seductiveness, Deutsch warns, the little girl might not be successfully "bribed" into becoming a properly submissive female: "The masochistic ingredient in relation to the father appears in active games with him, which later assume an increasingly erotic character . . . When this seduction on the part of the father is lacking, the girl will encounter difficulties in her feminine development."[25]

The common product of female socialization under patriarchy is an adult woman who may deeply resent her feminine identity but does not doubt it, and who seeks confirmation of her importance in sexual relations with men who are more powerful than herself and in the care of others who are younger, smaller, and weaker than herself. Her capacity for full erotic expression may be considerably blunted, but her ability to nurture, to sympathize with others, and to express affection is highly developed. Hence the fact that women rarely molest children, in spite of the extensive opportunity provided by daily intimacy.

In short, nothing in the psychological functions of the incest taboo explains its differential observation by men and women. Rather, the structure of the patriarchal family, in which child care is relegated to subordinate women, determines that men and women internalize the taboo very differently. In a family where fathers rule and mothers nurture, the most strictly observed incest taboo must be the prohibition on sexual relations between mother and son; the most frequently broken taboo must be that on relations between father and daughter.

The third and final major school of thought in anthropology explains the incest taboo primarily as a social law, regulating marriage. From this point of view, the incest taboo is identical with the law of exogamy, which requires marriage outside the family group. The function of the taboo is the creation not of the family alone, but of kinship relations among families. By preventing marriage within the family group, the incest taboo interferes with this group's natural tendency to isolate itself. Compelled to exchange members through the arrangement of marriage, family groups are organized into a society through the operation of the incest taboo. Marriage outside the family group becomes the fundamental form of social alliance.[26]

Seen in this light, the incest taboo is also a special case of a more general principle of social organization, which Levi-Strauss calls the "rule of the gift."[27] Cooperative social life is created, according to this view, through the mechanism of a regulated exchange of gifts. This exchange results in the formation of special relationships of trust and mutual aid. The exchange of objects and produce is governed by rules of trade or rituals of friendship. The exchange of people in marriage, the most serious and lasting kind of gift-giving, is governed by the rule of exogamy or the incest taboo.

The strength of the social theory rests in its ability to explain the wide variety of incest taboos, which in many cultures extend far beyond the confines of the immediate family to numerous and remote relatives. It also explains why incest prohibitions tend to be most elaborate and complex in so-called primitive cultures whose economic and political life is organized through kinship, and why these prohibitions tend to contract in scope in Western, industrialized cultures, where the economic and political importance of kinship is diminished.[28]

Like the biological and psychological theories, the social theory in its purest form is sex-neutral. The incest taboo or exogamy law simply requires the exchange of people between family groups. Nothing inherent in the rule itself requires the exchange of women only or prevents the exchange of men. In practice, however, the arrangements of exchange are almost always conducted by men, and the objects of exchange are women. In the words of Levi-Strauss: "The total relationship of exchange which constitutes marriage is not established between a man and a woman, but between two groups of men, and the woman figures only as one of the objects in the exchange, not as one of the partners . . . This remains true even when the girl's feelings are taken into consideration, as, moreover, is usually the case. In acquiescing to the proposed union, she precipitates or allows the exchange to take place. She cannot alter its nature.[29]

The asymmetry in the incest taboo thus results not from any abstract requirement of gift-giving, but from the fact that the givers and receivers are men, and the gifts given are women. Wherever women are considered the property of men, the incest taboo becomes a rule governing their exchange. Since the rule is made and enforced by men, without the active participation of women and children, it expresses the predominant interests of men alone, not the interests of the social group as a whole.[30]

In patriarchal societies, including Western society, the rights of ownership and exchange of women within the family are vested primarily in the father. These rights find their most complete expression in the father's relationship with his daughter. In every other relationship, the rule prohibiting the sexual use of female relatives is reinforced by the claims of other kinsmen. Thus incest with the mother is most strenuously forbidden, because it is an affront to the father's prerogatives. Incest with a sister is also an offense against the father's rights, which in this case do not include the right of sexual use but do encompass the rights of ownership and exchange. Similarly, the aunt and cousin are forbidden because they belong to the uncle; the sister-in-law and niece because they belong to the brother, the daughter-in-law and granddaughter because they belong to the son, and so forth. But the daughter belongs to the father alone. Though the incest taboo forbids him to make sexual use of his daughter, no particular man's rights are offended, should the father choose to disregard this rule. As long as he ultimately gives his daughter in marriage, he has fulfilled the social purpose of the rule of the gift. Until such time as he chooses to give her away, he has the uncontested power to do with her as he wishes. Hence, of all possible forms of incest, that between father and daughter is the most easily overlooked.

It is no doubt for this reason that the biblical injunction against incest omits any specific reference to sexual relations between father and daughter, while almost every other conceivable breach of the incest taboo is explicitly named and condemned:

> None of you shall approach to any that is near of kin to him, to uncover their nakedness: I am the Lord.
> The nakedness of thy father, or the nakedness of thy mother,

shalt thou not uncover: she is thy mother; thou shalt not uncover her nakedness.

The nakedness of thy father's wife shalt thou not uncover: it is thy father's nakedness.

The nakedness of thy sister, the daughter of thy father, or daughter of thy mother, whether she be born at home, or born abroad, even their nakedness thou shalt not uncover.

The nakedness of thy son's daughter, or of thy daughter's daughter, even their nakedness thou shalt not uncover: for theirs is thine own nakedness.

The nakedness of thy father's wife's daughter, begotten of thy father, she is thy sister, thou shalt not uncover her nakedness.

Thou shalt not uncover the nakedness of thy father's sister: she is thy father's near kinswoman.

Thou shalt not uncover the nakedness of thy mother's sister, for she is thy mother's near kinswoman.

Thou shalt not uncover the nakedness of thy father's brother, thou shalt not approach to his wife: she is thine aunt.

Thou shalt not uncover the nakedness of thy daughter in law: she is thy son's wife; thou shalt not uncover her nakedness.

Thou shalt not uncover the nakedness of thy brother's wife: it is thy brother's nakedness.

Thou shalt not uncover the nakedness of a woman and her daughter, neither shalt thou take her son's daughter, or her daughter's daughter, to uncover her nakedness, for they are her near kinswomen: it is wickedness.

Neither shalt thou take a wife to her sister, to vex her, to uncover her nakedness, beside the other in her life time.[31]

The biblical law is addressed to men. It is assumed without question that men initiate and women submit to sexual relations. The wording of the law makes it clear that incest violations are not offenses against the women taken for sexual use but against the men in whom the rights of ownership, use, and exchange are vested. What is prohibited is the sexual use of those women who, in one manner or another, already belong to other relatives. Every man is thus expressly forbidden to take the daughters of his kinsmen, but only by implication is he forbidden to take his own daughters. The patriarchal God sees fit to pass over father-daughter incest in silence.

To recapitulate, nothing known about the origin and functions of the incest taboo explains why, in practice, mothers and fathers observe the taboo so differently. The incest taboo may be understood as a biological law which prevents inbreeding, as a psychological law which creates the family, as a social law which creates kinship, or as the sum of all these. However it is understood, the incest taboo in its abstract form applies equally to both sexes. It is the refraction of the incest taboo through the institutions of male supremacy and the sexual division of labor which results in the asymmetrical application of the taboo to men and women. Only under male supremacy do women become objects of exchange. Only male supremacy determines that men have the right to give women for marriage or concubinage, while women have no comparable rights either in men or in themselves. Only under male supremacy do incest taboos become agreements among men regarding the disposition of women.

The man who has the power to give a woman away also has the power to take her for himself. That power can be contested only by other men, not by the women who are given or taken. No kinsman, and certainly no man outside the family, is in a position to challenge a father's power over his daughters. Thus the rule of the gift is breached most commonly where it is least capable of enforcement, that is, in the relationship between fathers and daughters.

Whereas male supremacy creates the social conditions that favor the development of father-daughter incest, the sexual division of labor creates the psychological conditions that lead to the same result. Male supremacy invests fathers with immense powers over their children, especially their daughters. The sexual division of labor, in which women nurture children and men do not, produces fathers who are predisposed to use their powers exploitatively. The rearing of children by subordinate women ensures the reproduction in each generation of the psychology of male supremacy. It produces sexually aggressive men with little capacity to nurture, nurturant women with undeveloped sexual capacities, and children of both sexes who stand in awe of the power of fathers.

Wherever these conditions obtain, father-daughter incest is likely to be a common occurrence. In any culture, the greater the degree of male supremacy and the more rigid the sexual division of labor, the more frequently one might expect the taboo on father-daughter incest to be violated. Conversely, the more egalitarian the culture, and the more the childrearing is shared by men and women, the less one might expect to find overt incest between father and daughter. The same logic applies to particular families within any one culture. The greater the domination of the father, and the more the caretaking is relegated to the mother, the greater the likelihood of father-daughter incest. The more democratic the family and the less rigid the sexual division of labor, the less likely that fathers will abuse their daughters.

This hypothesis cannot be confirmed or disproved by cross-cultural studies of the prevalence of incest, since no reliable data are available for comparison. But it can be validated by the study of incestuous families themselves, which show father-daughter incest to be but one manifestation of a despotic paternal rule.

Two
DAUGHTERS' LIVES

5

Incestuous Fathers and Their Families

These fathers . . . tend toward abuses of authority of every conceivable kind, and they not infrequently endeavor to secure their dominant position in the family by socially isolating the members of the family from the world outside. Swedish, American, and French surveys have pointed time and again to the patriarchal position of such fathers, who set up a "primitive family order." —*Herbert Maisch*, Incest, 1972

Forty women who had had incestuous relationships with their fathers shared their stories with us. Most were young women in their twenties or early thirties. At the time we met them, most had already married and some had already divorced; half had children. They worked at common women's jobs; they were mothers and houseworkers, typists and secretaries, waitresses and factory workers, teachers and nurses. About half came from working-class and half from middle-class families.[1] Their ethnic and religious backgrounds reflected the predominant Catholicism of the state of Massachusetts, where most of them lived (see Tables 5.1 and 5.2). To all appearances, they were an ordinary group of women.

All of the informants were white. We made the decision to restrict the interviewing to white women in order to avoid even the possibility that the information gathered might be used to fuel idle speculation about racial differences. White people have indulged for too long in discussion about the sexual capacities, behaviors, and misbehaviors of black people. There is no question, however, that incest is a problem in black families, as it is in white families. Many of the first, most daring, and most honest contributions to the public discussion of incest were made by black women, and much of our work has been inspired by theirs.[2]

Table 5.1. Demographic characteristics of incest victims and comparison group[a]

Demographic characteristic	Incest victims		Comparison group	
	No. = 40	%	No. = 20	%
Age				
18–25	23	57.5	11	55
26–30	7	17.5	6	30
31–35	5	12.5	2	10
36 +	5	12.5	1	5
Mean	27.7		26.8	
Marital status				
Single	15	37.5	11	55
Married	14	35.	4	20
Separated or divorced	11	27.5	5	25
Children				
Yes	20	50	5	25
No	20	50	15	75
Religious background				
Catholic	17	42.5	8	40
Protestant	14	35	9	45
Jewish	5	12.5	3	15
n.a.	2	5		
Educational level				
Advanced degree	3	7.5	6	30
B.A.	12	30	7	35
Some college	11	27.5	7	35
High school graduate	10	25	0	0
< twelfth grade	4	10	0	0

a. Comparison group for tables 5.1–5.3 and 5.5 are daughters of seductive fathers.

All of the informants were outpatients in psychotherapy. Some allowed their therapists to discuss their histories with us; others agreed to be interviewed in person as well; and a few, having heard of our study, carried on a correspondence with us. We chose to restrict the study to women who had therapists because we believed that our work could not be carried out without causing pain. Every interview we conducted was

Table 5.2. Family background of incest victims and comparison group

Family background	Incest victims		Comparison group	
	No. = 40	%	No. = 20	%
Father's occupation				
Working class	19	47.5	11	55
Middle layers or self-employed	21	52.5	9	45
Mother employed outside home				
Yes	9	22.5	6	30
No	31	77.5	14	70
Parents separated or divorced				
Yes	9	22.5	5	25
No	31	77.5	15	75
Victim's place in family				
Only daughter	15	37.5	11	55
Oldest daughter	17	42.5	4	20
Other	8	20	5	25

stressful, both for the informants and for ourselves. As one woman commented, "Every time I tell about it, I hurt in a new place." By limiting the study to patients in therapy, we made certain that the informants had at least one safe place in which to deal with their renewed memories.

Informants were located primarily through an informal network of therapists in private practice in the Boston area. Cases were initially discussed with the therapists, who exercised some preliminary judgment about which patients should be approached. Patients who were in severe distress or who had not established a good therapeutic alliance were generally screened out of the study. The therapists then informed their patients about our research and invited them to participate. It is our impression that those who accepted, and especially those who agreed to be interviewed in person, had already dealt with the incest trauma to a certain extent in their therapy.

Information was gathered according to a semistructured interview protocol which covered the patient's present work and personal life, a detailed description of the patient's family of origin, a history of the incestuous relationship, and an assessment of the long-term effects of the incest. Interviews generally lasted two to three hours. Case discussions with therapists were recorded in the form of extensive notes; interviews with patients were recorded verbatim. The forty interviews were collected over a period of four years, beginning in 1975.

Though all the informants were patients in psychotherapy, they were not in any obvious manner a disturbed group of people. Most functioned quite well in their daily lives, and some had achieved remarkable success, particularly in their work. They were special, perhaps, only in that they had admitted to themselves that they had problems in their personal lives and were trying to do something about it. Our method of locating the informants tended to select for a relatively healthy group of patients.

Our definition of incest reflected a predominantly psychological rather than a biological or social concept of the taboo. Incest was defined to mean any sexual relationship between a child and an adult in a position of paternal authority. From the psychological point of view, it does not matter if the father and child are blood relatives. What matters is the relationship that exists by virtue of the adult's parental power and the child's dependency. In fact, most of the informants (thirty-one, or 78 percent) had been molested by their biologic fathers. Five had been molested by stepfathers, and four by adoptive fathers.

We further defined a sexual relationship to mean any physical contact that had to be kept a secret. From a biological or social point of view, only contact which might lead to defloration or pregnancy, that is vaginal intercourse, is dignified with the name of incest. This narrow definition is reflected both in the criminal codes of most states and in the popular thinking on the subject. From the point of view of the adult male, sexual activity that stops short of penile penetration is often described as "unconsummated," as though somehow it does not "count." But from a psychological point of view, especially from the child's point of view, the sexual motivation of the contact, and the fact that it must be kept secret, are far more significant than the exact nature of the act itself. From the moment that the father initiates the child into activities which serve the father's sexual needs, and which must be hidden from others, the bond between parent and child is corrupted.

The composite portrait of the incestuous family which emerged from the testimony of the informants is only one version of a complex reality. It is, first of all, a retrospective portrait, with all the simplification and distortion that inevitably degrades an adult's memory of childhood. Second, it is a portrait drawn from the perspective of the victim alone.

Nevertheless, as the investigation progressed, we gained increasing confidence in the accuracy of the informants' accounts. Each individual's testimony had the vividness and integrity of well-preserved memory, and the accounts of many informants were so similar that they tended to validate each other. Finally, the general picture which emerged from the collective testimony of the informants has been corroborated in many respects by other researchers who have directly observed incestuous fathers, mothers, or entire families.

The families in which the informants grew up were conventional to a fault. Most were churchgoing and financially stable; they maintained a facade of respectability. They were for the most part unknown to mental health services, social agencies, or the police. Because they conformed to traditional family norms, their private disturbances were easily overlooked:

> *Marion:* Yes, we were what you call an intact family. My mother lived at Church and Church functions. My father sang in the choir, and he molested me while my mother was at Sunday School class parties. There was no drinking or smoking or anything the world could see. Only God knows.

The informants described their fathers as perfect patriarchs. They were, without question, the heads of their households. Their authority within the family was absolute, often asserted by force. They were also the arbiters of the family's social life and frequently succeeded in virtually secluding the women in the family. But while they were often feared within their families, they impressed outsiders as sympathetic, even admirable men.

The daughters themselves were often impressed, for their fathers did have many strengths. Most took their responsibility to provide for the family very seriously. Their daughters knew them to be hard-working, competent, and often very successful:

> *Yvonne:* My father was a jack of all trades. Throughout his life he did many interesting things. He was manager of a state agency, foreman of a construction company, and even a politician; he ran for the State Senate. He was likable and could talk anyone into helping him out when he was in a jam. I remember him as a big man, about six feet tall, and very good-looking.

> *Christine:* My sisters and I used to feel really proud to see our father dressed up in his uniform. Or when he was called away on flight duty we'd be very excited to hear him talk about bombs and how he was going to protect our country.

Thirty-one of the forty fathers were the sole support of their families. Two policemen, three military officers, two physicians, and two college professors were included in their number, as well as an assortment of businessmen, storekeepers, and skilled tradesmen. Many worked long hours and held more than one job. Their role as family breadwinner was honored with almost ritual solemnity:

> *Lily:* No matter what had gone on that week, every Friday my father would bring home his paycheck. He'd take my mother's hand and put the check in it and close her hand over it without saying a word.

The competence in work and social life of incestuous fathers has also been documented in many previous studies. I. B. Weiner, in a clinical study of five fathers referred for outpatient treatment, observed that the fathers all had "successful work histories" and their families were not in "economic distress."[3] Herbert Maisch, in his study of 72 cases reported to the German courts, characterized the offenders as working-class men with average or above-average levels of skill.[4] Several investigators remarked as well on the fathers' above-average intelligence.[5] Noel Lustig, in his study of six military men who committed incest, described the fathers as "strongly motivated to maintain a facade of role competence as the family patriarch in the eyes of society." The men were well thought of outside their families.[6]

In addition, the families of our informants adhered rigidly to the traditional sexual division of labor. Most of the mothers were full-time houseworkers who depended entirely upon their husbands for their livelihood. Six mothers did some part-time work outside the home. Only three mothers had full-time jobs. None of the mothers had the working skills or experience which would have made independent survival a realistic option.

The mothers were considered inferior to the fathers, not only in their work achievements, but also simply in their status as women. These were families in which sex roles were rigidly defined, and male superiority was unquestioned:

Christine: My father just thought women were stupid. He had a very, very low opinion of women, and he never made my mother feel like she was worth anything. Nothing she could do was any good.

The preference for males was expressed in countless ways. Boys in the family were given more freedom and privileges than girls, or were excused from household chores. Some families paid for the education of their sons but not their daughters. One daughter recalled that with each of her mother's numerous pregnancies, her father proudly informed the relatives that his wife was expecting a boy.

In many families, it was considered a male prerogative to supervise and restrict the activities of the females. Fathers exercised minute control over the lives of their wives and daughters, often virtually confining them to the house. The boys in the family were sometimes enlisted as deputies in this policing role. Many daughters reported that their fathers discouraged their mothers from driving a car, visiting friends, or participating in activities outside the home:

Yvonne: My mother was a secretary when she met my father, and she became his secretary. After they were married, my parents moved away from my mother's birthplace, to Vermont. My father told my mother she should not work or drive there because it was too cold and too dangerous in the snow. She never drove or worked again.

Daughters were also deterred from establishing any independent social contacts. The fathers consolidated their power within the family by isolating their wives and children from the outside world:

Sheila: We had no visitors. My father was very exclusive, and my mother was afraid to let people in when he had been drinking. People just didn't come to our house. I remember my best friend who lived across the street from me: people would float in and out of her house like it was Grand Central Station. I used to think, wouldn't it be nice to be able to do that.

One of the most significant distinguishing characteristics of the incestuous fathers was their tendency to dominate their families by the use of force. Half of the informants reported that their fathers were habitually violent and that they themselves had seen their mothers beaten (see Table 5.3). Other children in the family were often beaten as well. The fathers were selective in their choice of targets: one child was often singled out as a scapegoat, while a more favored child was spared. This lesson was not lost on the daughters, who quickly recognized the advantages of being in their fathers' good graces:

> *Esther:* My father is an extremely macho and egotistical person, an educated elitist who always felt that he married beneath him. In fact, he is extremely intelligent and artistically creative. I have always admired his superior intellect and his talent. But he is also a very willful and childishly demanding person who has always had his own way. He is and always was subject to fits of irrational violence, and the whole family is scared to death of him. Except for me, that is.

This violence, though terrifying to the mothers and children, did not exceed certain clear limits. No family member was injured seriously enough to require hospitalization, though there were some close calls, and no outside intervention was provoked. Although the fathers often appeared completely out of control in the privacy of their homes, they never made the mistake of attacking outsiders. They were not known as bullies or troublemakers; in the presence of superior authority, they were generally ingratiating, deferential, even meek. In this, as in many other aspects of family life, they seemed exquisitely sensitive to the bounds of the male prerogative, and did not exceed the socially condoned limits of violence.

Many previous studies have recognized the dictatorial role of fathers in incestuous families. One explained the father's "dominant position" as resulting from his "intimidation and control of the family."[7] Another described the father as "the authoritarian head of the house."[8] Still another observer indicated that "in an overwhelming majority of all cases, the family structure was formed by . . . the dominating influence of the husband and father."[9]

Other observers, however, have described the same fathers as "ineffectual and dependent," "inadequate," or "weak, insecure and vulnerable."[10] Far from appearing as tyrants, these fathers emerge as rather pitiful men, sometimes even as victims of a "domineering or managing wife."[11] The solution to this apparent contradiction lies in the fathers' ability to assess their relative power in any situation and to vary their behavior accordingly. In the presence of men much more powerful

Table 5.3. Distinguishing characteristics of incestuous families and comparison group

Family characteristic	Incest families No. = 40	%	Comparison group No. = 20	%
Father violent[a]				
Yes	20	50	4	20
No	20	50	16	80
Father alcoholic				
Yes	15	37.5	7	35
No	25	62.5	13	65
Mother ill[b]				
Yes	22	55	3	15
No	18	45	17	85
Mother-child separation[b]				
Yes	15	37.5	0	0
No	25	62.5	20	100
Daughter's family role[b]				
Maternal	18	45	1	5
Mediator	6	15	3	15
Nonmaternal	16	40	16	80
Children in family				
1	6	15	4	20
2	9	22.5	6	30
3	8	20	4	20
4	10	25	3	15
5	2	5	2	10
6	0	0	0	0
7	0	0	1	5
8	3	7.5	0	0
9	1	2.5	0	0
10–13	0	0	0	0
14	1	2.5	0	0
Mean	3.6[c]		2.85	

a. Differences between the two groups were significant at the $p < .05$ level.
b. Differences between the two groups were significant at the $p < .01$ level.
c. Difference between this mean and the national mean of 2.2 was significant at the $p < .01$ level.

than themselves, such as police, prosecutors, therapists, and researchers, the fathers knew how to present themselves as pathetic, helpless, and confused. Only in the privacy of their homes, where they knew they would encounter no effective opposition, did they indulge their appetites for domination. Face to face with men of equal or superior authority, they became engaging and submissive.

Male professionals who are not themselves intimidated often find it hard to imagine how women and children might be. As one expert on child abuse admits: "Many sexually abusive fathers are described as tyrants in the home . . . Professionals who have worked with sexual abuse frequently encounter a father who has been described in these terms. When he enters the office for an interview, the professional is astonished to find this "violent and unpredictable" man to be 5'7", 150 pounds and neatly dressed. He is of a calm disposition and appears to be a rather anxious, harassed and overburdened man, puzzled by recent events."[12] A 5'7", 150-pound man out in public and on good behavior may not seem at all frightening to a larger man in a position of authority. But the same man may be quite large enough to terrorize his wife and children behind closed doors.

Alcoholism was another common characteristic of the incestuous fathers of our informants, though not a distinguishing one. Over a third of the informants considered their fathers to be problem drinkers. Like the violence, however, the fathers' drinking was effectively concealed from outsiders. Family relationships were often severely disrupted by the father's excessive drinking, and in a few cases the father's health was seriously affected, but most fathers retained their ability to work and to conform to normal standards of public behavior. If the father's drinking problem was recognized at all, it usually fell into the category of "a good man's failing." Very few fathers received any medical or psychiatric treatment for alcoholism or, for that matter, for any other problem.

Alcoholism has frequently been associated with incestuous behavior. In one study of imprisoned sex offenders, for example, 46 percent of the incestuous fathers were diagnosed as alcoholic, a figure that approximates our own. But as that study points out, although sex offenders who are alcoholic often commit their crimes while drunk, it is naive to attribute the offense to demon alcohol. The sexual assault, more often than not, is planned in advance. On careful questioning, offenders often admit that they drink in order to gather courage for the approach.[13]

While the fathers of our informants preserved a facade of competent social functioning, the mothers were often unable to fulfill their traditional roles. Over half of the informants (55 percent) remembered that their mothers had had periods of disabling illness which resulted in frequent hospitalizations or in the mother's living as an invalid at home. Over a third (38 percent) of the daughters had been separated from their mothers for some period of time during childhood. The separations occurred because their mothers either were hospitalized or felt unable to cope with their child care duties and temporarily placed their daughters in the care of relatives. Three mothers died before their daughters were grown, one by suicide. Another mother committed suicide after her daughter left home.

Depression, alcoholism, and psychosis were among the most common causes of the mothers' disability. Many daughters remembered their mothers as suffering from mysterious ailments which made them seem withdrawn, peculiar, and unavailable. One daughter reported that when she was ten, her mother developed the delusion that she was dying of cancer and took to bed for a year. Many other daughters commented on their mothers' strange maladies which seemed to elude definition:

> *Janet:* She was almost like a recluse. She was very alone. It was obvious to me by the time I reached high school that my mother was really strange. My sisters and I used to joke about it.

As in the case of the fathers, the mothers' psychiatric and medical problems usually went undiagnosed and untreated.

If the cause of the mother's ailment sometimes seemed obscure, in other cases it was only too obvious: repeated enforced pregnancies. The average number of children for this group of mothers was 3.6, well above the national mean of 2.2. Seventeen mothers had four children or more, and five had eight or more children (see Table 5.3). Although some daughters reported that their mothers loved babies and had always wanted large families, in many cases the pregnancies were more or less imposed on women who felt helpless to prevent them:

> *Rita:* I blame my father for her death, to a certain degree. After the seventh child, they found out she had cancer, and they told her not to get pregnant again. But she couldn't control it, my father being the man he is. He felt, if you're going to have sex, you have to have the child. And he was the type of man who would say, if I can't get it from my wife, I'll go elsewhere. He's also the

type of man where, if she didn't want to open her legs, he'd pinch her thighs.

Whether or not they wanted to have many children, the mothers of large families often suffered physically from their multiple pregnancies and became overwhelmed with the burden of caring for many small children:

> *Christine:* Now I know she was only 98 pounds at the age of twenty-five. She was yellow, jaundiced; she had some kind of kidney infection; and she was sick with every one of her pregnancies. We were barely a year apart, and I think having kids in such rapid succession, my mother was really tired out.

Four of the mothers also had severely handicapped children, whose care absorbed virtually all their energies.

Numerous researchers have commented on the surprisingly large number of children found in incestuous families. In Maisch's German study, the average number of children was 3.48, compared to a national average of 1.8.[14] Studies of other populations have found even higher averages. For example, a study of an American inner-city population, found an average of 4.7 children of incest families, compared to a mean of 3.9 in a comparison group.[15] A study of imprisoned incestuous fathers reported that they had an average of 5.1 children.[16] And a study of a rural Irish population reported an average of seven children in incestuous families, as compared to a county average of 4.5.[17] Only one researcher, however, apparently understood the connection between the large size of the family and the relative powerlessness of the mother: "The finding relating to more children in the home of incest families . . . suggests an overburdened mother, possibly tired because of early and prolonged childbearing . . . Perhaps it gives us some insight into the mother's general forbearance and passive acceptance of the incest offender's peculiar behavior in the home."[18]

Economically dependent, socially isolated, in poor health, and encumbered with the care of many small children, these mothers were in no position to challenge their husbands' domination or to resist their abuses. No matter how badly they were treated, most simply saw no option other than submission to their husbands. They conveyed to their daughters the belief that a woman is defenseless against a man, that marriage must be preserved at all costs, and that a wife's duty is to serve and endure.

Most of our informants remembered their mothers as weak and powerless, finding their only dignity in martyrdom. The few who described their mothers as strong meant by this that there was apparently no limit to their capacity for suffering:

> *Rita:* She held on because that's all she had. Everything she did was self-sacrifice. She made sure there was food on everyone's plate—whatever we left behind, that's what she ate. She went around in the same housedress and a pair of loafers day after day—never any new clothing. She never wore makeup, never colored her hair, never spent money on herself. Her kids came first.

> *Anne-Marie:* She always said, give with one hand and you'll get with the other, but she gave with two hands and always went down. She was nothing but a floor mat. She sold out herself and her self-respect. She was a love slave to my father.

None of the fathers adapted to their wives' disabilities by assuming a maternal role in the family. Rather, they reacted to their wives' illnesses as if they themselves were being deprived of mothering. As the family providers, they felt they had the right to be nurtured and served at home, if not by their wives, then by their daughters.

Thirty-two (80 percent) of the informants were the oldest or the only daughters in their families.[19] Before the age of ten, almost half (45 percent) had been pressed into service as "little mothers" within the family. They cared for their younger sisters and brothers and took on responsibility for major household tasks. Many became astonishingly competent in this role. Pride in their accomplishments as little adults became their compensation for loss of childhood:

> *Christine:* I could see that my mother needed help, but she wouldn't ask for it; she'd nag and bitch, and that would turn my sisters off. My sisters were very unproductive. So I'd pitch in without being asked. I'd vacuum, I'd do the laundry, I'd wash the dishes, I'd do this, I'd do that. This was from the time I was, oh, nine. I still think I can do a lot of things better than my mother.

Whether or not they were obliged to take on household responsibilities, most of the daughters were assigned a special duty to "keep Daddy happy." They mediated parental quarrels and placated their fathers when their mothers dared not approach them. They became their fathers' confidantes and often shared their grievances and secrets.

In their special roles as little mother or as father's consort, the daughters believed that they bore the responsibility for holding the family together. None of the informants thought that her parents were happily married; many were well aware that their parents were miserable together. Though a few daughters wished devoutly that their parents would divorce, most dreaded this possibility, and did whatever they could to avert it. They lived in terror that their fathers would desert the family and that their mothers would fall apart completely.

Since it was their duty to provide a sympathetic audience for their fathers, many daughters heard about their parents' marital troubles in great detail. The fathers' complaints were monotonously simple. They considered themselves deprived of the care to which they felt entitled. In their estimation, their wives were not giving enough: they were cold; they were frigid; they refused sex; they withheld love.

These complaints seemed plausible enough to the daughters, who themselves often felt deprived of maternal affection. Some daughters were additionally aware that their mothers had highly negative sexual attitudes:

> *Janet:* My mother is a terrible prude. I don't remember any of her sayings, but I remember the feeling behind them. It was so ugly, it made sex sound like the dirtiest thing around.

In retrospect, however, most daughters felt that their fathers' complaints wore a little thin and that their parents' problems must have been more complicated than their fathers' accounts had led them to believe. As adults, they puzzled over what went wrong and who was most at fault:

> *Marion:* In my case I put most of the blame on my mother. She is a cold person—cannot show love to anyone except babies. She started a large family and ignored my father from the day she got pregnant. I have seen her many times shove Daddy away from her. I feel she drove my Dad to this thing. He was starved for affection. Still, he may have had a deeper problem; I'll never know. He couldn't seem to keep his hands to himself. I never brought a girlfriend home. He would squeeze all the neighbors'

wives in the wrong places. He didn't seem to care if we saw him or not. He made me sick at my stomach.

Janet: He would just talk in very personal terms about how deprived he was. But then my mother says she always did have sex with him, so I don't know who was telling the truth.

At the time, most of the daughters took their fathers' side. It was easy enough to sympathize with the fathers' feeling of deprivation, for most of the daughters themselves felt slighted or neglected by their mothers. Though many could see that their mothers were ill or overwhelmed with their own problems, few, as children, could afford the luxury of compassion. They knew only that they bore the burden of their mothers' shortcomings and were obliged to nurture others while their own longings for nurture went unsatisfied. In these circumstances, the daughters could not escape feeling profoundly disappointed in their mothers.

At best, the daughters viewed their mothers ambivalently, excusing their weaknesses as best they could. The one daughter out of the forty who cherished a positive image of her mother did so on the basis of a fantasy which she created after her mother's death. Though her mother had endured savage beatings herself and had been helpless to prevent the abuse of her children, this daughter clung to the belief that her mother would have taken protective action, had she lived.

At worst, the relations between mother and daughter were marked by active hostility. Many of the daughters remembered their mothers only with bitterness and contempt. They described the women who had borne them as selfish, uncaring, and cruel. In their moments of despair, these daughters felt the absence of the most primary bonds of caring and trust. They believed they had been unwanted from the moment of their birth, and they cursed their mothers for bringing them into the world:

Esther: My mother was extraordinarily rejecting. I was born ten months after my brother, and I was clearly an "accident," greatly regretted.

Paula: She's an asshole. I really don't like my mom. I guess I am bitter. She's very selfish. She was seventeen when she had me, and her mother put her in a home. She blames me for ruining her life because she got pregnant with me. But I'm not the one who spread my legs.

Sandra: Why do people bother having kids? Why did my mother have me? I'm sure in those days people knew how to get rid of them. She seemed to know how. I wish she was dead so I could forget about her—or that I was dead so that she'd suffer. Why does God allow people like her to live?

Other authors have also remarked on the alienation between mothers and daughters which seems to prevail in incestuous families. Maisch found that 61 percent of the mothers and daughters in his study had a distant or hostile relationship which preceded the onset of overt incest.[20]

By contrast, most of our informants had some fond memories of their fathers. Although they feared their fathers, they also admired their competence and power. Many described their fathers as gifted, likable, and intelligent, terms that they rarely applied to their mothers. Some remembered that, as children, they had frankly adored their fathers:

Sheila: It was nice having a father who did things with you. He loved to take us on trips and show us around. He was fun to be with.

Lenore: We had long intellectual conversations. My father lectured me about history. I was a captive audience. I was so impressed. He was my idol.

Feelings of pity for the fathers were also common. With few exceptions, the daughters seemed more tolerant of their fathers' shortcomings and more forgiving of their failures than they were toward their mothers, or themselves:

Esther: I find that most of my anger is toward my mother rather than my father. I know that is not quite rational, but I can't help feeling that the bond between mother and child ought to be such that a child is assured protection. I somehow do not expect that fathers are as responsible for the welfare of offspring as mothers are.

All of the daughters received favored treatment from their fathers, in the form of gifts, privileges, or exemption from punishments. Many spent long hours in the exclusive company of their fathers, often on adventures which were kept secret from the rest of the family:

Christine: He used to call me his mama-san, and I used to massage his feet. He used to take me to stag bars. I thought that was great. I used to really like him. I was definitely Daddy's girl.

In the special alliance with their fathers, many daughters found the sense of being cared for which they craved, and which they obtained from no other source. The attentions of their fathers offered some compensation for what was lacking in their relations with their mothers.

Mothers were often suspicious and resentful of this special relationship. They perceived, correctly, that what bound father and daughter together was in part a shared hostility toward themselves. The mothers' resentment made the daughters feel guilty, but could not entirely extinguish the pleasure they derived from their favored status. Some even exulted in their mothers' mortification:

Paula: Face it, she was just jealous. The man she loved preferred me!

These daughters, in short, were alienated from their mothers, whom they saw as weak, helpless, and unable to nurture or protect them. They were elevated by their fathers to a special position in the family, in which many of the mothers' duties and privileges were assigned to them. They felt obligated to fulfill this role in order to keep their families together. Moreover, their special relationship with their fathers was often perceived as their only source of affection. Under these circumstances, when their fathers chose to demand sexual services, the daughters felt they had absolutely no option but to comply.

Most of the daughters (80 percent) were under thirteen years of age when their fathers first approached them sexually. The average age was nine (see Table 5.4). The sexual contact was limited at first to fondling and gradually proceeded to masturbation and oral-genital contact. Most fathers did not attempt vaginal intercourse, at least until their daughters had reached puberty. Force was rarely used. It was not necessary:

Yvonne: The first time I remember any sexual advances, I was about four or five. I hadn't started school yet. My parents were having a party—that is, my mother was entertaining some women. My father took my brother and me to bed to be out of the way. My brother lay on one side of him, me on the other. I re-

Table 5.4. Incest histories

History	Number	Percentage
Child's age at onset		
< 5	4	10
5–6	5	12.5
7–8	8	20
9–10	9	22.5
11–12	4	10
13 +	8	20
Unknown (< 13)	2	5
Mean	9.4	
Duration		
Single incident	7	17.5
0–2 years	13	32.5
3–5 years	8	20
> 5 years	9	22.5
Unknown	3	7.5
Mean	3.3	
Repetition with sisters		
Yes	11	27.5
Unknown	10	25
No	6	15
No available sisters	13	32.5
Secrecy broken with child at home		
Yes	17	42.5
No	23	57.5
Mean duration before secrecy broken		3.8 years
Agency intervention		
Yes	3	7.5
No	37	92.5
Court intervention		
Yes	3	7.5
No	37	92.5

member him curling up beside me, pressing me to him from behind and touching my vagina. I also remember him playing with
my ass. I only remember lying there and him telling me that was
what Adam and Eve did, so it was okay.

Those authors who restrict their definition of incest to intercourse find
that the daughters are somewhat older, on the average, at the onset of
the relationship. In Maisch's study, the average age of the daughter was
12¼ at the time intercourse began.[21] Other researchers who define incest, as we do, to mean any sexual contact find, as we do, that most relationships begin when the children are grade-schoolers. The girls in one
study were five to fourteen years old; those in another were between the
ages of six and fourteen.[22]

The father's explanations to our informants, if any were offered, always sounded silly in retrospect. Younger girls were told, "This is how
we learn about the birds and the bees," "This is our special game," or
"Don't you want to make Daddy feel good?" Older girls were told, "I'm
getting you ready for your husband," "You should feel comfortable about
sex," or "You need me to teach you the facts of life." Many of the fathers
seemed to consider it their parental prerogative to introduce their
daughters to sex.

Sometimes the sexual encounter took on the aspect of an initiation
rite. By introducing their daughters into secret and forbidden knowledge, the fathers compelled their daughters to leave girlhood behind and
taught them something about their place in the world as women:

> *Jackie:* That was the year I grew up. I got my period, and I gave
> up my dolls and stopped being a tomboy.
>
> *Sara:* As a child I thought, why would someone that I love and
> who loves me do anything wrong to me. There seemed to be no
> other answer but ... this is natural, and this is the way it is. I
> thought maybe, just maybe, this was my personal indoctrination
> into womanhood.[23]

Seven of the daughters could remember only a single incident in
which they were molested by their fathers. But the majority recalled that
once begun, the sexual contact was repeated whenever the father could
find an opportunity. On the average, the incestuous relationship went on

for three years. Other studies agree that the majority of incestuous relationships are of long duration.[24]

Although many of our informants were too young to have a clear idea of the significance of the father's behavior, the father's furtive attitude usually indicated to the daughters that there was something wrong with what they were doing:

> *Lenore:* When I was around seven, that's when the first sexual incident happened with my father. They used to have us kids in bed with them sometimes, and he continued this after mother was in the hospital. I got more favored attention. One time he called me in. He had a hard on and he had a rubber on. He told me to jerk him off. He told me to squeeze it and he came. I was a pretty innocent kid, pretty isolated. I didn't know what it was. I can't remember whether he told me not to tell, but it was intense and hurried and he was ashamed. He sent me away right after he came. I knew he would deny it, but I have a vivid memory of it.

Few of the daughters had anything positive to say about the sexual contact itself. Though many enjoyed other aspects of their special relationship with their fathers, most dreaded the sexual encounters and invented whatever pitiful strategies they could to avoid them:

> *Rita:* I hated it all the time; it was like a nightmare. There was nothing I could do. I went along with the program. I don't know why he went along with it, because I never responded. Every time I'd say, "Daddy, I gotta go pee." You know, anything to get out of it.

Fear, disgust, and shame were the feelings most commonly remembered. Most of the daughters coped with the sexual episodes by mentally dissociating themselves from them. They "froze up" or pretended that "it wasn't really happening":

> *Sheila:* My head just died then. It was an impossible thing for me to handle, so I just didn't handle it. It's like it never happened. Every time I try to talk about it, my mind goes blank. It's like everything explodes in my head.

A few informants remembered that they had experienced some pleasure in the sexual encounters, or that they had sometimes initiated the contact once the routine of the sexual relationship had become established. These memories only exacerbated their feelings of confusion and shame:

> *Paula:* With my father, I was the aggressor. He'd come in my bed and cuddle me and eat me; then he'd threaten me not to tell. He loved me very much. He just had a sickness. He was a good man in every other way. He went to church and worked six days a week. Maybe I did go up to my father and cuddle him, but I was a child; you don't make anything of it.

In these few instances, the fathers might have been able to convince themselves that their daughters desired and enjoyed their sexual attentions. But in most cases, the fathers persisted in their sexual demands even in the face of their daughters' obvious reluctance. Why they chose to do so is a matter of speculation. Presumably, they experienced their own needs as so compelling that they chose to ignore their daughters' unhappiness.

Some researchers who have studied incestuous fathers directly emphasize the father's unfulfilled dependent wishes and fear of abandonment. In the father's fantasy life, the daughter becomes the source of all the father's infantile longings for nurturance and care. He thinks of her first as the idealized childhood bride or sweetheart, and finally as the all-good, all-giving mother. The reality, that she is the child and he the adult, becomes quite immaterial to him. In the compulsive sexual act he seeks repeated reassurance that she will never refuse or frustrate him.[25]

In addition, the father must experience the sexual act itself as powerfully rewarding. He can structure the sexual encounter exactly to his liking, with no fear that his performance will be judged or ridiculed. His excitement is heightened by the need for secrecy and the sense of indulging in the forbidden. The sexual contact becomes like an addiction, one which, unlike alcohol or other drugs, leaves no morning hangover other than possibly a guilty conscience. The incestuous father can indulge his habit repeatedly and suffer no bodily consequences; if there are any, it is the daughter who suffers them.

Finally, in some cases the daughter's unhappiness actually contributes to the father's enjoyment. Many researchers have noted that incest, like other sex crimes, fulfills the offender's hostile and aggressive wishes. Power and dominance, rather than sexual pleasure, may be the primary motivation. One researcher, who administered psychological tests to convicted incest offenders, concluded that the incest was an expression of hostility to all women, and that the daughter was selected as the victim because she was perceived as the woman least capable of retaliation.[26]

Most of our informants were warned not to tell anyone about the sexual episodes. They were threatened with the most dreadful consequences if they told: their mothers would have a nervous breakdown, their parents would divorce, their fathers would be put in jail, or they themselves would be punished and sent away from home. One way or another, the girls were given to understand that breaking secrecy would lead to separation from one or both of their parents. Those who remembered no warnings simply intuited that guarding the incest secret was part of their obligation to keep the family together:

> *Janet:* I just knew there would be dire consequences if I told. My mother would fall apart, or they would separate. I didn't even want to imagine what would happen.

In some cases, the fathers threatened severe bodily harm:

> *Maggie:* He told me if I told anyone he would have me shot. I believed him because he was a cop. I'm thirty years old and I'm still afraid of him.

The majority of the daughters (58 percent) never explicitly told their mothers, or anyone else, of the incest as long as they remained at home. Nevertheless, they longed for their mothers to come to their rescue. Often they tried, indirectly, to indicate to their mothers that something was wrong. Many had vague symptoms of distress: they complained of abdominal pains or pain while urinating; they became fearful or withdrawn; they had nightmares. Such "nonspecific" symptoms are typical of incestuously abused children, in the observations of many clinicians.[27] A few of our informants as children developed compulsive, ritualized sexual behaviors that would have alerted any knowledgeable observer to the fact that something was wrong. For instance, one girl, at the age of five, began approaching male acquaintances and unzipping their pants. Others "experimented" sexually with younger children, subjecting them to the same assaults to which they themselves had been subjected. These and numerous other indirect cries for help were ignored or misunderstood by the mothers. Many daughters believed that their mothers knew, or should have known, about the incest, and they bitterly resented the fact that their mothers did not intervene:

> *Sheila:* One day she was at work, and she was so worried that something really bad was happening at home that she actually left work and came home. When she got home, I was locked in the bathroom crying, and I remember her saying to my father, "What's the matter with her?" I guess I have a hard time reconciling the fact that that happened and she still didn't realize I was in trouble. How come she never asked *me* what was happening to me? How come she never tried to find out how *I* felt?

> *Christine:* My mother's philosophy is to ignore things and hope they'll go away. She's always a victim; even in little things she always finds stupid reasons why she can't do anything about the situation. She knew about the incest; there's no way she couldn't have known. But she's never acknowledged it. She just says men are that way and there's nothing she could do about it.

Those daughters who did confide in their mothers were uniformly disappointed in their mothers' responses. Most of the mothers, even when made aware of the situation, were unwilling or unable to defend their daughters. They were too frightened or too dependent upon their husbands to risk a confrontation. Either they refused to believe their daughters, or they believed them but took no action. They made it clear to their daughters that their fathers came first and that, if necessary, the daughters would have to be sacrificed:

> *Yvonne:* The last time my father made these advances I was about eight or nine. My mom caught us again and my dad promised he wouldn't do it again. Then he got very drunk, went outside, and lay under a tree at night. My mom woke me up and told me my dad was drunk under the tree and wouldn't come in. She wanted me to ask him to come in before he got pneumonia. I got up, went out on the porch—it was damp and cool out—and did as my mother asked. I asked my dad to come in. He did. I decided after that that they were both pretty nuts.

Only three mothers, on learning about the incest, responded by separating from their husbands, and even in these few cases the separations were brief. The mothers found life without their husbands too hard to bear, and they took them back within a matter of months. Three other mothers, on discovering the incest secret, sent their daughters away from home:

> *Paula:* She was afraid I'd become a lesbian or a whore. So she put me in a mental hospital. It was a good excuse to get rid of me.

In general, those daughters who told their mothers had reason to regret it. Sensing correctly that no protection would be forthcoming if they told, most of the daughters bore the incestuous relationship in silence, biding their time until they were old enough to leave home.

Some of the daughters developed close relationships with adult women outside the family, which partially compensated for their disappointment with their mothers. Though few dared to confide their secrets to these outsiders, the relationships helped the daughters to endure the misery of their family life:

> *Marion:* My mother's sister was the only person in my childhood that I remember relating to at all. She lived on a farm with her three children, and I used to go there in the summer. I love the outdoors and that is where I would play most of the time. I never stayed at home if I could help it. I didn't tell her about my Dad, but we talked about Mom and how funny she acted sometimes. She said if I knew how they had been brought up, I would understand. She never explained it. I remember wishing she was my mother.

> *Sandra:* My best friend's mother used to take me in when my mother threw me out. If it weren't for her, I'd be sleeping in hallways. Anyone with half a brain and half a heart would open their doors, but not too many really do it. I was well off there; I lived with them till I had my first labor pains. Marriage was a change for the worse. I wish I'd stayed with them.

The girls who found surrogate mothers were among the most fortunate. All of the women longed for a mother who could be strong, competent, and affectionate. Many desperately envied their friends and classmates who appeared to have normal mothers:

Lenore: When I hear other women complaining about their mothers, I feel like screaming, "You stupid idiot, don't you realize how lucky you are?"

Some of the daughters expressed their disappointment in both parents by elaborating the fantasy that they were adopted and that their true parents would one day find and rescue them. Others simply resigned themselves to the fact that, from an emotional point of view, they were orphans:

Janet: I remember very clearly at age nine I decided that if they did get divorced, I didn't want to live with either one of them.

As the daughters reached adolescence, they often became more assertive and rebellious. The fathers responded with intense jealousy, bordering on paranoia. They did whatever they could to seclude and isolate their daughters and to prevent them from developing normal relationships with peers. They saw the outside world as filled with sexual dangers and opportunities, and they often regarded their daughters as untrustworthy little bitches who needed to be closely guarded. Many daughters reported that their fathers would tear up their clothes, forbid lipstick or makeup, and refuse to allow parties or dates:

Sheila: He would raise the roof because of the clothing that I wore or how I looked. I think I was the last kid in my whole group to start wearing lipstick. I didn't really understand what it was all about. All I knew was my father was telling me I was very bad for some reason and it all involved *that.*

Other fathers eventually accepted the inevitable and permitted their daughters to have some social life, but insisted on interrogating their daughters about their sexual activities:

Lenore: He would tell me not to throw myself away on some boy and sacrifice my intellect. I got the message loud and clear that you can't be sexual and have your intellect too. Later I realized that he wanted to keep me for himself. I was Daddy's little girl. When I hit high school, around age fifteen, I started screwing around a lot. I had been so isolated I never made friends. This seemed like an easy way to make contact with people. As soon as my father found out, he would find an excuse to beat the crap out of me. It happened whenever I had a new boyfriend. Supposedly his attitude was very libertarian. He wanted to hear about what I was doing. He was kind of lecherous about it.

As the fathers' jealousy and sexual demands became more and more intolerable, the daughters began to try to escape from the family. Thirteen girls ran away from home at least once (see Table 5.5). Most of the attempts were short-lived, for the girls quickly realized that they were not equipped to survive in the street, and they reluctantly returned home. Only two girls managed to make good their escape. From mid-adolescence, they supported themselves as strippers or prostitutes:

> *Paula:* I ran away to New York. I was on my own at age sixteen. I never had a pimp; I wasn't that crazy. I knew a lot of women in the business and I did a lot of speed and downs. If I hadn't met up with my boyfriend, I'd be dead today.

Three girls who ran away were pursued, caught, and committed to hospitals on "stubborn child" complaints. Their incest history did not come to light during these hospitalizations. Three others tried to get away from home by requesting foster placements or admission to residential schools. They, too, were unsuccessful:

> *Esther:* The way I was able to get away from my father was by running away with an older man. Before that I had tried to get professional help with the aim of being placed in a girls' residence. I had several sessions with a social worker to whom I was unable to reveal the reason for my intense desire to leave home. She met with my father, and she was favorably impressed with his great love and concern for me. She refused to help me gain admittance at that girls' residence.

Just as the girls' childhood distress symptoms had been ignored, their adolescent escape attempts were misunderstood. None of the professionals with whom these girls came into contact undertook to find out why they were so desperate to get away from their families.

Sooner or later, most of the daughters realized that the only way to escape from their fathers was to find another powerful male protector. A

Table 5.5. Distress symptoms in incest victims and comparison group

Distress symptom	Incest victims		Comparison group	
	No. = 40	%	No. = 20	%
Adolescent pregnancy[a]				
Yes	18	45	3	15
No	22	55	17	85
Runaway attempt				
Yes	13	32.5	1	5
No	27	67.5	19	95
Major depressive symptoms				
Yes	24	60	11	55
No	16	40	9	45
Sucide attempt				
Yes	15	37.5	1	5
No	25	62.5	19	95
Drug or alcohol abuse				
Yes	8	35	1	5
No	32	65	19	95
Sexual problems				
Yes	21	55	10	50
No	19	45	10	50
Promiscuity				
Yes	14	35	3	15
No	26	65	17	85
Victimization				
Yes (rape)	6	15	3	15
(beatings[a])	11	27.5	0	0
No	24	60	17	85
Self-image[b]				
Predominantly +	3	7.5	2	10
Dual or confused ±	13	32.5	16	80
Predominantly –	24	60	2	10

a. Differences between the two groups were significant at the p < .05 level
b. Differences between the two groups were significant at the p < .02 level

great many became pregnant or married prematurely. Eighteen of the forty women (45 percent) became pregnant during adolescence. In most cases, they had no particular desire for children, and the pregnancies were unintended. Planned or not, however, the pregnancies usually did put an end to the incest.[28]

For many of the daughters, marriage appeared to be the passport to freedom. Some confessed the incest secret for the first time to their husbands or fiancés. A number of the men responded in a very caring and appropriate manner: they were angry at the fathers and concerned about the harm that had been done to the daughters. Women who were lucky enough to find men who responded in this way usually felt extremely grateful.

As the fathers felt their daughters slipping out of their control, they began to cast about for substitutes. If there were younger sisters in the family, the fathers often transferred their sexual attentions to them. In eleven families (28 percent), incest was repeated with younger sisters. In another ten families (25 percent), the daughters suspected that their sisters had been molested but could not be positive about it. In one third of the families, there was no repetition of the incest because there were no available sisters. The phenomenon of the father's "moving on" to a younger daughter has been observed by many authors, some of whom report even higher proportions of families in which this occurs.[29]

Brothers were not molested, according to our informants. However, a number of brothers were physically abused, and several developed assaultive and abusive behavior in identification with their fathers. One of the daughters was molested by her brother as well as her father; she felt that her father, in breaching the incest taboo, had given her brother tacit permission to do the same. Others suspected that their brothers were carrying on the family tradition in the next generation:

> *Marion:* In all your research do you think it's inherited? I hate to say this, but I think my brother has the problem. I remember we had a cottage at the ocean when his little girl was three or four. I caught them in bed one time when we were all supposed to be gone. I saw him fondling her and it made me sick. After that I saw very little of him until recently. He has two granddaughters now. I feel he's abnormally proud of the one; I can't explain it, but it's there. This I have never told anyone.

In several families, the fathers deserted once the daughters had left home. This outcome confirmed the daughters' belief that they had been responsible for keeping the family together, and that the parents' marriage depended upon the incestuous relationship for its survival.

In no case was the incestuous relationship ended by the father. The daughters put a stop to the sexual contact as soon as they could, by whatever means they could. But most felt that in their fathers' minds, the incestuous affair never ended, and that their fathers would gladly resume the sexual relationship if they were ever given an opportunity. Though all the daughters eventually succeeded in escaping from their families, they felt, even at the time of the interview, that they would never be safe with their fathers, and that they would have to defend themselves as long as their fathers lived.

6

The Daughter's Inheritance

My father had forever deserted me, leaving me only memories which set an eternal barrier between me and my fellow creatures ... [His] unlawful and detestable passion had poured its poison into my ears, and changed all my blood, so that it was no longer the kindly stream that supports life but a cold fountain of bitterness corrupted in its very source. It must be the excess of madness that could make me imagine that I could ever be aught but one alone; struck off from humanity; bearing no affinity to man or woman; a wretch on whom Nature had set her ban. —*Mary Wollstonecraft Shelley*, Mathilda, *1819*

Many years had passed in the lives of our informants since their incestuous relationships had ended. All of the women we interviewed had been living on their own for several years, and many had raised families of their own. All had attempted, as best they could, to put their incest experiences behind them and to get on with their lives. But the memory of incest persisted, shaping their relations with others and their image of themselves. All, without exception, felt somehow branded or marked by their experiences:

Marion: How do you get over this? I know it eats away at your very gut level. I think I have forgotten it until some little thing reminds me. Then I relive it again.

The most common complaint was a feeling of being set apart from other people. Many of the women described themselves as "different" or stated that they knew they could never be "normal," even though they might appear so to others. The sense of being an outsider, cut off from ordinary human intercourse, often reached extreme proportions:

Yvonne: I felt like no one would ever want a girl who had something wrong with her, like me.

Christine: I used to think because I'm so different, I must be special, there must be something God had planned for me. I used to feel superior to everyone. I needed that, because I didn't have any friends.

Sandra: I used to think I was one step beyond . . . in another world from the others. I dreamed once about a little girl who fell under the bed. They looked for her but they couldn't find her. She was in another dimension. She was upset and crying. She screamed, but nobody heard.

Many women made an explicit connection between their feelings of isolation and the incest secret. Although they had been helpless as children to prevent the incest, they nevertheless felt that they had committed an unpardonable sin which left them permanently stigmatized. The feelings of shame did not dissolve easily once the incestuous "affair" had ended but persisted into adult life. Many women felt that what set them apart from others was their own evilness. With depressing regularity, these women referred to themselves as bitches, witches, and whores. The incest secret formed the core of their identity:

Yvonne: I feel the relationship between me and my father was wrong, and that it has colored the whole of my life. It left me feeling bad and unworthy to live a normal life.

Marion: You just feel dirty inside.

Sandra: I'm nothing but a little dressed-up whore.

Some women even embraced their identity as sinners with a kind of defiance and pride. As initiates into forbidden sexual knowledge, they felt themselves to possess almost magical powers, particularly the power to attract men. They seemed to believe that they had seduced their fathers and could therefore seduce any man:

Sandra: There's nothing I haven't done! I'll see how far I can go leading a guy on. I have the upper hand in the situation. I get them to the point where they say, "I love you." Then I say, "Chalk another one up."

So spoke a woman who in reality was repeatedly beaten, exploited, and deserted by her lovers. Her boastfulness served as a defense against feelings of utter helplessness. The belief that she was possessed of a diabolical power which drove men mad and caused them to mistreat her was easier to bear than the humiliation of powerlessness.

Several other women also spoke of feeling that they had extraordinary powers over others, especially sexual powers over men, and destructive powers over both men and women. One woman described herself as a "bad witch" and expressed the fear that she could cause other people to sicken with her thoughts. These fantasies uniformly dated back to the incestuous situation in childhood. In part they represented a defense against the feeling, which these women had so often experienced, of being dominated and overwhelmed by their fathers. In part they were expressions of the sense of specialness and privilege which they had derived from being their fathers' favorites. Finally, these fantasies represented the reality that for many years these women had had the potential power to destroy their families. As guardians of the incest secret, they had been warned time and again that they could bring disaster upon their families by revealing what they knew. All children, no doubt, have fantasies of secret powers that could be used to destroy their parents. Few children, however, are in possession of knowledge that could make this fantasy come true.

In addition, the fantasy of having extraordinary ability to attract men often received some confirmation in reality, for many women had learned that men found their incest histories sexually exciting. Seven women had been sexually approached by other relatives as well as their fathers. It was as though, even without explicitly revealing the incest secret, the fathers had communicated to other family members that their daughters were the object of special sexual interest. The experiences of repeated molestation simply confirmed in the daughters' minds the belief that they must have unconsciously "asked for it." Once free of their fathers, many women had learned that their incest histories could be used to attract male attention. One woman made an explicit connection between her use of the incest history to entice lovers and the prostitute's manipulation of male fantasy to excite her "johns":

Christine: Every time guys found out about it, it turned them on. I'll never know why. I read this book about a Victorian prostitute, Nell Kimball. She talked about how her customers always wanted to know how she got into the trade. They didn't want to hear the real nitty-gritty story. They wanted to hear something horrible, how she was used, how she was led astray. I guess even then men were turned on by their own cruelty.

The feeling of being malignantly marked, of being placed outside the covenant of normal social intercourse, caused many of the women intense pain. They complained bitterly of loneliness, which they recognized as partly of their own making:

> Yvonne: I often feel depressed for no apparent reason and have trouble letting the people I'm with know me and get really close to me. I never share my innermost thoughts and pain with anyone.
>
> Vivian: I put a vault around myself.

Sixty percent (25) of the incest victims complained of major depressive symptoms in adult life. Thirty-eight percent became so depressed at some point in their lives that they attempted suicide (see Table 5.5). Twenty percent had times when they became alcoholic or drug-dependent. Most described their drug abuse episodes as ineffective attempts to cope with feelings of loneliness and depression. Several women had despaired of human understanding and sought comfort only in a personal relationship with God. One woman felt so sinful that she would not enter a church. She felt that the church, as a human institution, had rejected her, but she wrote private letters to God. Another woman briefly entered a convent, hoping that the nuns would be able to discover and exorcise her hidden evilness. She left disappointed, for no one perceived her inner turmoil:

> Sheila: I wasn't afraid of God's judgment. I thought, "Well, He knows. He's the *only* one who knows what I feel like inside." He was the only one I ever talked to. It was the people in this world that I just couldn't open up to.

The isolation these women felt was compounded by their own difficulty in forming trusting relationships. The legacy of their childhood was a feeling of having been profoundly betrayed by both parents. As a result, they came to expect abuse and disappointment in all intimate relationships: to be abandoned, as they felt their mothers had abandoned them, or to be exploited, as their fathers had exploited them. Given these possibilities, most women opted for exploitation.

At the same time that these women had little hope of attaining a rewarding relationship with anyone, they desperately longed for the nurturance and care which they had not received in childhood. Thus they often made desperate attempts to capture even a fleeting feeling of closeness and warmth. Their experience with their fathers had taught them that sex was the one sure way of getting attention. Many women had developed a repertoire of sexually stylized behavior which appealed to their fathers, and it usually worked on other men as well.[1] The incest experience had left them feeling that they were good for little else besides sex. The result was often a series of brief, unsatisfying sexual relationships. One third (35 percent) of the women had periods in their lives when they were sexually promiscuous, by their own definition of the word. Many oscillated between periods of compulsive sexual activity and periods of asceticism and abstinence.

When these women did form lasting love relationships, they were often stormy and tormented. Never having learned to protect themselves, they seemed to have a predilection for men who were at best aloof and unreliable, and at worst frankly exploitative:

> *Christine:* Sometimes my husband would rape me. That might sound odd, but sometimes he'd rape me. He took advantage of me cleaning the house. He took advantage of my money. He wanted me to sell myself for extra money. He pressured me so much; he made me feel so guilty, like I was such a square, I wasn't with it, I wasn't hip, because I didn't want to do it with just any guy. It would shock me. He also wanted me to go to bed with other guys so he could watch. I did do that a few times. I felt stupid because I knew better, but I was in love with him.

At the time they were interviewed, twenty-five of the forty women (63 percent) had been married at least once, and fourteen (35 percent) were still married. Very few, however, were reasonably contented in marriage. Their most common complaint was the feeling that their husbands did not really value or respect them. Many women felt obliged to be grateful to their husbands for marrying them at all, knowing that they had already been used by their fathers. By admitting their husbands into the knowledge of the incest secret, they ceded a great deal of power to their husbands, for the secret could be used to shame them and put them in their place.

Other women complained that they seemed unable to choose husbands or lovers whom they themselves respected. As one informant put it, "I'm better off with a bum. I can handle that situation." Another woman made a direct connection between her incest experience and her unhappy marriage:

> *Esther:* I married at a very young age, and I have regretted it ever since. Nevertheless, I have so far found it impossible to leave my husband. He is a man whom most people regard as beneath me. He is unable to hold a job or to support the family. I have been the only significant parent in my children's lives. I see a clear and definite relationship between my incestuous relationship and my need to punish myself by staying with a man who is such a drain on my life.

Eleven women repeatedly endured beatings from their husbands or lovers. In many cases, they seemed to feel that they deserved to be beaten:

> *Yvonne:* My husband and I weren't getting along at all. He started hitting me—at my provocation, so we deduce.
>
> *Paula:* Our fights were incredible. I had black eyes. Sometimes I deserved it. I have a mouth.

Having seen their mothers beaten, the incest victims seemed to take it for granted that their men would mistreat them and that they would have to put up with it. A number of women tolerated extremes of abuse in their marriages, and took steps to protect themselves only when their lives were clearly in danger. An association between a history of incestuous abuse and later victimization has also been reported by Rainbow Retreat, a shelter for battered women in Phoenix, Arizona. Twenty three percent of their clients had had a sexual encounter with a parent or a close relative before age fifteen.[2]

Six of our forty informants had been raped as well as beaten. Three had been raped more than once. In some cases, the women had been clearly placed at greater than ordinary risk for rape by the incestuous family situation. Two women, for instance, had been raped during runaway episodes, when they were wandering the streets:

> *Lenore:* I was raped the first time at age fifteen. I was taken to a hospital because I had been cut. My parents were out of town. It was during one of my runaway attempts. The police were very hostile after they saw I had underwear and a package of pills in my purse. I didn't want my parents called but they had to, and then I had to tell them the story. They didn't believe me. My stepmother did at first, but my father never did. It happened again after I left home. I got raped and some teeth were knocked out. I had to ask for money for the dental bills. Again they didn't believe it; they thought my boyfriend did it. My father told my brother and sister I was so obnoxious I probably deserved it.

Although the incidence of rape among these women seems quite high, it may not in fact be significantly different from the incidence in the general population of women. Estimates of the incidence of rape vary greatly, depending upon what is included in the definition. In one study of college students, for example, 24 percent of the women reported they had had a "forced sexual experience" after the age of twelve.[3] More striking than the actual incidence of rape among our informants was their attitude toward being raped. Only the minority felt angry. Most reacted to the assaults as if they were deserved punishments. One woman, who was raped by a man whom she had picked up at a bar, married her assailant a week after the attack.

Though many of these women did not express overt anger about the ways they were mistreated, the repeated instances of abuse deepened their distrust of other people and increased their isolation still further. Thus a vicious cycle was created, for with each disappointment, the women grew more embittered and yet more desperate for closeness and understanding. Few women had the opportunity to learn from their mistakes; rather, they seemed doomed to repeat them.

In spite of repeated mistreatment, the majority of the incest victims did not express a great deal of hostility toward men. Most of them occasionally lapsed into complaints, expressing sentiments such as, "Men are no damn good" and "They only want one thing":

> *Stephanie:* When I ride the bus, I look at all the men and think, "All they want to do is stick their pricks into little girls."

Only three women, however, expressed a predominantly hostile or fearful attitude toward men, or avoided men entirely.

The majority of the incest victims, in fact, tended to overvalue and idealize men. In their pursuit of sexual intimacy, they sought to recapture the specialness that they had felt in the relationship with their fathers. Many had affairs with much older or married men, in which they relived the secrecy and excitement of the incestuous relationship. As the "other woman," however, they had little power to define the terms of the relationship, and they had to content themselves with lovers who were capricious and often unavailable. Some of the women seemed to feel that it was only natural to be completely dominated by the men they loved. In submitting to their lovers, they attempted to fulfill their unsatisfied childhood longings for protection and care. One woman described her lover explicitly as a parent:

> *Anne-Marie:* He has me hypnotized. He has power over me. I feel like I'm addicted; I have to see him. He seems like he's ten feet tall. He's a tower of strength. He says I should take care of myself; he buttons up my coat collar for me. I feel that he loves me like a mother and father.

Whatever anger these women did feel was most commonly directed at women rather than at men. With the exception of those who had become conscious feminists, most of the incest victims seemed to regard all women, including themselves, with contempt. At times, remembering their privileged position as their fathers' favorites, they exempted themselves from their general condemnation of women. In adult life, their only possible source of self-esteem was to maintain an identification with their powerful fathers. But more often, on a deeper level, they identified with the mothers they despised, and included themselves among the ranks of fallen and worthless women.

The incest victims' hostility to women generally prevented the development of supportive female friendships. Women were seen as potential rivals who would betray their friends for a man, as vicious gossips, or simply as empty, inadequate people who had nothing to offer.

For many of the incest victims, the overt hostility toward women masked a deeper longing for a relationship with a caring woman. This longing was rarely expressed, for most of the informants had simply despaired of having any sort of satisfactory relationship with a woman. Some of the informants did express a fantasy of finding an idealized

female protector and teacher, a woman worthy of emulation and respect:

> *Regina:* I wish I could meet an older woman, about fifty, some-
> one who had been through a lot but was really a wise woman, the
> kind of woman my mother never was. Just knowing she was there,
> I'd feel better.

A small minority of the incest victims experimented with lesbian relationships. In these relationships, they expressed their intense desire for
female nurturance and their wish that sexual relations could be mutually
satisfying rather than exploitative:

> *Sandra:* Everyone's waiting for me to go gay again. Saturday
> night I went to a gay bar with my old girlfriend. I hadn't done it
> since I was nineteen. At first I was very apprehensive, but once I
> was there, nothing shocked me. I felt comfortable and I had a
> good time. Maybe they're not sick. I feel more in common with
> them, they have better relationships. If I didn't have three kids, I
> would do it.

Other researchers have commented on the possible connection between a history of incest and the later development of a lesbian identity.
In one clinical study, over a third of the incest victims developed a lesbian orientation.[4] A nationwide survey of 225 lesbian women conducted
by another psychologist found that a significantly higher proportion of
these women reported childhood rape or molestation, compared with a
matched control group of heterosexual women.[5] Our study does not bear
out this connection, at least not in terms of numbers. Only two of the
forty incest victims developed a confirmed lesbian identity. Three others
considered themselves bisexual. The vast majority of the victims remained steadfastly, even doggedly heterosexual. Yet the two women who
did become lesbians felt strongly that their incest experience had influenced their sexual orientation. They believed, moreover, that in developing a lesbian identity, they had to some degree mastered their childhood traumas and achieved a healthier and more rewarding personal life
than would otherwise have been possible:

> *Lenore:* I feel I would have been bisexual—I think everybody is,
> naturally—but for the shit from my father. It made it impossible

for me to relate to men sexually. I found myself in relations with men casting myself in the role of a sickie. As soon as I was with a man, I would become crazy and fall apart. The men reinforced it. This was a direct product of my father's little messages. I don't repeat that with a woman, or if I do, I can stop it and control it.

For these women, development of a lesbian identity seemed to be an adaptive and positive way of coming to terms with the incest trauma.[6]

Regardless of sexual object choice, over half (55 percent) of the incest victims complained of impairments in sexual enjoyment. Many of the informants reported that their pleasure in sex was minimal or even entirely absent. The memory of incest was intrusive and often paralyzing. Some women complained of disturbing "flashbacks," or memories of the incestuous sexual acts, in the midst of their love-making:

> *Janet:* For a long time, I couldn't make love at all. Steve would approach me, and I'd remember my father. I'd cry all the time. I couldn't stand for him to come near me. Even now, whenever I feel pushed into making love, or even if it's my idea, if he starts making moves that remind me of my father, I have to stop. I tell myself it's not my father, it's Steve, it's all right, but it's not all right.

Others so thoroughly associated sex with the feeling of being dominated and controlled that they were unable to relax:

> *Lenore:* I had a lot of sexual problems too. I thought I was fucked up not to have orgasms. I was depressed about it and would make a big confession about how I couldn't have an orgasm. I was afraid to lose control. That was my father's whole trip: if you're sexual, you lose control, you lose yourself and become that person's slave. So I would never allow myself to have orgasms. I'm still pretty tense about sex. I think it is a direct consequence of the scene I grew up in.

In spite of their unhappiness in their personal lives, the women who had survived incestuous abuse displayed some impressive strengths. Accustomed to hard work and responsibility since childhood, many became highly disciplined, dedicated, productive workers. Even in adverse circumstances, their accomplishments were often remarkable. One woman, who had been self-supporting from the age of fifteen, put herself through college and a doctoral program. Another was a well-known figure in local politics while she held down two jobs, represented her union, and paid for the education of her younger sisters and brothers. A third, the mother of five children, not only held down a full-time factory job but also organized most of the charity and social acivities in her neighborhood. A fourth ran her own small business while raising two children alone. The work achievements of these women were all the more noteworthy in contrast to their generally unrewarding personal lives.

In adult life, a great number of the incest victims also continued the caretaking role that had been imposed upon them in childhood. Several provided a home and refuge for their younger sisters, or took in runaway teenagers or other homeless children. Many dedicated themselves to raising children with the determination that their sons and daughters would not have to suffer what they themselves had suffered:

> *Esther:* Part of my reason for marrying was my desire to have children so that I could be a better mother than mine was.

A number of the incest victims expressed the feeling that only their work and their obligations to their children kept them anchored to life:

> *Marion:* I really think my work has helped me more than anything. I love people and I listen to all their problems, and through the years I guess I felt my problem wasn't any worse than others. I'm really a workaholic. I loved my work and had my shop in my home so I could provide a good home for my two children. I always was there when they came home from school and always had well-balanced meals for them. They felt secure. I did get into some terrible trouble in marriage, but I think I did right in putting my children first and getting out.

In spite of their devotion, many of the incest victims who became mothers were tormented by the fear that they would be bad mothers to their children, as they felt their mothers had been to them:

> *Paula:* I want to be a good mother and also party it up. There are two sides of me. I feel very guilty because I yell at my kid sometimes. If I put her through what my mother put me through, I'll kill myself.

Many set for themselves highly unrealistic standards of parental conduct; and when, inevitably, they failed to meet these standards, they felt worthless and intensely guilty. Emulation of the image of perfect sainted motherhood offered the only alternative to the identity of the fallen woman or wicked stepmother. It was as though the incest victims lacked any internal representation of an adequate, satisfactory mother, and could only imagine either the ideal mother they wished they had had or the neglectful mother of their childhood experience.

In addition to the fear that they would be bad mothers to their children, many of the incest victims had a more specific fear that they would not be able to protect their daughters from sexual abuse. Very few were able to trust any man, including their husbands and lovers, around their daughters:

> *Esther:* Recently, a lover of many years married another woman after I turned him down. My reasons are varied and complex, but probably the most significant reason is the fact that I have two pretty teenage daughters, and I feared to bring a man into the house who might possibly take advantage of them. Realistically speaking, this is very unlikely—the man in question is a highly ethical and very kind person.

In a few instances, these fears were well founded. Several women married men who were physically abusive toward their children, and one woman married a man who was sexually abusive. In addition, three women had episodes in which they themselves became violent with their children. In most cases, however, the mothers' worries and feelings of inadequacy were out of keeping with the reality of the situation. Most were able to protect and care for their children far better than they took care of themselves.

In general, these women rarely enjoyed the benefits of their hard labor or derived much satisfaction from their competence and strength. Capable of moving heaven and earth to serve others, especially their children, they were virtually incapable of fighting on their own behalf:

> *Sandra:* I feel I have a sign on me saying, "Walk all over me." I'm afraid to fight; I could lose. I don't know what my rights are.

Yet these women alone suffered the consequences of their psychological impairments. Almost always, their anger and disappointment were expressed in self-destructive actions: in unwanted pregnancies, in submission to rape and beatings, in addiction to alcohol or drugs, in attempted suicide.

Thus did the victims of incest grow up to become archetypally feminine women: sexy without enjoying sex, repeatedly victimized yet repeatedly seeking to lose themselves in the love of an overpowering man, contemptuous of themselves and of other women, hard-working, giving, and self-sacrificing. Consumed with inner rage, they nevertheless rarely caused trouble to anyone but themselves. In their own flesh, they bore repeated punishment for the crimes committed against them in childhood.

7

Seductive Fathers and Their Families

The attitude of the father contains another element of decisive importance in feminine development. He appears, without being conscious of it, as a seducer, with whose help the girl's aggressive instinctual components are transformed into masochistic ones.
—*Helene Deutsch,* Psychology of Women, *1944*

Twenty women whose fathers had been seductive, but not overtly incestuous, told us their stories. Their class, ethnic, and religious backgrounds were similar to those of the incest victims whom we interviewed (see Table 5.1). Like the incest victims, most were young white women in ordinary women's occupations. Like the incest victims, all were patients in psychotherapy.

We defined seductiveness on the part of fathers to mean behavior that was clearly sexually motivated, but which did not involve physical contact or a requirement for secrecy. For example, some fathers constantly talked about sex with their daughters, confiding the details of their love affairs and ceaselessly interrogating their daughters about their own sexual behavior. Others habitually left pornographic materials for their daughters to find. Others exhibited themselves to their daughters or spied upon them while they were undressing. Still others courted their daughters like jealous lovers, bringing them presents of flowers, expensive jewelry, or sexy underwear. Although all these behaviors stopped short of genital contact, they clearly betrayed the fathers' intrusive sexual interest in their daughters, which was a form of covert incest.

We chose to compare these two groups of women for three reasons. First, we consider overt incest to be only the most extreme form of a traditional family pattern. For every girl who has been involved in an incestuous relationship, there are considerably more who have grown up in a covertly incestuous family. In reconstructing a picture of this kind of family, we expected to find many similarities with the families of incest victims, and thus to establish the concept that overt incest represents only the furthest point on a continuum—an exaggeration of patriarchal family norms, but not a departure from them.

The second reason for comparing these two groups of women was our hope of defining family characteristics that seem to increase the risk of overt incest, as well as those characteristics that seem to protect against this development. The final reason for comparing the two groups was to identify specific long-term consequences of incestuous abuse, and to assess the relative harmfulness of overt and covert incest. Since both groups of informants were patients in psychotherapy, differences in their adult psychological functioning could not be attributed to the incest victims' patient status.

Like the incestuous families, the families with seductive fathers had an ordinary appearance. They were often prosperous and highly regarded in their communities. Whatever private troubles they had escaped the detection of friends or neighbors and were certainly unknown to social agencies or the police:

> *Carla:* My parents are very security-conscious, neighbor-conscious. Appearances are everything.

Puritanical and negative sexual attitudes were common in these families, as they were in the incestuous families. Sex was a taboo subject, and sex education was virtually nonexistent. The parental relationship was usually perceived as tense and cold. Physical displays of affection between family members were uncommon and uncomfortable. Bodies, particularly women's bodies, were considered dirty, and great emphasis was often placed on cleanliness, dress, and appearance. The romance between father and daughter flourished, not in the warmth of tolerant and affectionate family life, but in the chilly climate of distrust and scarcity.

Traditional sex roles also seemed to prevail, as they did in the incestuous families. The seductive fathers were in most cases the sole financial support of their families. They were steady workers in offices and factories; they were businessmen and salesmen, physicians and engineers. The mothers occasionally did part-time office work or "helped out" with the family business, but in the main they defined their primary role as wives and homemakers. Marriage was the center of their lives.

As in the incestuous families, the fathers were without question the heads of their households. However, significantly fewer of the fathers felt entitled to resort to violence to enforce their dominant position. Only 20 percent of these daughters, as opposed to 50 percent of the incest victims, reported that their fathers had been habitually violent (see Table 5.3). As seen by their daughters, many of these fathers were quite authoritarian and intimidating. Certainly they had the capacity to rule their families by force, but in contrast to the incestuous fathers, they rarely used it:

> *Mary:* He's a very high-tempered angry man who needs to control everybody. But he also needs to be loved.
>
> *Charlene:* He's a large, bearish man, very righteous and domineering.
>
> *Susan:* My father is very strict and opinionated about morality, very authoritarian, but also very charming.
>
> *Merrill:* He's very overbearing and stubborn. But he's an honest, hard-working, self-made man.

Unlike the incest victims, only one of whom described her father as a "milk toast," many of the daughters of seductive fathers saw their fathers as able to control and restrain their aggression. Some described their fathers as mild-mannered, reserved, gentle, or even meek:

> *Penny:* He's an angel, a thoughtful, soft-spoken, quiet man.

Although the threat of violence was not nearly as extreme in these families, the threat of paternal abandonment loomed in the minds of these daughters, as it did in the minds of the incest victims. The seductive fathers were able to control their families less by intimidation and force, and more by withdrawal and unavailability. Like the incest victims, these daughters saw their fathers as unhappily married and feared that their fathers would desert the family.

Unlike the incestuous fathers, the seductive fathers were often womanizers. They made no secret of their marital dissatisfaction and often made little effort to conceal their extramarital affairs from their wives. If the affairs were kept secret, the favored daughters were privy to the information and in this way were involved in a conspiratorial relationship with their fathers. A few fathers had affairs with very young women during their daughters' adolescence—in two cases, with the daughters' girl-friends.

Like the incestuous fathers, many of the seductive fathers were problem drinkers. In fact, there was no significant difference between the two groups on this point: about 35 percent of the women in both groups thought that their fathers drank excessively. This is a significant finding, for it indicates that intoxication may not be sufficient to explain the incestuous fathers' loss of control. The seductive fathers, though they abused alcohol to the same extent as the incestuous fathers, did not coerce their daughters into an overtly sexual relationship. Nor did they resort to violence against other family members to the same degree as the incestuous fathers.

One can only speculate on the reasons for the seductive fathers' greater self-restraint. It may well be that these men had better developed adult personalities and more highly elaborated inner controls. But since neither group of fathers was interviewed directly, there was no way to confirm such a judgment. It may also be that the controlling factor was not the personality of the fathers, but the personality and social resources of the mothers.

For the daughters of seductive fathers described their mothers very differently from the incest victims. In general, the mothers appeared to be healthier, more assertive, more competent, more socially active, and less isolated than the mothers in incestuous families. Only 15 percent had ever been seriously ill, as compared to 55 percent of the mothers of incest victims. There were no maternal illnesses severe enough to necessitate separation of mother and daughter, and no maternal deaths in this group. The mothers also had fewer pregnancies. The mean number of children in this group of families was 2.85, a number which is not significantly higher than the national average, as compared to 3.6 in the incestuous families. With fewer children to care for, the mothers were less overwhelmed with their household duties, and only one daughter of the twenty was pressed into service as a deputy mother in the family.

Like the mothers of the incest victims, these mothers were described as submissive to their husbands and grimly determined to preserve their marriages at all cost. They did not, however, tolerate the extremes of abuse that the mothers of incest victims did. The mothers put up with verbal denigration and abuse, they managed without respect or affection, and they chose to overlook their husbands' drinking or philandering as long as there was not too much gossip. But they did not put up with beatings, they did not allow themselves to be secluded in their homes, and they did not submit to enforced pregnancy.

Because they were better able to protect themselves, these mothers seemed to be better able to protect their daughters from overt sexual abuse. This was true in spite of the fact that in most cases, the mother-daughter relationship was marked by deep estrangement. From the daughters' point of view, at least, there was little affection, cooperation, or trust between mother and daughter. Many of these informants, like the incest victims, described their mothers as implacably cold and hostile:

> *Mary:* My mother was an ice maiden, cold, ungiving. She had condemned me to hell.

> *Molly:* My mother never touched me. I have no memory of ever being kissed by her. I knew she never wanted me in the first place.

> *Beth:* She's the family's self-appointed martyr and sufferer: "Everything happens to me." In fact she is sick a lot, and I've always tried to please her and take care of her, but she's never satisfied. My sister was her favorite. She was Miss Goody-two-shoes. In my mother's eyes, she could do no wrong and I could do no right.

Three out of the twenty daughters reported identical family myths, namely, that they had seriously damaged and hurt their mothers in the process of being born. This legend was invoked to explain and rationalize the mother's rejection of her daughter, and it came to symbolize the deep conflict in the mother-daughter relationship:

> *Beth:* She never failed to remind me how I had messed her up inside. I used to feel terribly guilty about it. But then I learned that she could have had an operation to repair the damage. It wasn't even a very serious operation, but she refused to have it done. She'd rather walk around with something wrong with her and hold that over my head.

Overt competition was also a prominent feature of the relationship between many of these daughters and their mothers. The mothers conveyed to their daughters the belief that the most, perhaps the only important project in life was getting and keeping a man, and that feminine worth was determined entirely by success in attracting masculine attention. They impressed upon their daughters the idea that in this world men came first, and it was every woman for herself:

> *Molly:* If I ever got close to a man, she was right there, trying to horn in on my territory.

Rivalry for the father's attention was particularly intense:

> *Penny:* My mother's a bitch and a nag. I don't know why Daddy stays with her; she makes his life miserable. Daddy and I really understand each other. If my mother doesn't like it, too bad.

These competitive feelings often concealed a deeper longing for maternal care and protection. Like the incest victims, many of these women felt that their mothers had in some degree sacrificed them to their fathers. While overtly the mothers resented the special relationship between father and daughter, covertly, the daughters felt, their mothers promoted or at least acquiesced in the relationships:

> *Barbara:* At the time my father wanted to divorce my mother and marry another woman. He had been womanizing for some time. My mother didn't want to divorce him because she didn't want the status of a divorced woman, or for other women to get the money, since she had been with him when he was poor, helped him build up a business, and wanted to reap the fruits. She also had some rhetoric about "the children," but since she is still with him, "the children" have little to do with it. At some point—I think I was fourteen—I had the definite feeling that he was going to stay (it was almost impossible to get a divorce without the wife's consent) but that I was thrown in as part of the deal.

Like the incest victims, the daughters of seductive fathers experienced their relationships with their fathers as privileged and special. Unlike the incest victims, these women did not have to bear the burden of secrecy about the relationship itself, for their fathers generally made no effort to hide their favoritism. Within their families the daughters were often known as "Daddy's princess" or "Daddy's special girl." Their fathers often spent more time with them than with other children, or with their mothers; and when their fathers were angry or upset, they turned to their daughters for solace and comfort.

Although the daughters generally enjoyed their special status, they felt ambivalent about it for a number of reasons. First, no matter how much attention they received from their fathers, they were always aware that these favors could be withdrawn at any time:

> *Eileen:* I'm not comfortable being his daughter. It's almost like I never was. When I was older, I felt like his wife. I think that was just his way of being a father. I never knew when he was going to be there or not. I didn't even expect him to be consistent. I didn't have his attention; I had to win it. The only way to win it was to be a charming little girl.

The daughters sensed that their fathers' special interest in them did not develop in response to their own need for parental nurturance but rather expressed the fathers' needs. In the person of the favorite daughter, the fathers found a wholly dependent being who would serve and flatter them and whom they could control. The favorite daughter also served as a pawn in the marital struggle. By flaunting the special relationship, the fathers revenged themselves upon their wives for real or imagined grievances and kept their wives actively competing for their attention.

Because the daughters were drawn into the marital conflict in the role of mother's rival, they often felt deeply torn. In effect, they felt as though they could please their fathers only at the expense of alienating their mothers. They paid for their special status in the family by suffering the jealousy and resentment of their mothers, and often of other siblings as well.

In one family, the myth that the mother-daughter rivalry had begun at birth assumed life-and-death proportions, because of the father's outright rejection of his wife and preference for his daughter:

> *Mary:* Supposedly I almost killed my mother when I was born. My father said, "If it's a choice between the mother's life and the daughter, save the daughter."

This terrifying version of the family romance illustrates the extreme alienation between mother and daughter, and the degree to which the daughter assumed responsibility for it ("I almost killed my mother"). It also illustrates the degree to which all family members felt that the father had the power to control their fate, even to decide who should live or die.

This issue of control also raised conflicts for the daughters, for the special relationship with their fathers often interfered with their strivings for independence and autonomy. Even when the daughters enjoyed and appreciated their fathers' attentions, they felt some resentment at their fathers' efforts to monopolize their time and control their activities:

> *Beth:* He'd seclude himself with me. Sometimes we'd have our meals separately from the rest of the family. I had to come straight home from school every day because he'd be waiting for me. We'd go for rides together and cuddle. I liked the attention, but sometimes I didn't want to come right home. I wanted to play with other kids.

Often the fathers' interest in their daughters extended to minute supervision of their clothing and appearance. The daughters felt that their bodies were not their own:

> *Mary:* One time my mother cut my hair, and my father went crazy. He acted like it was his hair, not mine, and I had no right to have it cut off.

The feeling of being invaded was most intense when the father's expressions of sexual interest were most overt:

> *Carla:* I always felt nervous being alone with him. He would get sloppy and maudlin when he was drunk. He'd come in my room and sit on the bed and kiss me and tell me how much he loved me. Once he pinned me down on the bed. He was breathing heavily and I could smell the liquor on his breath. It was disgusting. I felt, "Get this drunken man off me."

These conflicts, already present in childhood, intensified as the daughters reached adolescence. Like the incestuous fathers, the seductive fathers often reacted intensely to their daughters' increasing sexual maturity. Many became extremely jealous and attempted to restrict or monitor every aspect of their daughters' social lives:

Sally: Dad followed me around in cars when I dated. I would be having a pizza with a boy and all of a sudden there would be my father. It was no coincidence.

Barbara: My father didn't physically violate me, although I remember I didn't want to wash dishes because then he would slobber all over me with "affection," but he held an inquisition every Sunday morning over exactly what I had done the night before. He also competed with my boyfriends, coming into the room where they were and showing off his muscles. He also told me: 1) he would find me a boyfriend when the time came; 2) I would end up walking the streets; 3) no man would marry a nonvirgin; and 4) if I got pregnant, I would not have to run away from home.

The rationale for this monitoring was a puritanical abhorrence of sex. The fathers conveyed to their daughters the sense that sex was evil and shameful, at the same time that they continued to display their own sexual preoccupation with their daughters. Some daughters perceived that their fathers were essentially blaming them and holding them responsible for the sexual interest they aroused:

Charlene: Dad would say, "I don't want you trotting your pussy all over town."

Mary: When I was twelve, my father found me drinking. It gave him a perfect excuse to take the door off my room. He said it was to keep an eye on me. He sure did, especially when I was undressing.

A number of the seductive fathers who were not habitually violent became violent during their daughters' adolescence. Others, perhaps in order to avoid becoming violent and paranoid, completely withdrew from their daughters when they began showing sexual interest in boys their own age. They reacted to their daughters' emerging sexuality either with an attempt to establish total control or with total rejection. The message they conveyed to their daughters was, in effect, "As long as you remain my little girl, everything will be fine; but if you try to grow up, there will be hell to pay":

Donna: When I started becoming a woman, we lost our closeness. He never liked any of my boyfriends, he was always critical.

He seemed frightened of me, like I was something not to be messed with. I interpreted it as total rejection and wondered what I had done wrong.

Daughters of seductive fathers thus learned that they had two choices in life. They could remain their Daddy's good little girls, bound in a flirtatious relationship whose sexual aspect was ever present but never acknowledged, or they could attempt to become independent women, without any assistance from their mothers, and in the process risk their fathers' anger or rejection. They reached adult life schooled in the complicated art of pleasing a man and knowing virtually nothing about how to please themselves. In short, they were well prepared for conventional femininity.

In spite of the increased family stress during their adolescence, the daughters of seductive fathers did not become as desperate as the incest victims. The tension in their homes was uncomfortable but not unbearable, for unlike the incest victims, these women did not go to extremes to get out of their families. Only one of the twenty women made a runaway attempt, as opposed to thirteen of the forty incest victims. None of the women tried to get herself placed in a residential school or foster care (see Table 5.5). In contrast to the incest victims, these women also more successfully avoided early pregnancy and marriage. Only three of the twenty became pregnant during adolescence (15 percent, as opposed to 45 percent of the incest victims), and the majority of the women remained single into their twenties. At the time of the study, though the mean age of the two groups of women differed by less than a year, over half the daughters of seductive fathers had not yet married, while 63 percent of the incest victims had done so. Because the seductive fathers did not demand an overt sexual relationship, they did not drive their daughters into the arms of the first man who seemed capable of protecting them. They gave their daughters a little more time in which to grow up.

Because this group of women were not forced prematurely out of their families, they were also able to continue their education without early interruptions. As a result, their academic achievements were considerably greater than those of the incest victims. Thirty percent of this group had graduate degrees, compared to only eight percent of the incest victims. This was true in spite of the fact that the two groups came from similar class and religious backgrounds, and both groups came from families where women's achievements were not encouraged. The discrepancy is all the more striking in view of the incest victims' impressive capacity for work. The daughters of seductive fathers, unlike the incest victims, had sufficient social support during adolescence and early adulthood so that they were able to complete formal academic programs. The incest victims, in spite of their abilities, were simply not in a position to do so.

In adult life, the daughters of seductive fathers generally fared better than the incest victims, both materially and psychologically. They generally did not feel themselves to be branded, marked, or irrevocably cut off from normal society. They did not have a confirmed negative identity. They did not describe themselves as witches, bitches, or whores. Though many complained of depression, their depressive symptoms were not as severe as those of the incest victims. Only one of this group of twenty women (5 percent) abused drugs or alcohol, and only one ever made a suicide attempt, as compared to 35 percent and 38 percent, respectively, of the incest victims.

As a group, these women also proved better able to protect themselves from extremely abusive or destructive relationships. None of the women tolerated beatings from a husband or lover, compared to 28 percent of the incest victims. Three of the women (15 percent) were victims of street rape, which means that the overall incidence of rape in this group was the same as in the group of incest victims. Their reactions to their rapes were quite different, however; during the crisis period, these women generally reached out more to others for help and expressed more anger at their assailants than the incest victims. Their coping strategies after rape were clearly more adaptive than those of the incest victims.[1] They did not feel they deserved to be raped.

Although the daughters of seductive fathers in many ways fared better than the incest victims, they did not escape their family experiences entirely unscathed. Many of their problems seemed to be similar to those of the incest victims, but milder in degree. For example, though they were not, on the whole, as severely depressed as the incest victims, the majority (55 percent) did have major depressive symptoms. And though only 10 percent had a predominantly negative self-image, compared to 60 percent of the incest victims, a similarly low percentage described themselves in predominantly positive terms. The majority (80 percent) had a dual or confused self-image; they fluctuated between thinking of themselves as "good girls" and "bad girls." On the one hand, they saw themselves in the idealized role as "Daddy's princess"; on the other hand, they were never entirely able to suppress the covertly incestuous elements in their relationships with their fathers, and they saw themselves as little temptresses who had aroused their fathers' prurient interest and their mothers' jealous hostility.

Many women spoke of themselves as leading "double lives," and some in fact developed a secret sexual life. One woman, for instance, alternated between a job in a massage parlor, which was concealed from her family and friends, and an unpaid job in her father's business. The implication was that she felt prostituted in both situations. Another woman developed highy dissociated "good" and "bad" personalities, each having a different name, different clothes, habits, and friends. The "good" girl was subdued, compliant, and eager to please; she liked to stay home and cook for her husband. The "bad" girl liked to go to dating bars, get drunk, and pick up men. She was vivacious, aggressive, and tough. This woman experienced her two selves as constantly at war and felt unable to control which personality would dominate at any given moment. Unlike a classic case of multiple personality, however, she did not have amnesia for her conflicting personality states.

Thus in adult life, the daughters of seductive fathers maintained the dual identity that had originated in their families. They were the "good girls" who had dutifully served and pleased their fathers, and who had fulfilled the implicit task of keeping the family together, yet at the same time they were the "bad girls" who had flirted dangerously with adult sexuality and had come dangerously close to violating the incest taboo. As grown women, they remained confused and uncertain as to which was their "real" self. Most tried to live up to the image of the "good girl," often imposing upon themselves impossible standards of achievement. All were haunted by the fear that beneath the facade lurked a contemptible person who would eventually be exposed or gain the upper hand.

While the incest victims often seemed to have been forced into abrupt and premature separation from their families, the daughters of seductive fathers often seemed not to have separated at all. Even after they had married or established independent homes, many of the women in this group maintained close ties with their fathers. Some never succeeded in putting an end to the original seductive relationship. As grown women they continued to return home to serve and care for their fathers, or they allowed their fathers to interfere in their personal affairs. Because the sexual nature of the relationship was harder to define, it was often harder for the daughters to put an end to it. One daughter finally tried to set some limits on her father's courtship behavior when she was in her mid-twenties and had been living on her own for several years:

> *Susan:* Once a month he'd appear at my apartment with flowers and presents. He'd want me to prepare a candlelight dinner and wait on him like a courtesan, while he told me about his love life. When I told him I didn't want to do it any more, he reacted like an indignant Pasha.

Others simply acquiesced in the continuance of the "affair" or clung to it even after they were married:

> *Penny:* I'll never be too old to sit on Daddy's lap.

Some women who had managed to put some physical distance between themselves and their fathers still felt their fathers' continued presence in their fantasy life. One woman repeatedly dreamed that her father was pushing his way into her apartment. Another, whenever she was with a man, fantasized that her father knew what she was doing and would appear at any moment to drag her back home. Many women felt as if they had never established any privacy or boundaries where their fathers were concerned; the sense of being watched over, invaded, or surrounded was constantly with them. Those women who did achieve a sense of autonomy felt that they had to be constantly on guard against their fathers' efforts to draw them back into an infantilizing relationship:

> *Amanda:* He was always telling me to get an education, but when I got my Master's, he didn't even write to congratulate me. He wouldn't come to my wedding, but he offered all his help when I got divorced.

Like the incest victims, the daughters of seductive fathers also had difficulties in their personal relationships. They, too, tended to overvalue men and to devalue women. Female friendships were superficial or absent entirely. At best, women were seen as people to talk with about men; at worst, as a competitive threat. Many informants became involved in triangular situations with other women:

> *Odile:* She was my best friend, I trusted her, and now she's seeing my husband. He does the same to her as he did to me. I know that I should be happy to be rid of him, but I'm more jealous of her.

In their relationships with men, many of these women continued to seek for a powerful, charming protector, a "good daddy." Most of the men they actually met failed to live up to this idealized image. The result was a repetitive pattern of romantic infatuation followed by disappointment and anger.

Though these women did not tolerate the same degree of abuse as the incest victims, many did establish a pattern of highly unsatisfactory relationships with men. They found themselves attracted to men who were either distant and aloof, or controlling and domineering. Many were conscious of the resemblance between their lovers and their fathers:

> *Donna:* I didn't have a hell of a lot of choice. When my husband first met me, he said we were going to get married. That made me feel relaxed. I picked a man who was extremely dominant. He provided enough irritation to keep me growing.

> *Carla:* My boyfriend was just like my father. He was very dominating, ordered me around. I felt like scum. After he left me, I used to get these incredible crushes on men who were unavailable. I seemed only interested in that type.

One woman described how her intense relationship with her father adversely influenced her choice of men:

> *Donna:* I chose sexual partners who were emotionally unstable, motorcycle riders. It was a way to stick it to my father.

Only men who were unavailable or domineering seemed sufficiently attractive to be worth pursuing. As a result, few women were able to establish relationships with men based on mutuality. Their love affairs tended to recapitulate the pattern of their parents' marriages. Many found themselves repeating the behavior of the mothers they so disliked and concentrating all their efforts on the project of cajoling a capricious, difficult male:

> *Eileen:* My mother always told me how important it was to have a man take care of you. I think I'm still looking for the perfect man, a combination of a mother and a father. I still play the flirtatious little girl.

Similar to the incest victims, many of the daughters of seductive fathers (50 percent) also complained of sexual problems. The memories of their fathers' intrusiveness and their mothers' disapproval combined to inhibit sexual responsiveness:

> *Eileen:* My first knowledge of sex was, sex is bad. I felt I had to deny my sexuality. I'm obviously responsive in bed, and men say I'm sexy. But I don't have orgasms. If I get very aroused, I end up crying.

As in the case of the incest victims, the syndrome observed in the daughters of seductive fathers has been described by other clinicians, not in controlled studies, but anecdotally. In 1934, the psychoanalyst Karen Horney described "a common present-day feminine type," which bears a striking similarity to many of the daughters of seductive fathers: "The central problem here consisted not in any love-inhibition, but in an entirely too exclusive concentration upon men. These women were as though possessed by a single thought: 'I must have a man.'—obsessed with an idea overvalued to the point of absorbing every other thought, so by comparison all the rest of life seemed stale, flat, and unprofitable."[2]

Horney observed further that the genesis of this kind of personality problem lay in a family history of intense rivalry between mother and daughter and in early sexual stimulation of the daughter by a father or older brother. Although she did not apply the word *seductive* to the fathers of her patients, her descriptions make it clear that in at least some of the cases, she too was dealing with daughters of that type of father: "In still another case the father had made sexual advances to the patient from her fourth year, which became more outspoken in their character at the approach of puberty. At the same time he not only continued to be extremely dependent upon the mother . . . but was likewise very susceptible to the charms of other women, so that the girl got the impression of being merely her father's plaything, to be cast aside at his convenience."[3]

Finally, Horney maintained that successful therapy with these women followed from the "uncovering and working through of the destructive drives directed against women" and of the feelings of guilt that these hostile wishes engendered.[4] We have found the same to be true in the therapy of incest victims and daughters of seductive fathers. Only when the daughters have overcome their bitterness toward their mothers can they begin to respect all women, including themselves.

In general, having grown up with a covert or mild form of incest, the daughters of seductive fathers exhibited a mild form of the incest-victim syndrome in adult life. Like the incest victims, they tended to feel contempt for women and to hold men in excessive regard. Like the incest victims, they had many difficulties in establishing rewarding personal or sexual relationships, difficulties that were ultimately related to their own lack of self-respect. Unlike the incest victims, however, they did not develop a confirmed negative identity as the guardian of a malignant secret. They did not think of themselves as irredeemably evil and did not feel doomed to exclusion from normal society. As a result, they were spared some of the worst punishments of the incest victim. They felt obliged neither to submit to physical abuse from others, nor to make attempts to destroy themselves.

Comparison of the testimony of these daughters of seductive fathers with that of the incest victims yields other important differences. In particular, it demonstrates the importance of the power of mothers as agents of child protection. The families in which mothers were rendered unusually powerless, whether through battering, physical disability, mental illness, or the burden of repeated childbearing, appeared to be particularly at risk for the development of overt incest. In families where a more nearly equal balance of parental power was preserved, overt incest did not develop, even though the fathers' sexual interest in their daughters was quite apparent. The mothers who were able to function competently in their traditional roles, and who did not themselves submit to physical abuse, effectively protected their daughters from incest, even though they and their daughters were often bitterly estranged. The most effective barrier to overt incest thus appeared to be not the father's impulse control, but the degree of social control exerted by the mother.

Yet the similarities in all of the daughters' descriptions of their families were striking. Both groups of women came from traditional patriarchal families. Physical and economic control of the family rested with the father. Sex roles were rigidly and traditionally defined. Conservative religious attitudes and sexual morality, including a rigorous double standard of sexual behavior, prevailed. The two types of family differed not in kind but in degree, the overtly incestuous family representing a pathological extreme of male dominance, the covertly incestuous family representing the more commonplace variety. In both types of families, daughters learned that fathers rule, that mothers submit, that the ordinary female condition is contemptible, and that exceptions can be made for the favorite of a powerful male. Far from being unusual, these lessons are part of the ordinary experience of girlhood.

The testimony of the daughters in both types of families also made it clear that overt incest was in many ways more destructive than covertly incestuous behavior. In contrast to the incest victims, the daughters of seductive fathers did not show symptoms of extreme distress in childhood and adolescence. Though they might have been deeply unhappy and uncomfortable in their homes, they were not prematurely driven out of them. The normal course of their maturation was impeded, certainly, but not foreclosed.

For both groups of women, the destructive psychological effects of the disturbed father-daughter relationship could be observed lasting into adult life. The pathological effects of overt and covert incest were similar in nature and differed mainly in degree, the daughters of seductive fathers exhibiting in milder form many of the same symptoms that in the incest victims were developed to great severity. From these observations it can be concluded that both overt and covert incest were harmful to the daughters, but that overt incest was worse.

The similarities between the incest victims and the daughters of seductive fathers once again confirm the contention that incest represents a common pattern of traditional female socialization carried to a pathological extreme. Covert incest fosters the development of women who overvalue men and undervalue women, including themselves. Overt incest fosters the development of women who submit to martyrdom and sexual slavery. Those who consider masochism, selflessness and deference to men desirable attributes of mature womanhood may be unable to recognize the harmfulness of incest, and may even consider a little bit of paternal seduction desirable for proper feminine development. But for those who aspire to an image of free womanhood, incest is as destructive to women as genital mutilation or the binding of feet.

Three
BREAKING SECRECY

8
The Crisis of Disclosure

*We're not just a churchgoing family, we have very strong faith and be-
lief and conviction. So for this to come out was really a shock. I could
not believe what my children were telling me. It was like watching some
wild horror movie. I felt like I wasn't just in the valley, I was down in
the pit.*   —*a mother, 1977*

Most incest victims both long and fear to reveal their secret. In
childhood, fear usually overcomes any hope of relief; most girls dread
discovery of the incest secret and do not reveal it to anyone outside the
family. They believe that no recourse is available to them and that disclosure of the secret would lead to disaster. But as the daughters grow
up, the burden of secrecy becomes increasingly difficult to endure. The
child who has remained silent for many years may finally be driven to
seek outside help.

Unfortunately, given the current state of law enforcement, child protective services, and the mental health professions, the child victim has
good reason to fear exposure. Too often, because of bias and ignorance
within the helping professions and the criminal justice system, the intervention of outsiders is destructive to both parents and child. The victim
who reveals her secret implicitly challenges a traditional and cherished
social value, the right of a man to do as he pleases in his own home. And
in effect, if not by intention, society punishes the child who has the te-
merity to accuse her father. In a rural county in Idaho, for example, a
team of child protective workers observed that the general community
response to discovered cases of incest was initially a punitive reaction,
followed by avoidance and inaction:

> While the reaction of the community has been volatile and un-
> predictable . . . little, if any thoughtful planning has been initiated

... Most often, the community's response initially is one of extreme anger with frequent comments to the effect that "they should castrate the bastards; they ought to take them out and kill them; they are all crazy and they should be locked up." In the more protracted involvement with these families ... these initial intense emotions eventually evolve to either conditional acceptance or avoidance. We have seen spouses, lawyers, judges, and doctors assertively question the possibility of such distasteful acts having occurred when more than a preponderance of the evidence supports the legitimacy of the allegation ... The same avoidance mechanism which disallows the mother/spouse from conscious awareness is also operational in the community at large.[1]

This common reaction of initial shock and outrage followed by denial disrupts and threatens the family, provoking the father's wrath, without offering any adequate protection to the child. Thus the child is left even more at the mercy of her father than she was before she dared to disobey him. The picture is not uniformly bleak, however. In the past few years, comprehensive programs for the treatment of incest victims and their families have developed independently in a number of centers. Organized by a few dedicated and imaginative mental health workers, these programs appear to offer a more promising model for social intervention when an incestuous family is discovered.

In order to learn from their experience, we visited five treatment centers across the country. They were chosen because each had been in existence for a number of years, and each had developed a distinct approach to the problem of intervening in incestuous families. At each center we interviewed staff members, and in some we also observed therapy groups and interviewed individuals who had participated in the treatment program. The oldest and best known is the Child Sexual Abuse Treatment Program in San Jose, California. This program, based in the Juvenile Probation Department of an urban county court, has treated upward of one thousand families in the past eight years and has been given a mandate by state and federal child protective agencies to teach professionals how to deal with sexual abuse. The four other programs, though smaller than the one in San Jose, have each developed an effective, systematic way of intervening in incestuous families. Two programs—the Harborview Sexual Assault Center in Seattle, Washington, and the Center for Rape Concern in Philadelphia, Pennsylvania—grew out of rape crisis centers in private institutions. The two others—the Sexual Trauma Treatment Program in Hartford, Connecticut, and the Child Protective Service in Tacoma, Washington—developed within the state agencies that have mandatory authority to deal with child abuse. The mere fact of their existence is encouraging, for it demonstrates the possibility of a more enlightened and humane institutional response to the child victim.

The five treatment programs vary considerably in their theoretical base, their ideology, their internal structure, their staffing, and the populations they serve. Nevertheless, they have developed a remarkable degree of commonality in their practice. From observations of these programs, as well as from interviews with other clinicians and from our own experience, it has been possible to develop recommendations for the treatment of incestuous families. These suggestions are offered tentatively, as they are based upon impressionistic data in a field which is new and developing rapidly. Still, they represent a decided improvement over the most common current practices.

Whatever their background or theoretical orientation, professionals who have worked extensively with incestuous families appear to agree on three essential points: the need to restrict and control the excessive power of incestuous fathers, the need to reinforce and foster the power of mothers, and the need to restore the mother-daughter relationship. These points of consensus bear out our own analysis of the dynamics of father-daughter incest.

All experienced workers agree that the disclosure of the incest secret initiates a profound crisis for the family. Usually, by the time the secret is revealed, the abuse has been going on for a number of years and has become an integral part of family life. Disclosure disrupts whatever fragile equilibrium has been maintained, jeopardizes the functioning of all family members, increases the likelihood of violent and desperate behavior, and places everyone, but particularly the daughter, at risk for retaliation.

The precipitant for disclosure is often a change in the terms of the incestuous relationship which makes it impossible for the daughter to endure it any longer. When the daughter reaches puberty, the father may attempt to initiate intercourse. This new intrusion, and the risk of pregnancy which it entails, may drive the daughter to attempt to end the relationship at any cost. Another common precipitant for the breaking of secrecy is the father's attempt to seclude his adolescent daughter and restrict her social life. As the father's jealous demands become more and more outrageous, she may at last decide to risk the retribution which has been so often threatened rather than submit. Finally, the daughter may decide to break secrecy in order to protect younger siblings even more helpless than herself:

> *Rita:* My younger sisters were growing up, and I was afraid he might start on them. I couldn't see that. I could put up with it for myself, I was willing to tolerate it, but I couldn't see him starting up with my sisters. That's when I went to the authorities.

Once the decision to break secrecy has been made, the daughter must find a person to confide in. Often the daughter is too alienated from her mother to trust her with this secret. In an effort to ensure a protective response, she frequently bypasses her mother and seeks help from someone outside the family. In a series of ninety-seven incest cases seen at the Harborview Sexual Assault Center in Seattle, for example, slightly over half (52.5 percent) of the children first reported the incest to a friend, relative, babysitter, neighbor, or social agency. The remainder (46.5 percent) first told their mothers.[2]

For the mother, whether or not she suspected the incestuous relationship, disclosure of the secret is utterly shattering. First of all, she feels betrayed by her husband and her daughter. But in addition to her personal feelings of hurt and outrage, she must cope with the knowledge that her marriage and livelihood are in jeopardy. If her daughter's accusations are true, she faces the prospect of divorce, single parenthood, welfare, social ostracism, and even the possibility of criminal proceedings against her husband. These possibilities would be terrifying to any woman, even one in good health who was confident of her ability to manage alone in the world. How much more frightening, then, must such a future appear to a woman who is physically or mentally disabled, worn down by childbearing, intimidated by her husband, or cut off from social contacts and supports outside of her family. Small wonder that many a mother, faced with the revelation of the incest secret, desperately tries to deny her daughter's accusations. If she believes her daughter, she has nothing to gain and everything to lose.

For the father, the disclosure is likewise a threat to his entire way of life. He stands to lose not only the sexual contact he craves, but also his wife, his family, his job, and even his liberty. Faced with this overwhelming threat, most commonly the father adopts a stance of outraged denial. He does whatever he can to discredit his daughter and to rally his wife to his side. All too often, this strategy succeeds. Although the

mother may believe the daughter initially, she soon succumbs to the bar-
rage of entreaties, threats, and unaccustomed attentions from her husband.

Without active outside intervention, then, the daughter is greatly at
risk within her family once the incest secret has been revealed. By defy-
ing her father's orders to maintain secrecy, she has in effect made him
her enemy. Her mother was never a strong ally, and in a crisis she cannot
be depended upon. If nothing is done to protect the daughter, the
chances are great that the parental couple will unite against her and virtually drive her out of the family.

For this reason, the person to whom the incest secret is revealed bears
a heavy burden of responsibility. The very fact that the secret is out
means that the family is in crisis, the daughter is in danger, and something must be done. But outsiders are often no more prepared than family members to respond appropriately. Most friends, relatives, neighbors,
and even helping professionals find it hard to conceal their shock and distress when first learning about incest. As one social worker admitted
candidly: "It makes me feel so upset, I really don't want to hear about it.
I can only give you an unprofessional reaction: Ugh!" Even professionals
who work with abused children every day have a hard time with incest.
A survey of the Child Protective Services staff in Florida, for example,
disclosed that almost a third (31 percent) of the workers felt uncomfortable working with sexual abuse cases and preferred not to do so. The
same workers perceived father-daughter incest as the most difficult type
of case.[3]

Every state in the United States has a law making it mandatory to report cases of child abuse to an appropriate agency, usually the state child
protective service. State laws vary in their specifications of persons required to report and in the mandated procedure for reporting. The state
of Idaho, for example, requires that "any person having reasonable cause
to believe that a child under the age of eighteen years has been abused
. . . shall report . . . within 24 hours . . . to the proper law enforcement
agency."[4] The Massachusetts statute, by contrast, requires only professionals to report and stipulates that the report shall be made to the Department of Public Welfare.[5] Almost all state laws specify that the privilege of confidentiality which exists between professional and client,
except the lawyer-client privilege, is not grounds for failure to report.
Mandated reporters are generally given immunity from civil action as
long as the report is made in good faith. Yet many professionals who
learn of incest do not report it, even though they know they are required

to do so by law, and even though they are often at a loss for what else to do. Professionals confronted by the reality of incest often react with the same kind of denial and avoidance mechanisms as mothers and other family members. They do nothing and hope the problem will go away.

Mental health professionals, accustomed to working in an atmosphere of confidentiality, may feel particularly uncomfortable about reporting, especially if, as is frequently the case, the child pleads for secrecy. Not uncommonly, professionals who work with sexually abused adolescents attempt to improvise their own system of intervention, avoiding the official child protective apparatus. A nurse in a community mental health center, who had extensive experience with adolescent girls, explained one such personal system:

> I don't report it initially. The kids don't want me to, and I respect that, and besides, I don't think the Child Protective Service is very concerned or handles the cases well. But I do call up the mother and tell her what the kid has told me, and I say I believe it and if it doesn't stop I will report it. The mothers are very often furious with me. They say I'm crazy, I've got a dirty mind, the kid's got a wild imagination and so on. Usually the kids predict what the mothers will say. Everybody denies it, but I think once there's been a confrontation, the abuse stops. Then I just work with the kids. I help them make plans to get out as soon as they can.

This woman spoke out of a feeling of loyalty and dedication to her clients, and her arguments are persuasive. Nevertheless, this approach, and any approach which fails to report incest to the legally designated authority, creates more problems than it solves. First, it is not at all clear that a simple confrontation, such as a phone call to the mother, is sufficient to put a stop to the sexual abuse. Second, even if such an intervention is sufficient to protect the one child in treatment, it does nothing to ensure the safety of other children in the family. Third, the use of the reporting option as a threat casts the child protective service in an entirely punitive role. If, as frequently happens, the sexual abuse continues and eventually has to be reported, the possibility of a positive alliance with the protective service caseworker is already seriously reduced. Workers in the agencies which are mandated to intervene in abusive families particularly resent being cast in this role. As one caseworker complained,

"People don't know how to report. That's the biggest error therapists make. They say if you don't come back, or if you do it again, we'll report you to Child Protective Service. That's blackmail. We are set up as punishment. It's very frustrating."

Finally, and this is perhaps the most serious objection of all, failure to report sexual abuse places the outsider in complicity with the father. Any relationship the outsider establishes with the daughter, the mother, or the whole family must be compromised by the fact that the outsider, by withholding knowledge of the incestuous offence, is tacitly protecting the father and breaking the law.

For all these reasons, any helping professional who learns about an incestuous situation should report it. The person making the report can explain to the child and the family that the report is not a punishment but a routine matter of policy and a constructive step toward establishing a safe atmosphere in the home. The child protective service worker who receives the report should be approached as a potentially helpful person, not as a mindless minion of the state waiting to swoop down upon the family and take away the children. As one experienced therapist observed:

> Most of the child protective service workers are so glad to have somebody cooperate with them instead of just dumping on them. Because normally, what professionals do is let them do their thing, and then bitch about what they did. People don't like to be the heavies. It's easier to let somebody else be the heavy and then you do all the nice stuff. So there's a built-in resentment between protective workers and most mental health professionals. I think that's why we have credibility with the protective workers, because we don't mind being the heavies. We consider that's part of the deal if you're going to work with abused kids of any kind.

We advocate the reporting of sexual abuse in spite of the fact that the agency mandated to receive the report may not always respond effectively or appropriately. The reality is that most state child protective services are severely overburdened and understaffed. According to a survey by the American Humane Association, "no state and no community has a protective service program adequate in size to meet the service needs of all reported cases of child neglect and abuse."[6] This observation was made in 1967, even before increased public awareness of child abuse and the passage of mandatory reporting laws resulted in a massive increase in the number of reports. In some states, child abuse and neglect reports have increased over tenfold within a few years. Between 1976 and 1977, the total number of reports received by the National Study of Child Abuse and Neglect Reporting increased by 23 percent, from 412,-972 to 507,494. In seven states, increases of over 100 percent were recorded in a single year.[7]

These overwhelming increases in reporting have nowhere been accompanied by corresponding increases in the staffing of child protective agencies or the training of protective service workers. As a result, it is virtually impossible for many child protective agencies to fulfill their mandated responsibilities. Many agencies function in a permanent state of emergency. Inexperienced workers, inadequately supervised and burdened with huge case loads of abuse and neglect, are expected to respond quickly, usually within twenty-four hours, to each new report, to make rapid assessments of situations that may be life-threatening, and to intervene effectively in families at their most desperate and explosive moment. Not surprisingly, caseworkers frequently become demoralized and "burnt out," and agencies are plagued with high staff turnover and an atmosphere of exhaustion and instability.[8]

For workers preoccupied with the need to rescue children who have already been battered or who are in imminent danger of physical assault, sexual abuse cases cannot be assigned the first priority. As one Massachusetts protective service worker lamented: "We have such a backlog of cases that we're constantly making decisions we shouldn't have to be making. Is a two-year-old with a broken arm worth a four-year-old with a cigarette burn? The ones we put on lower priority really get to me."[9] And because only a small fraction (5.8 percent) of all abuse and neglect cases are initially reported specifically as sexual abuse, it is unusual for a worker within any one agency to develop special familiarity or expertise with such cases.[10] As a result, the response to sexual abuse reports is often haphazard and idiosyncratic. Occasionally, a worker or supervisor may respond in a panicky, overly aggressive manner, needlessly removing the child from her home. But more commonly, when errors are made, they are errors of omission rather than commission. Child protective service workers, who like the rest of the public are made uncomfortable by reports of incest, may find excuses not to investigate too carefully or too deeply.

One mother of our acquaintance, for example, decided to report her husband for incest to the state authorities. The decision cost her much anguish, and the whole family awaited a response with great anxiety.

After a considerable delay, a caseworker visited the home. The worker complimented the mother on her clean house, admired her carpets, and assured her that her family was "not the type we usually see," apparently meaning that they were not poor. The children were not interviewed. No further action was taken. The father remained in the home, where he continued to pursue his daughter. A call to the agency several months later revealed that the case file had been lost, and that no one had the slightest interest in finding it.

Given the limitations under which most protective agencies labor, such inaction is all too common. In Massachusetts, for example, a study of child protective service response to sexual abuse reports indicated that in 26 percent of the cases, no one bothered to validate the report by interviewing the child, and in one third of the cases (32 percent), no home visit was made. Workers were significantly more likely to interview the child and parents in reported cases of neglect or physical abuse. Follow-up counseling was recommended to the families in only half of the sexual abuse cases (52 percent). However, in 39 percent of the cases, the child was ultimately removed from her home as a result of the investigation. It seems apparent from this data that the state agency lacked a capacity for effective intervention short of the drastic step of removing the child.[11]

In spite of the near impossibility of their task, some child protective workers have evolved effective and creative methods for intervening in incestuous families. One dedicated individual or a small cohesive group can sometimes improvise a system that works, more or less. A common feature of all these empirically developed systems is their focus on rapid, appropriate crisis intervention. There is underlying agreement that as soon as secrecy is broken, the child and mother need immediate and intensive support. As one worker advised: "If you have limited resources, put them into that first day, that first week. It beats trying to pick up the pieces later on."

The daughter, once she has revealed her secret, needs a great deal of reassurance. She needs to be told, first, that others believe her story; second, that she is not to blame; and third, that she will be protected from further sexual abuse and from her father's retaliation for breaking secrecy. She should be praised for her courage in coming forward and should be assured that her confession will, in the long run, help the whole family. She should be questioned regarding her safety at home, and all the options available for her protection should be explained to her.

Once the devastating news of exposure reaches the mother, she may need even more support than the daughter. Torn between her husband

and her daughter, and terrified of the consequences of disrupting her marriage, the mother may be virtually paralyzed and incapable of taking action alone. Unless she finds a sympathetic and helpful ally outside the family, she is likely to submit to her husband's direction and influence and to withdraw from her daughter. As one worker observed: "The mothers don't know what to do. They're in shock. They need instruction, they need guidelines. They don't need eighteen options or a nondirective approach. It's useless to people in that situation. They will tend to drift toward their husbands because they see themselves as not being able to make it on their own. You don't ever want to put them in a position where they have to choose sides against their kids."

Intensive support for the mother may mean daily contact during the first week and almost as frequent contact during the second week after disclosure. Practical matters, such as the decision to separate from the father, the decision to file criminal charges, and financial or babysitting arrangements, should be taken care of as rapidly as possible during this time. The sooner these issues are dealt with, the sooner the crisis will abate and the sooner the processes of healing and reconstruction can begin.

Most experienced workers agree that during the crisis period, father and daughter should not be under the same roof. Even if the father confesses immediately following disclosure, it is simply too dangerous and too stressful for the daughter to have to return home, to face her father and to go on living under his authority.

For many reasons, it is more desirable to have the father leave home rather than the daughter. First of all, as he is an adult, he is far more capable of finding alternative living arrangements. He does not need to be placed in foster care; all he needs is to get a room somewhere. Second, many temporary shelter arrangements for girls are either inappropriate or unsafe for incest victims. If the daughter is sent to a juvenile detention center or receiving home, it is hard for her to escape the feeling that she, rather than her father, is being treated as the criminal. If, alternatively, the daughter is placed in a foster family, she runs the risk of repeated sexual victimization. Once a girl has been branded as an incest victim, many men will find her sexually interesting and treat her like public property. As a result, it is not unusual for the daughter to be subjected to sexual attentions from foster fathers and other members of the foster families.

Finally, even if an ideal placement is found for the daughter, she is bound to feel punished if she is excluded from her family while her father remains at home. Removing the daughter from the home reinforces the tendency of the parental couple to ally against her, whereas removing the father gives the daughter a chance to repair her relationship with her mother and gives the mother an opportunity to function on her own.

Excluding a man from his own home, however, is an enormous challenge to male dominance. As such, this course of action usually meets with resistance, not only from the fathers themselves, but from almost every existing social institution. A father can be compelled to leave his home only upon court order. To obtain such an order, the daughter, and usually therefore the mother also, must be willing to file a criminal complaint against the father. The police must be willing to act on this complaint to arrest the father. At the arraignment, the judge must be willing, as a condition of release pending trial, to issue a vacate order instructing the father to leave the home, and a restraining order forbidding him to initiate contact with his daughter. Finally, the police must be willing to enforce these orders once they have been issued. Even in those few cases where criminal complaints are filed by the daughter, the police and the courts cannot be counted upon to see the wisdom of removing the father from his home. Twenty-seven states now provide civil remedies for victims of domestic violence, making it possible in some instances to obtain vacate and restraining orders against an offender by filing a civil rather than a criminal complaint. However, numerous procedural barriers to removing a father from his home remain.[12]

State child protective services have no authority to compel a parent to leave the home. They are empowered only to remove the child, and even this power is limited and dependent upon the cooperation of the family or juvenile court. Thus, outsiders who intervene in incestuous families are often forced to remove the daughter, even though they recognize that it would be far better for the father to leave temporarily. As one child protective worker commented:

> Our primary goal when the information comes to us would be to ask or some way persuade the father to leave the home. The separation must occur as soon as possible. The preferred way is to have the father leave so the child doesn't have to be removed. But it doesn't work many times because the fathers are so adamantly opposed to admitting any of this, and also because the mothers are so dependent, they feel they can't function alone. The child becomes sensitive to being the homebreaker, and the father is very much invested in putting the pressure on everyone at home, to

prevent them from making a statement and getting him out. So often we end up having to go to court for protective custody. We don't like to do it, but sometimes we have to.

In spite of their limited powers, child protective workers have devised their own strategies to induce the fathers to leave home voluntarily. Those programs in which participating parents are organized into self-help groups are at a definite advantage in this situation, for another offender is often more persuasive to a newly discovered father than a professional can possibly be. In the Child Sexual Abuse Treatment Program in San Jose, for example, the father is visited within twenty-four hours by another father who is already involved in the program. The parent volunteer is often able to persuade the father that he has more to gain by cooperation than by maintaining a stance of belligerent denial. The father is not asked to cooperate for altruistic reasons, such as to spare his daughter hardship, but for his own self-interest. He is told that it will look better in court if he confesses immediately and if he does whatever he can to make life easier for his daughter.

Persuasion succeeds best when it is backed up with a display of strength. This requires the active cooperation of the police. In Bonner County, Idaho, sexual abuse reports are investigated by a child protective service worker accompanied by a plainclothes police officer. Faced with the possibility of arrest, most fathers reportedly confess on the spot and agree at once to a contract for family treatment supervised by the juvenile court.[13]

In one program where the child protective service enjoys very strong support from law enforcement, fathers are required by the program to plead guilty to a felony charge in order to qualify for treatment. In return, the fathers can be reasonably confident that they will receive considerate treatment by the police and lenient sentencing by the court. No arrests are made, and the fathers arrange to give their statements by appointment.

In programs where good working relations with law enforcement are not well established and where volunteer parent groups are not available, child protective workers are forced to rely on bluff rather than persuasion. In one program, for example, the initial contacts with mother and daughter are carefully kept secret from the father, until the workers feel that a strong alliance with the mother and daughter has been established. The goal of the workers is to prepare the mother and child to make a complaint to the police before the father realizes that the incest has been discovered. This strategy climaxes with the surprise arrest of the father. The goal with the father is to catch him at a vulnerable and undefended moment, so that he will confess, and so that he may agree to leave home voluntarily even if the court does not order him out.

This last approach may seem at best underhanded, and at worst a violation of due process of law. No one, least of all those child protective workers who practice it, consider it an ideal strategy. But almost any approach which breaks through the family pattern of denial and submission to the father is preferable to inaction. All members of the family, especially the father, must be convinced that the breaking of secrecy is irreparable, that there can be no going back. The more rapid and decisive the crisis intervention, the more quickly the family can begin the work of reconstruction.

In some instances, even when crisis intervention has been intensive and appropriate, the mother and daughter are already so deeply estranged at the time of disclosure that the bond between them seems irreparable. In this situation, no useful purpose is served by trying to separate the mother and father and keep the daughter at home. The daughter has already been emotionally expelled from her family; removing her to protective custody is simply the concrete expression of the family reality. These are the cases which many agencies call their "tragedies." This report of a child protective worker illustrates a case where removing the child from the home was the only reasonable course of action:

> Division of Family and Children's Services received an anonymous telephone call on Sept. 14 from a man who stated that he overheard Tracy W., age 8, of [address] tell his daughter of a forced oral-genital assault, allegedly perpetrated against this child by her mother's boyfriend, one Raymond S.
>
> Two workers visited the W. home on Sept. 17. According to their report, Mrs. W. was heavily under the influence of alcohol at the time of the visit. Mrs. W. stated immediately that she was aware why the two workers wanted to see her, because Mr. S. had "hurt her little girl." In the course of the interview, Mrs. W. acknowledged and described how Mr. S. had forced Tracy to have relations with him. Workers then interviewed Tracy and she verified what mother had stated. According to Mrs. W., Mr. S. admitted the sexual assault, claiming that he was drunk and not accountable for his actions. Mother then stated to workers that she banished Mr. S. from her home.

I had my first contact with mother and child at their home on Sept. 20 and I subsequently saw this family once a week. Mother was usually intoxicated and drinking beer when I saw her.

I met Mr. S. on my *second* visit. Mr. S. denied having had any sexual relations with Tracy. Mother explained that she had obtained a license and planned to marry Mr. S.

On my *third* visit, Mrs. W. was again intoxicated and drinking despite my previous request that she not drink during my visit. Mother explained that Mr. S. had taken off to another state and she never wanted to see him again. On this visit mother demanded that Tracy tell me the details of her sexual involvement with Mr. S.

On my *fourth* visit, Mr. S. and Mrs. S. were present. Mother explained that they had been married the previous Saturday.

On my *fifth* visit, Mr. S. was not present. During our discussion, mother commented that "Ray was not the first one who had Tracy." After exploring this statement with mother and Tracy, it became clear that Tracy had been sexually exploited in the same manner at age six by another of Mrs. S.'s previous boyfriends.

On my *sixth* visit, Mrs. S. stated that she could accept Tracy's being placed with another family as long as it did not appear to Tracy that it was her mother's decision to give her up. Mother also commented, "I wish the fuck I never had her."

It appears that Mrs. S. has had a number of other children all of whom have lived with other relatives or were in foster care for part of their lives. Tracy herself lived with a paternal aunt from birth to age five. Mother is very accepting of court action at this time.

In summary, it is the opinion of the Division of Family and Children's Services that the above named child is *at risk* and in need of care and protection.

For many people, the shock of sexual abuse pales before the shock of this mother's statement, "I wish the fuck I never had her." So thoroughly is motherhood sentimentalized that the mother who wishes to be rid of her child is considered a monster. In reality, women have always greeted the burden of motherhood ambivalently, even in the best of circumstances, and many women bear children involuntarily. But the opprobrium which attaches to any woman who willingly gives up her child is so great that some mothers will keep and mistreat their children rather than admit that they cannot care for them. Sometimes, the revelation of maternal neglect constitutes a plea for outside intervention, signaling the fact that a mother wants to be relieved of the duty to care for her child. In these cases, the mother deserves to start a new life, and the daughter deserves a new home.

The outcome of the crisis of disclosure depends, ultimately, on the status of the mother-daughter relationship. If, in spite of everything, the mother still feels some tenderness for her daughter, then every effort should be made to keep mother and child together and to foster the restoration of the bond between them. But if their relationship has already been destroyed, then mother and daughter should be parted.

9

Restoring Families

*To extend the hand of friendship, understanding, and compassion, NOT
to judge or condemn.*
*To better our understanding of ourselves and our children through
the aid of the other members and professional guidance.*
*To reconstruct and channel our anger and frustrations in other direc-
tions, NOT on or at our children.*
*To realize that we are human and do have angers and frustrations;
they are normal.*
To recognize that we do need help, we are all in the same boat . . .
*To start each day with a feeling of promise, for we take only one day
at a time . . .*
*To become the LOVING, CONSTRUCTIVE, and GIVING PARENTS or PERSON
that we wish to be.* —"Parents United Creed," 1975

After the crisis of disclosure comes the slow, laborious task of putting lives back together. For all family members, the time of reconstruction is a time of extreme anxiety. Return to the *status quo ante* is impossible, yet particularly for the parents, it may be equally impossible to
conceive of a new way of life. The incestuous father has immense difficulty imagining how life can be bearable if he loses control over his wife
and children and sexual access to his daughter. He cannot be expected to
give up his accustomed power and privileges without a fight. If he meets
with determined resistance from his wife and daughter, his distress will
be extreme. Desertion, suicidal gestures, and homicidal threats are not
uncommon during this time. Two mothers testify on the father's reaction:

> He wanted to get back together, and I think he thought all along
> that eventually I'd take him back. When I filed for divorce, he

couldn't believe it. He really went crazy. He started driving past our house every night. The kids were scared, and I told them if he ever tried to get in the door to call the police right away. One night he came to the house drunk and threatened us with a knife. The kids and I got out the back way and ran to a neighbor's house. When he saw he couldn't get us, he stood on the doorstep and slit his wrists.

We had been in the women's shelter for two weeks, and I kept my daughter out of school because I didn't know what he'd do if he found her. One day a man I had never seen before came up to me on the street and gave me a wooden cross. He told me it was from my husband. That night they moved us to a shelter in another state.

The mother, too, is under extreme stress. She feels more alone at this time than she has ever been in her life. In addition to coping with the father's pressure and threats, she is compelled to shoulder the responsibility for her family alone, something she does not want to do or feel capable of doing. And she is sacrificing whatever financial or emotional security existed in her marriage, for the sake of a daughter who has often seemed more like a rival than a child. She is overcome by feelings of despair, panic, and rage. However hard she tries to avoid blaming her daughter, there may be times when she quite simply hates her.

The daughter, once the initial crisis has passed, may not feel the relief she hoped for. True, the sexual abuse has been stopped, but nothing else has changed. Her parents are usually in such distress that they are no more able to respond to her needs than they ever were; in fact, once the sexual bond which held the family together has been broken, there is nothing to disguise the enormity of the gulf between the child and both her parents.

Rebuilding the family begins with restoration of the mother-daughter bond. On this point, there was unanimity among experienced therapists in all five treatment programs visited, even those who were most committed to reuniting the parental couple. As Henry Giarretto, director of the Child Sexual Abuse Treatment Program in San Jose, California, put it: "We feel the essential nucleus is the mother and daughter. As soon as the mother communicates to the daughter that she [the daughter] wasn't to blame, the repair process has begun.[1]

In order to give her daughter the kind of protection and support that she was unable to give in the past, the mother needs a kind of support that she herself has never had: she needs concrete help in the day-to-day tasks of running a household, a safe place to express her own feelings and to develop her own goals, and more contact with her peers. Unless she comes to see that she has something to gain for herself, it is useless to expect her to do anything for her daughter. She does not need anyone to teach her how to be a martyr; she needs an ally. This may be a caseworker, another mother who has been through similar turmoil in her own life, or ideally both.

Some treatment programs, such as the one in San Jose or the Child Protective Services in Tacoma, rely heavily on parent organizations to provide an intense, corrective, nurturing social experience. These groups, called Parents United in San Jose and Families Re-United in Tacoma, are organized on a partial self-help model. They are incorporated and governed by the parents themselves, but they do not exclude professionals, as true self-help organizations do. Meetings are led jointly by professional counselors and parents who have reached an advanced stage in the program.

The advantages of parent support groups for mothers are numerous. First, they provide comfort and practical help in a much more complete way than any counselor, however tireless, possibly can. Parents United, for example, offers financial aid, legal and medical referrals, babysitting and temporary shelter for children, help with transportation problems, and employment resources, as well as 24-hour availability for emotional support. Second, parent support groups provide the mother with a new, constructive social network, bringing her out of her seclusion in the home. Third, they build self-esteem, not only by alleviating the mother's shame, because she is in the company of other women who have had similar experiences, but also by giving the mother the opportunity, when she is ready, to let others benefit from her experience. Thus, though she is given a great deal of help when she needs it most, she is not restricted to the role of patient.

An essential element in parents' self-help groups is the concept of sponsorship. A mother entering the program for the first time is "adopted" by another mother who has made sufficient progress in resolving her own problems that she is ready to offer help as well. The importance of the sponsor is illustrated by one mother's experience:

> I was in that orientation meeting, and I was too far from the door to get to it, and even if I had been next to it, I don't know if I'd

have had the strength to get up, but if ever I felt like I wanted to leap through a plate glass window, that was the time. I came out of that room practically running, and someone grabbed me and said, "I know this is your first time. I've been through it too." If it hadn't been for her sitting and talking to me and holding my hand, I might have never—most likely would have never come back to the program. But out of that program—it's given me a whole new direction in life.

Given adequate protection and support, many mothers can take advantage of this unwanted disruption in their lives to make remarkable gains. Often this is the first time that their neglected physical or emotional problems have received any attention, and the first opportunity they have ever had to develop their own aspirations outside of their family role. Concrete gains for mothers are measured by such criteria as improved physical health, increased social contact, and new skills, such as learning to drive a car. Return to school or to the paid work force are frequent outcomes.

Successful programs provide mothers with the opportunity to develop competence and skill within the structure of the program itself, by becoming sponsors to newcomers and by helping to educate the wider public. In the Tacoma program, for example, advanced parents participate in a "presentation," in which they share their experiences privately with a newly admitted family or publicly in a consciousness-raising forum. In the San Jose program, advanced parents are invited into a leadership training group, which helps to lead orientation groups and to organize new chapters of Parents United. Such activities liberate an enormous amount of creative energy and build up a sense of accomplishment and power in the participants.

As the mother develops increased self-confidence and a sense of well-being, she is less willing to return to an oppressive marriage. Only when she feels capable of making it on her own can she freely choose whether to reconcile with her husband or to divorce him. Strengthening the mother also diminishes the rivalry between mother and daughter. When the father is no longer seen as the source of all sustenance, the competition for his favors becomes less desperate.

During the time that the mother is in treatment, the daughter also needs intensive support. As in the case of the mothers, an individual ally is essential, and peer group support, if available, is desirable. Involvement in a group not only diminishes the shame associated with the sexual abuse but also offers the daughter a safe place to vent her feelings about her mother. Often the focus of treatment moves quickly from the sexual issue to the daughter's longing for her mother's care and to her frequent disappointments in her mother. The group provides consolation as well as practical, problem-solving help.

Group support is extremely useful, not only for adolescents but also for younger children. In Tacoma, The Child Protective Service and the Rape Relief Program jointly run a group, the Sunshine Girls, composed of thirty girls, ages eight to twelve, who meet weekly after school. The group has two co-leaders, a male and female therapist. Transportation to and from the group is organized by parent volunteers, all mothers. The mothers are also present in the meeting to provide consolation and hugs to the girls as needed, to serve food, and to direct play activities. The children learn to share their experiences with astounding openness. As visitors, we were not only welcomed without embarrassment, but urged to start a similar program in our own community because, as one ten-year-old put it, "There are probably a lot of kids involved in incest there, and they probably feel all alone."

The goal of treatment for the daughter is similar to that for the mother: to relieve guilt, to increase self-esteem, to break down the child's isolation, to develop her autonomy, and to teach her that she has the right to protect herself. Peter Coleman, of the Tacoma Child Protective Service, defined his program's treatment objectives:

> In the groups assertiveness is the paramount learning, defined as stating your needs and getting them met, if possible, without infringing upon the needs or feelings of others. This attacks the continuum of battering, abuse, control, dominance, compliance, submissiveness, and helplessness. I insist that the facilitators be strong women and gentle men. We are truly seeking to liberate these little girls. However, it causes friction in schools and families when formerly docile little dolls become assertive.[2]

As both mother and daughter begin to feel more self-confident, the process of reconciliation can begin. Joint counseling sessions with mother and daughter are often useful in restoring the bond between them. The relationship is restored when the daughter feels that she has access to her mother, when she can turn to her mother with her problems, and especially when she is sure that her mother will take immediate protective action if her father attempts to renew sexual contact or harasses her in any way.

In some programs, particularly those with a strong feminist orientation, treatment ends with the restoration of the bond between the mother and her children. The fate of the father is considered more or less irrelevant, once mother and daughter are able to defend themselves. Helping professionals who take this position argue against devoting scarce resources to the treatment of offenders when the outcome of such treatment is questionable, and when excluding the fathers from their families seems a much safer strategy than trying to rehabilitate and reintegrate them. As the feminist social worker Florence Rush puts it: "Has anyone thought of the fantastic notion of getting rid of the father?"[3]

The problem with this suggestion is that there is no way of "getting rid of" the fathers. They may desert or be expelled from their families, but this does not necessarily put an end to their abusiveness. New victims do not seem to be in short supply, as this mother testified:

Out of what you may term "sheer desperation," I am writing to you. First of all, I would like to tell you, I agree wholeheartedly that incest must be brought out of society's closet. The fear, frustration, and shame that surround this problem must be broken through once and for all so that work can be done and help can be found. Ignorance abounds on this subject even in the medical profession. Before you label me "bitter" over that last statement, let me explain my situation.

Four years ago, I met my present husband. I had just been divorced, and I had three children, two boys and a girl. The man who became my husband had just been divorced from his first wife also. I found out shortly after I met him, the reason for his divorce was incest. He was being treated by a psychiatrist at the time and asked me to talk to his doctor. I did, and was told the following:

"Tom has been involved in an unhappy marriage with a wife who has been demanding and domineering in every way, especially sexually. He felt so threatened by this (and his morals were too high to turn to another woman), that he turned to his daughter for love and understanding. I feel sure that if he were involved in a happy, loving marriage, this could never happen again."

On this premise I continued to date him and two years ago we were married. Our marriage has been a very happy, loving, and fulfilling one and that did not prevent it from happening again! Two months ago, my nine-year-old daughter came to me and confided that Tom had been "doing things to her that she didn't think were right." With a little questioning, I found out that he had indeed been molesting her. Of course, I was sick at heart.

I confronted him and consulted another psychiatrist. This time I got a completely different story from the first one. I find out now that this condition my husband has is "incurable." There are no treatment programs known that can really work in curing child molesters. It may work for a while but sooner or later the compulsion will return and it will happen again. Consequently, I have been put in the position of "policeman" in my own home. I can never allow my daughter to be alone with my husband. I can never for a minute, trust him in this respect again. And he must learn to live with the knowledge that I can't trust him and he can't trust himself. He loathes his problem and is bewildered by it.

I do indeed feel bitter towards the doctor who, I feel, misinformed me on the subject at a time when I desperately needed intelligent and precise information. And this is why I feel it is so important for more work to be done—more research teams such as yourselves and more people such as myself to step forward and get some positive action going on this matter.

This mother's letter raises two important points. First, it argues for the necessity of treating offenders, if not for their own sake, then for the sake of the women and children who will inevitably be involved with them. Second, it illustrates the dangers of improper evaluation and ineffective treatment. This mother was unusual in her determination to find help for herself and her husband; her failure to find it was not at all unusual.

It is easy to make mistakes in treating sex offenders. Those schooled in a traditional model of psychotherapy may find themselves hopelessly lost. Traditional therapy presumes a patient who suffers inner distress, who seeks treatment voluntarily, and who agrees to confide in his therapist to the best of his ability, holding nothing back. The therapist, in turn, agrees to listen and intervene in a nonjudgmental manner and to keep the patient's communications confidential. The goal for the patient is increased self-awareness and inner change. This model is absolutely useless when applied to sex offenders. Incestuous fathers are generally not in distress as long as they have sexual access to their daughters. They almost never seek treatment voluntarily, and they generally do not reveal the full extent of their offenses. Their goal is not to change themselves but to manipulate the therapist so that the therapist becomes an ally, protecting them from prosecution or even helping them to regain access to their victims. In this situation, insight-oriented psychotherapy is completely inappropriate.

A therapist who is not experienced in working with sex offenders can be thoroughly "conned." In one case, a psychologist in his fifties, who had had many years of clinical experience, requested consultation after his patient had been in treatment for six months because he felt that therapy was stagnating. The patient, a 35-year-old mechanic and the father of four children, had sought out the therapist on his own initiative after quitting a program specifically designed for offenders. Although he was under court order to undergo treatment, his probation officer apparently approved the change as long as the patient kept his appointments with his new therapist, which he did. At the time he began therapy, the patient was living apart from his wife and children but visiting them secretly in violation of the court order. The therapist did not report these violations. The patient had found a new girlfriend, who had a five-year-old daughter and who was unaware of the patient's history. The therapist did nothing to warn the mother or protect this child.

The patient's oldest daughter, aged fourteen, was living apart from her mother in a girls' residence. Although the patient had been convicted of repeatedly molesting her from the age of five, he acknowledged only one incident, when the girl was eleven. In the therapy sessions he spent most of his time talking about how miserable he was because he was not permitted to see this daughter. As the therapist admitted in consultation, the patient had succeeded in winning him over to his side completely:

> He puts his head down between his knees and says, "Oh Jesus, I don't think there's any way I can influence the court. I just can't see my daughter till she's fuckin' twenty!"—you know, really desperate. And I'm thinking to myself, Jesus Christ, can't you work out some way this guy can see his daughter with maybe a cadre of state police, you know, with guns drawn—at least let him *see* her, let him talk to her. Part of me wants to go to bat for him and suspend all my other activities. I think that's a kind of orneriness in me. I grew up in a family that's always been for lost causes, minority kinds of causes, so I've been kicked around a lot. I wonder if I'm looking for trouble here with this guy. I feel everybody's

against him so I'll be for him. And I'll tell you a funny thing. I would like him to see the girl, 'cause I can identify with this guy. Because maybe ten years ago, when my daughter was fourteen, I remember I would look when she would walk up the stairs in a short skirt. To me, that was kind of incestuous, borderline incestuous. I identify with him in terms of my fantasies.

The patient in this case ultimately persuaded the therapist to write a letter to the court, recommending that he be allowed visitation rights with his daughter. In spite of the fact that the daughter ran away from the receiving home when she learned her father was coming to visit her there, the therapist claimed that he "did not know" how the daughter felt about this recommendation. What he meant was that he really had not considered the daughter's feelings at all.

This case illustrates what psychoanalyst Robert Langs describes as a "corrupt misalliance" between patient and therapist.[4] The therapist is manipulated in the service of the patient's antisocial purposes, and no therapy takes place. Without a sophisticated understanding of sex offenders, many therapists find themselves similarly entrapped. The moral of the story should be clear: confidentiality has no place in the treatment of sex offenders; new violations must be reported at once. And before the therapist makes any recommendations on behalf of this patient, the effect on the entire family must be evaluated and understood.

Traditional family therapy, as developed by such theorists as Murray Bowen and Salvador Minuchin, is also inappropriate for the incestuous offender.[5] The tendency of this school of thought is to attribute a multitude of evils to the combination of a "domineering" mother and a "passive" father. Intervention usually takes the form of restoring male dominance, something that does not need restoration in the incestuous family. One eminent family therapist's complete misunderstanding of the dynamics of father-daughter incest is illustrated in this account of his work by a student observer: "N. sees these fathers as wimps, as one down, and the mothers as not interested in them. He takes the focus off the father and tries to spread the problem around. In one family, the father tried to strangle the mother. N. said to her, "What did you do to deserve it?" He told her, "You're a frigid bitch.""

This approach could hardly succeed in anything other than reinforcing the father's most sadistic and psychopathic tendencies. None of the successful programs we studied makes use of this treatment model. Even those programs most committed to the ideal of restoring the nuclear family recognize that a favorable outcome requires a drastic change in the balance of power within the family, in favor of the mother.

Therapists who have worked extensively with sex offenders appear to be unanimous in their insistence that treatment must be mandated and supervised by the courts. Without this incentive, the offender does not have the necessary motivation to participate in treatment. The need for court involvement has been stressed by four authorities on the subject, all of whom are noted for their compassion and skill in treating offenders:

> The authority of the criminal justice system has proved to be absolutely essential in treating incest. Most of the small number of "drop-outs" from the CSATP [Child Sexual Abuse Treatment Program] have been families who were not involved with the police.[6]
>
> Most offenders deny the act of incest to the detriment of themselves, the victim, and the family members. The drastic personality changes which are required demand that the power of the court support such commitment to change.[7]
>
> In brief, an offender population can hardly be treated in a clinic such as [ours] without the active participation of the court and its probation department. Any time spent initially cultivating court cooperation and educating probation officers about what psychiatry can and can not deliver facilitates subsequent teamwork. Failure to do so could result in program failure, either through distrust, sabotage, or ignorance, all of which reinforce the resistance of the anti-social offenders.[8]
>
> Without the court mandate, the fathers slip away.[9]

Therapists who undertake the treatment of sex offenders should have personal, working relationships with police officers, prosecutors who handle sexual assault cases, judges, and probation officers. Contact and case review should be frequent enough to ensure that the offender in treatment meets with a united front. If there are any divisions between the agencies involved in the case, the incestuous father will find them and take advantage of them.

Successful engagement of offenders in treatment seems to be directly related to the degree of cooperation between the treatment program and the criminal justice system. In the Child Sexual Abuse Treatment Program, for example, where all of the local judges and over half of the district attorneys support the program, roughly 90 percent of the fathers referred to the program are reported to be treatable.[10] In other programs, where such close institutional ties have not been fully developed, the results are much less favorable. In one program, for example, the staff estimated that only one third of the fathers were willing to participate in the initial phases of treatment, and only about ten percent completed the program.

Most successful treatment programs for sex offenders resemble programs for the treatment of addictions, with the added inducement of legal sanctions for failure to comply. The programs begin from the premise that the offender lacks the internal motivation to change or the capacity to control his behavior. Both motivation and external control are provided by a highly structured group process that sets firm limits and offers tangible rewards.

All programs rely heavily on peer confrontation, pressure, and support. In one program, for example, the offender is required to attend weekly group sessions, to keep a daily log of his activities with special attention to his sexual impulses and behavior, to write an autobiography detailing the development of his sexual deviation, and to read and summarize educational material. The log, autobiography, and book reports are presented to the group and subjected to criticism. Group rules emphasize self-control. Smoking is forbidden, and lateness and absence are not tolerated. If an offender persists in fantasizing about the forbidden sexual activity, he is pressured by the group to give up masturbation until he can substitute a more appropriate fantasy. The use of pornography is discouraged as long as it promotes fantasies of unacceptable sexual behavior. Participants in the program undergo a kind of aversive conditioning, in which they are taught, whenever they feel an unacceptable sexual impulse, to call up an image of the consequences they most fear. This "cognitive interference" is judged to be successful when the offender experiences autonomic nervous system symptoms, such as trembling, sweating, and nausea, instead of sexual arousal.[11]

The incestuous father experiences the requirements of such a program as a severe deprivation and a challenge to his way of life. In return for the gratifications that he is forced to renounce, the offender receives a great deal of support from the group members and the leader for making positive changes in his life. As in the case of the mothers' and daughters' groups, the offenders' group offers a sense of community and an opportunity to build self-esteem.

Groups provide incestuous fathers with a powerful reward by encouraging affectionate behavior that is neither exploitative nor sexual. In one Parents United group that we observed, for example, controlled, ritualized physical contact was an essential part of the group process. Members who showed intense feeling, such as trembling or sobbing, were comforted with hugs from other group members, and the meeting ended with the entire group forming a circle and embracing. For many fathers, such an experience is entirely novel, since they are accustomed to sexualizing all their wishes for closeness and intimacy. The controlled physical contact within the group not only provides some immediate gratification but also teaches the fathers that it is possible to give and receive affection outside of a sexual relationship.

At the same time that fathers are taught to distinguish between their sexual impulses and their desires for tenderness and affection, they are strongly supported and encouraged in the establishment of adult sexual relationships. Thus the fathers learn that they are not expected to suppress their sexual feelings entirely, but rather to express them in ways that are socially acceptable.

Besides providing a system of rewards and punishments, treatment groups attempt to inculcate in the offender a rudimentary awareness of the effects of his behavior on other people. In another Parents United group, the mother of a molested child was instructed by the group leader to walk around the room, telling each offender how she felt. Weeping, she stood in front of each man in the room and repeated, "I hurt." The group leader then asked the men to acknowledge the fact that they had hurt other people. Such direct, intense, and confrontive methods are necessary to break through the offender's preoccupation with his own wishes and needs and to make him aware of the consequences of his actions.

Like treatment programs for chemical addiction, many programs for sex offenders are organized in a series of graded steps. Some programs are explicitly modeled on the twelve steps of Alcoholics Anonymous.[12] In the early stages of treatment, it is recognized that the offender has lost control of his behavior; each promotion up the ladder represents his progress in establishing self-control and in accepting responsibility for his actions. In later stages of rehabilitation, the offender is asked not only to take full responsibility for his crimes but also to make restitution for them by helping and serving others. An especially significant form of restitution is a confrontation between the incestuous father and his daughter, in which the father takes full responsibility for the sexual relationship, acknowledges that he has failed his daughter as a parent, apologizes for the harm he has done her, and promises that he will never again sexually approach or abuse her, making this promise in the presence of the therapist and all family members.

The role of the leader is of major importance in offender groups. Such groups succeed best when the leader is an authoritative, somewhat charismatic figure, who takes on the role of the benevolent patriarch, enforcing the "rule of the gift." The leader must project a feeling of comfort with his own sexuality, kindness, empathy, and incorruptibility. Any sense that the leader secretly enjoys, excuses, or condones the offenders' behavior would be quickly detected by the group. In the presence of this kind of leadership, group members become zealous in confronting and exposing the lies, rationalizations, and manipulations of their peers. Experienced group leaders acknowledge that they could never hope to become as adept at recognizing a "con" as another offender.

In the absence of effective leadership, offender groups run the risk of reverting to the form of antisocial gangs, where offenders support each other's evasions and excuses. A therapist's observation of a prison therapy group illustrates the dangers inherent in the group process:

> First of all, they objected to being called sex offenders—"Makes us look like we did something bad." This is the manipulative approach that they're taking. One guy said, "Well, maybe some of us did bad things once." We all know that it was not once, and it was not maybe; it was definitely, and it was many, many times. But they're still, after two years in this group, saying things like "maybe!" Now where is the therapy? I think it can be done, but it has to be done in a very direct way. Every time one comes to the word "maybe," or minimizing in some way, one must jump on it immediately.

Because of the dangers of gang formation which are inherent in the group process, offenders should never be allowed to become leaders in treatment or self-help parent groups. It is all too possible for an offender with charismatic leadership qualities to dominate and corrupt a small group and to use it as a cover for his own continued depredations. The only protection against this kind of development is a structure that does not cede power to the offender. Therapy groups should be led by therapists, and self-help groups such as Parents United should be presided over by mothers or adult women with a history of childhood victimization, not by offenders.

This kind of intensive outpatient group treatment is appropriate for most incestuous fathers, but not for all. Those generally considered to have the best prognosis are men who are nonviolent, who have no history of other sex offenses, who admit to what they have done, and who express some degree of remorse and desire for change. A strong work history and the absence of other complicating problems, such as alcoholism, also improve the prospects for treatment. If the father is alcoholic, it is useless to attempt treatment while he is actively drinking; sobriety is a precondition for participation in any form of therapy.

These are the external, observable criteria of treatability. Some therapists also place great importance on the father's fantasy life and evaluate the degree to which the desire for sexual relations with a child has come to dominate the father's imagination. As one expert, whose specialty is in the evaluation of sex offenders, put it: "My hypothesis is, if they acted it out once and they have a lot of fantasy life, then they're going to act it out again. Hell, they're going to find a loophole somewhere. One of the standard questions I ask—I ask them for their wallets and I thumb through. If I see a picture of a young girl, I ask, 'Is this the one you masturbate with?' If they say 'yes,' prognosis is more on the guarded side."[13]

Some fathers are clearly unsuitable for outpatient treatment, and a few are beyond the reach of any known mode of therapy. Fathers who are sadistic, violent, or grossly perverse should not be at large in the community. Treatment of them, if attempted at all, must be carried out within the confines of a secure hospital or prison ward. In Seattle, where all convicted offenders are carefully evaluated and a well-coordinated network of services are available, about 80 percent of all convicted offenders are judged to be treatable in the community. Another ten percent are considered treatable in an inpatient setting, and about ten percent are judged to be untreatable.[14]

Estimates of an offender's prognosis in treatment are subjective at best, since there are no reliable data on treatment outcomes. The long-term effects of any therapeutic program are difficult to evaluate. Most studies of psychotherapy outcome lack an untreated comparison group from which it would be possible to estimate the rate of spontaneous improvement. It is also difficult to evaluate the degree to which the success of a new, experimental program is owing to the enthusiasm and dedication of the staff rather than to their methods. Most treatment outcome studies are also plagued by poorly defined measures of success or failure and by short follow-up times.

The traditional measure of success in the treatment of sex offenders is recidivism. By definition, rehabilitated offenders do not repeat their crimes. But data on recidivism are notoriously unreliable. Recidivism is measured by a second conviction for the same offense. Most offenders, even those who are reported, are never convicted of a crime once, let alone twice. It is possible that those offenders who do suffer exposure and are forced to undergo treatment merely learn to be more cautious and to cover their tracks better the second time around.

The only available outcome study of a treatment program for incest offenders is a report by Jerome Kroth, evaluating the Child Sexual Abuse Treatment Program in San Jose for the state of California. Kroth interviewed three groups of parents at the beginning, middle, and ending stages of treatment. There were nine offenders and eight spouses in each group. The group completing treatment had been in the program for about fourteen months, significantly longer than the average treatment time of eight and one half months. At the conclusion of treatment, all of the parents claimed that the sexual abuse had stopped, but the researcher made no attempt to verify these statements by interviewing the daughters. Moreover, seven of the seventeen parents acknowledged that if a repeat offense did occur, they "might keep it a secret." This disturbing finding represented a negative outcome, since over twice as many parents said they might conceal a repeated offense at the end of treatment as at the beginning. No follow-up of any kind was undertaken once the parents were discharged from the program.[15] On the basis of this kind of evidence, it seems premature to claim no recidivism.

Since recidivism is so difficult to document, it should not be used as the major criterion for judging the success of a treatment program. Rather, the progress in rehabilitation of incestuous fathers should be measured by the well-being of their wives and children. When no one in the family feels bullied, pressured, or intimidated by the father, when the daughter feels comfortable in his presence, and when the mother finds it possible to relate to the father as a mate rather than as an overlord, then therapy can be considered successful. The proper person to evaluate the offender's progress is not the offender himself but his victim.

The offender should never be considered entirely "cured." Just as the alcoholic never loses his suceptibility to addiction, even after years of sobriety, the incestuous father can never be expected to lose sexual interest in his daughter entirely. Even after he has acknowledged full responsibility for his crime and recognized the harm he has done to his daughter, he will still crave the incestuous relationship and may attempt to revive it in subtle ways. A man who has had many years of practice in concealing, excusing, and indulging an antisocial compulsion cannot develop secure inner controls in a few months of even the most intensive treatment.

Recognizing the tenacity of the father's incestuous wishes, some therapists have argued that it is naive to imagine that fathers can ever be safely reunited with their families. Even if the overt sexual behavior is brought under control, according to this line of reasoning, the father will never abandon his effort to dominate his family and to control his daughter's life. The well-being of the mother and children is not adequately protected if, as a result of therapy, an incestuous father is simply converted into a seductive one. As Lucy Berliner, a social worker at the Harborview Sexual Assault Center, observed: "In some of the families that I've seen where the parents want to stay together, the kids end up leaving as soon as they can, even though they are no longer being molested. A lot of the kids say it's still the same power trip, it's still the same power structure that made them uncomfortable in the first place."[16] According to this view, the interests of the mother and children are best served by a permanent separation from the father.

Yet many other therapists feel strongly that it is in the best interests of all concerned for fathers to return to their families. The very names of such self-help groups as Parents United or Families Re-United make it clear that the emphasis is on re-establishing the nuclear family. Those who espouse this point of view argue that children suffer greatly as the result of parental divorce and that the incest victim in particular is bound to become a scapegoat in her family if the disclosure of incest leads to a permanent rupture between the parents. As Peter Coleman, director of the Tacoma Child Protective Service, put it: "We recognize the need of the child to be socialized in her family. She has been victimized by sexual assault and other negative relationship factors, but she is twice victimized if a viable family is destroyed."[17]

This difference of opinion is not simply an academic controversy, for the outcome of treatment depends to a great extent on the program philosophy. Because the families are so thoroughly disrupted during the crisis of disclosure, they are, for a time at least, highly malleable. The resolution of the crisis may depend as much upon the goals of the treatment program as upon the wishes of the family members. In those programs where reuniting the parents is seen as a desirable goal, most couples in treatment reconcile. The Child Sexual Abuse Treatment Program, for example, reports that 76 percent of its couples are reunited at the end of treatment.[18] In those programs where keeping the parents together is not considered desirable, most parents separate.

The decision whether or not to reunite with the father properly belongs to the mother, after she has had an opportunity to find out that she can manage on her own, and after the mother-daughter bond has been restored. Premature pressure to reunite the parental couple should be avoided. Everyone has a sentimental longing for happy endings, but this feeling should not obscure the immense changes that are necessary in order to create a healthy family once the incestuous pattern has been established. Mothers must learn to become more dominant, while fathers must learn to become more submissive and nurturant. These changes run counter not only to entrenched family habits but also to traditional social norms.

In any case, fathers should not be readmitted into their families until three conditions have been met. First, the father should be under supervision of the court. Second, he should be actively involved in an appropriate treatment program. And third, he should have reached the point where he accepts complete responsibility for the incestuous relationship and has apologized to his daughter in the presence of the entire family. These conditions ensure at least a minimum degree of comfort and safety for the daughter.

Reuniting the parental couple should never be considered the end point of treatment or the criterion for success. The most meaningful index of family rehabilitation is the health of the mother-daughter relationship. If the father does re-enter the family, mother and daughter need to be assured of continued protection and support. Fathers who return to their families should therefore remain on probation for as long as their daughters remain at home. An arbitrary six-month or one-year follow-up is entirely inadequate.

The enormity of the changes required for the rehabilitation of the incestuous family cannot be overestimated. Fathers are asked not only to renounce a compulsive, pleasurable habit but also to give up power over their families and to become more responsive to the needs of others. Mothers long inured to submission and dependency are suddenly asked to become more independent and assertive. These changes challenge not only the tyranny of the individual father but the socially sanctioned system of male supremacy within the family. Such ambitious changes have a significance beyond the individual; they take on some of the aspects of a political or religious conversion.

A strongly religious atmosphere is in fact found in many treatment programs for offenders, particularly those that emphasize reuniting the family. The intensely emotional environment created by the group process, the emphasis on confession, expiation of sin, and spiritual renewal, and the rituals involved in the progression up the steps of the treatment ladder all contribute to the evocation of religious feeling. The attempt to create community, the veneration of the leader, and the zeal and dedication of the active membership in organizations such as Parents United give these groups the aura of an embattled religious sect. Many programs also share common features with systems of political re-education developed in revolutionary societies. Like political re-education programs, they are designed for men who have used their power to oppress and exploit others but who are judged not to be irremediably depraved. Like political re-education programs, they are coercive, they make use of intense peer group confrontation and support, and they require confession, apology and restitution. Like political re-education programs they attempt to create a "new man."

10
Criminal Justice

"What was the defendant wearing?" That was Mr. Freeman's lawyer.
"I don't know."
*"You mean to say this man raped you and you don't know what he
was wearing?" He snickered as if I had raped Mr. Freeman. "Do you
know if you were raped?"*
*A sound pushed in the air of the court (I was sure it was laughter). I
was glad that Mother had let me wear the navy-blue winter coat with
brass buttons. Although it was too short and the weather was typical St.
Louis hot, the coat was a friend that I hugged to me in the strange and
unfriendly place.*
—*Maya Angelou,* I Know Why the Caged Bird Sings, 1970

Sexual relations between adults and children are forbidden by law
in every state. Curiously, however, most incestuous relations between fathers and daughters do not meet the statutory definition of the crime of
"incest," but rather fall under the definition of somewhat lesser crimes,
such as "carnal abuse of a child," "indecent liberties with children," or
"corrupting the morals of a minor." Incest statutes are primarily concerned with prohibiting marriage and inbreeding among kin, not with
protecting children. The definition of incest is therefore usually restricted to sexual intercourse between blood relatives. Only five states
include sexual conduct other than intercourse in their incest statutes.
Eighteen states include intercourse between adoptive parent and child,
and twenty-four states include intercourse between stepparent and child
in their definitions of incest.[1]

Most states legally recognize a spectrum of sexual offenses against
children, other than incest, which are considered more or less serious depending upon the age of the child, the extent of sexual contact, and the

degree of coercion used. Almost every state reserves its most severe penalties for violent sexual assaults upon young children. Many states punish intercourse much more harshly than other sexual acts. In Alaska, for example, sexual penetration with a child under thirteen carries a maximum term of twenty years imprisonment. Sexual contact not involving penetration with the same child carries a maximum sentence of five years. Some states also make a strong distinction between sexual acts committed upon children and the same acts committed upon adolescents. In Kentucky, for example, sexual intercourse with a child under twelve is first-degree rape, punishable by ten to twenty years in prison. Intercourse between an adult and a child twelve to sixteen years old is third-degree rape, punishable by one to five years imprisonment. In Mississippi, carnal knowledge of a female under twelve is punishable by life imprisonment or even the death penalty; carnal knowledge of a chaste female over twelve and under eighteen is punishable by a fine not exceeding five hundred dollars, six months in the county jail, or up to five years imprisonment.[2]

On the books, the punishments for sexual relations with children often appear to be extremely harsh. In seventeen states, a man could theoretically receive a life sentence for intercourse with his prepubertal child, and in three states (Florida, Mississippi, and Oklahoma), it would be theoretically possible for him to receive the death penalty. In practice, however, these crimes are rarely prosecuted and even more rarely punished. The obstacles to enforcement of the laws against sexual abuse are numerous. The victim is usually afraid to complain. If she does complain, however, she puts herself at the mercy of a male-dominated criminal justice system which offers more comfort and protection to the male sex offender than to the female victim.

Females who press charges of sexual assault are often portrayed as spiteful and vindictive. In fact, most incest victims will endure almost any amount of abuse rather than subject their fathers to the punishments prescribed by law. The threat of severe penalties for sexual crimes does little to deter fathers from molesting their children; it does a great deal, however, to reinforce the secrecy of the forbidden relationship. Incestuous fathers are usually keenly aware that they are breaking the law, and often they enjoin their daughters to silence by portraying the terrifying punishments which will befall them if the secret is disclosed. No matter how miserable a daughter may be, she is likely to remain silent as long as she fears that a word from her will loose the full vengeance of the law upon her father, her family, and herself:

Rita: Although he was a no-good bastard, he did try to keep us together, which I knew was my mother's wish. And all I could do was picture my father in prison for years to come, without his kids, with nobody. All I could visualize was him sitting in a cell by himself, just thinking, you know. That hurt. I could picture my father going home from work, walking up the stairs to our apartment, opening the door expecting to find us kids running around, and there'd be nobody there. Then he'd turn around and there'd be two detectives waiting to take him to the police station. And I didn't like that picture. It seemed so cold, unfeeling, hard, something like that. That wasn't the type of person I was.

The daughter does not want to see her father punished. She wants him to stop abusing her, to start behaving like a trustworthy parent, and to make amends for his past mistreatment. If she is very alienated from her father or has despaired of his ability to reform, she may want him to leave the family; rarely does she want to see him in prison. She turns to the law only in desperation, when the incestuous relationship has become so unbearable that she is willing to take any risk in order to put an end to it.

It is difficult to estimate the percentage of incest cases which reach the stage of a formal complaint. In our study, three out of the forty victims (7.5 percent) filed charges with the police. In a similar study of clinic patients in California, seven out of thirty-eight cases (17 percent) reached the preliminary stages of court involvement.[3] Estimates that derive from general surveys rather than from clinical literature are even lower. In one study, only six percent of over three hundred women who had had sexual experiences with adults before the age of thirteen recalled that the incident had been reported to the police.[4] And in the state of Illinois, the Child Advocate Association of Chicago estimated that only about three percent of the approximately 22,000 cases of intrafamily sexual abuse are reported to the police each year.[5]

Even when legal proceedings are begun, the chances that an incestuous father will be convicted and imprisoned are remote. As a defendant charged with a sexual offense, he has vastly greater legal protection than the child who accuses him. First, he has the constitutional rights, guaranteed to all criminal defendants, to be considered innocent until proven guilty, to confront his accuser in a public trial, and to cross-examine any witness against him. These safeguards, designed for adversary proceedings between adults, give an enormous advantage to the defendant, where the only witness for the prosecution is a child, dependent on his care and habitually obedient to his authority. In addition, many states require corroboration of the victim's testimony against any person accused of sex offenses. Since the incestuous relationship almost always occurs in secrecy, this requirement makes conviction of the father virtually impossible.

For example, in *People* v. *Willmore* (1974), the Appellate Court of Illinois reversed the conviction of a father for aggravated incest with two daughters, on the grounds that the girls' uncorroborated testimony was "not convincing." The mother testified that her daughters had never complained to her, and the father unequivocally denied the charges. The parents' united stance, plus the daughters' inability to name specific dates on which sexual relations had occurred, led the judge to dismiss the case. If this precedent were followed, conviction of most incestuous fathers would be out of the question, since few daughters complain to their mothers, and even fewer keep track of the specific dates on which they are molested.[6]

Prosecution of a case of incest usually takes from four months to over a year. From the time of the initial complaint until final disposition of the case, the father is at liberty and, unless specifically restricted by the court, has free access to his wife and daughters. In no other criminal situation does the defendant have such power over the complainant. Though some fathers confess after the charge is made, many steadfastly deny the daughter's accusations and relentlessly pressure their daughters to retract the charges. Many mothers rally to the fathers' side. Even if they believe their daughters, they plead with them to drop the charges. If the daughter persists against her parents' will, she may be vilified, ostracized, and threatened with expulsion from the family. Few girls are strong enough to withstand this kind of pressure without wavering. A twelve-year-old girl, who recanted on the witness stand, explained her reasons: "We went to court and my mother told me to lie. I told her I'm not gonna tell no lie. But she said you better. I didn't know what she was gonna do, so I went ahead and told them it wasn't true. Then after that I had to go see a detective. He said he believed me, he knew my story was true. I cried about it because I couldn't change what I had done. Then my father came around and asked me to have sex with him again."

The daughter who manages to withstand intense pressure from her family may still collapse when she comes face to face with the judicial process in the person of detectives, prosecutors, attorneys, and judges.

She must be prepared to reveal the most minute and intimate details of her sexual experience to strange men who may be skeptical, indifferent, or overtly hostile to her. Detectives and prosecutors will interrogate her repeatedly, and they may deliberately subject her to bullying, insults, and humiliation, supposedly to test how well her testimony will hold up in the courtroom. If the case goes to trial, she must be prepared to endure public cross-examination by the defense attorney, who is obliged to try to discredit her. And if, by some incredible feat of endurance, she persists to the point of a conviction, she must be prepared to hear a lecture from the judge on the importance of keeping families together, to be asked sternly why she wants to throw her father in jail and her mother on the welfare rolls, and then to face her father's eventual return to the family with no further protection.

In the face of these obstacles, many victims retract or change their stories at some point. Yet law enforcement officers generally appear incapable of recognizing the intimidating effects of criminal procedures on child witnesses. The tendency of victims to vacillate simply reinforces the official suspicion that they are lying. All too commonly, complaints of incest are met with incredulity, whereas retractions are accepted on the flimsiest pretexts. One judge described with great satisfaction how he had "gotten to the bottom" of an alleged incest case. Under his astute questioning, the girl had admitted falsely accusing her stepfather in revenge for a strict curfew he had imposed on her. That a child would invent so serious a slander for so trivial a reason did not appear incongruous to the judge, nor did he see the relevance of the fact that the girl was still living under her stepfather's roof when she recanted.

In reality, false denials of incest are vastly more common than false complaints. Most young victims simply do not have the emotional strength to endure the ordeal of a criminal investigation and trial. Investigators who have gone to great lengths to validate complaints of sexual abuse report that unfounded cases are extremely rare. Henry Giarretto of the Child Sexual Abuse Treatment Program in San Jose, for example, estimated that fewer than one percent of all reports received by his program had proved to be false.[7] Another team which carefully evaluated forty-six families referred to a child protective agency in Albuquerque, New Mexico, concluded that only one allegation of incest was unfounded. In this case, the complaint served as a device to draw attention to a family which was troubled in other ways, and the child readily admitted fabricating the story as soon as she and her family received the psychiatric services they needed. The authors concluded that children were much more likely to back down from a true accusation than to invent a false one.[8]

With so many legal and psychological advantages, incestuous fathers have little to fear from the law. Even if a complaint is made, which is unlikely, the chances are slight that the case will ever go to trial, still slighter that the father will be found guilty, and even slighter that, if convicted, he will be sentenced to prison. The odds in favor of fathers may be judged from a study of 250 police reports of sexual assaults on children in New York City. In the majority of cases (75 percent), either no arrest was made (31 percent) or the accused was arraigned but never brought to trial (44 percent). Cases were dismissed for lack of corroborating evidence, or because the child, in the prosecutor's estimation, would not make a good witness, or simply to spare the child the rigors of a court appearance. Thirty-eight men pleaded guilty voluntarily to lesser charges, and an additional fifteen were found guilty after a trial. Of these 53 men convicted (21 percent), over half (30) received fines or suspended sentences with or without probation. Twenty-three men, or nine percent of the total, were sentenced to prison, the majority for one year or less.[9] On the books, then, the punishments for sexual abuse of children may be severe, but in practice they are almost never carried out.

In those few instances where fathers are convicted of their crimes, there is little evidence that enforcement of the law leads to any significant change. Placing the father on probation is usually a meaningless gesture, since few probation officers have the time or the inclination to supervise the fathers closely. And fathers who have succeeded in corrupting or intimidating their families usually have little difficulty with a probation officer. As one probation officer ruefully admitted: "The p.o.'s tend to get conned. First of all, they don't want to talk about the subject. Of if they do, it's really for their voyeuristic needs. It makes me sick the kinds of questions they ask the people. Mostly they just close their minds and say, 'We'll let bygones be bygones.' Or else, 'Jesus, how was it?' You know, I'm embarrassed even to tell you people about it."

A jail sentence is no more guarantee of reform than a period of probation. During the period that the father is incarcerated, the children may be protected, but after his release there is rarely any force stronger than his own conscience—already proven a thin reed—to prevent a new attempt to re-establish the old relationship. If anything, he may emerge from prison embittered and defiant:

Rita: He should have got rape to minors, statutory rape, and incest, but his lawyer got him down to a charge of attempted rape to a minor. He got two to five years, and he was out after eighteen months for good behavior with two years probation.

I don't feel sorry for my father, because after he got out of prison and married my stepmother—he could have had all the sex in the world he wanted with her—I went to him for assistance one time. I wanted to take a course so I could get a promotion, and it cost fifty dollars and I didn't have it, so I called him up and asked him if I could borrow it. I told him I'd pay him back ten or fifteen dollars a week: I wasn't asking for any handouts. He said, "Don't you know you can make that in one night, and all you do is lay back and enjoy your work?"

It was at that point I knew that if we had stayed together, he would have raised us girls to be his prostitutes, and he would have been our pimp. He came out and said that. If I didn't break up the family when I did—as far as I was concerned, I wasn't destroying the family, I was helping the family; I see it now.

When I asked him for the fifty dollars again, he propositioned me; he wanted another sexual relationship. By this time I was nineteen years old. I said, "Dad, you know, I'm a big girl now, I know right from wrong, and I know what I can do to you if you attempt it again." 'Cause I was still a minor; at that time the legal age was twenty-one. And it's still incest, no matter how old I get.

A year or so later, we talked about prison, what it was like, and about what happened at home, and who was responsible. He said, "Gee, you know, I really don't feel any remorse." He said, "I don't feel I've done anything wrong." I said, "What about prison, wasn't that hard to take?" "Oh no, prison was like a vacation. I didn't have to get up every morning, go to work, worry about feeding all those mouths, clothing all those backs." He doesn't have any conscience. If he could do it again, he would.

The judicial system, in summary, gives little solace to victims of incest. The laws as written are rarely enforced and, when enforced, rarely benefit the child. The threat of punishment does little to inhibit incestuous fathers, and the fact of punishment does nothing to rehabilitate them. In effect, the justice system serves to uphold and protect the authority of the father, no matter how abusive.

In the light of this dismal performance, many observers have argued that legal intervention in incestuous families inevitably does more harm than good, that the justice system cannot be expected to operate in the interests of children, and that victims and their families are best served by avoiding the justice system altogether.[10] We disagree. Deficient as the judicial system may be, it represents a potential limit to the abuse of paternal authority. In the laws against sexual abuse there are at least the rudiments of a social concern for the protection of children. At present, when the claims of parental privilege conflict with the child's right to protection, the balance of power in the justice system favors the father, and the law is therefore not enforced. But the balance of power in the justice system can potentially be modified so that the interests of children are better represented, and so that parental privilege does not automatically confer immunity from the law.

Conviction of an incest offender has a profound and generally salutary effect upon the child and the family. When a father pleads or is found guilty, the child victim is relieved of an enormous psychological burden. She is assured that the larger world does not condone incest, and that her right to the privacy of her body is respected. She also learns that others both believe in her truthfulness and hold her father responsible for the sexual relationship.

Conviction, or the threat of conviction, may also offer the best hope for the treatment and rehabilitation of offenders. Without the threat of punishment, most incestuous fathers simply do not have the motivation to change. Even after the abuse is exposed, most fathers will not voluntarily participate in treatment. They will do so, however, if treatment is ordered by the court as a condition of pretrial diversion, probation, or parole.

Legal intervention need not inevitably be destructive to children. Where the victim is treated with consideration and respect, where her complaints are taken seriously, and where police and court procedures are appropriately modified for children, the trauma of the legal process can be greatly reduced. This has been demonstrated with the development of advocacy programs for child victims.

Advocacy programs are a product of movements for social reform. A century ago, concern over the exploitation of children led to the founding of societies for the prevention of cruelty to children, a few of which still survive. The Brooklyn, New York, Society for the Prevention of Cruelty to Children, for example, has had a vigorous child advocacy program, offering special expertise in sexual abuse, since the 1880s.[11] In the past decade, the feminist movement has been largely responsible for the renewed development of child advocacy programs. Women who organized and staffed the rape crisis centers have been among the first to recognize the scope of the problem of child sexual abuse, to develop innovative services for abused children, and to fight for legal reforms. Where advocacy programs now exist, numbering in the dozens across the country, the legal system can be made less frightening to children and less injurious to families. Sometimes it can even be made to do what it is supposed to do: convict offenders.

A victim advocate is a person who understands both the emotional needs of the child and the intricacies of the legal system. For the duration of the court proceedings, she stands by the child and her mother, offering information, reassurance, and moral support. She accompanies the child to interviews with detectives and prosecutors and to court hearings. She explains what is happening and what is likely to happen. She acts as an interpreter of the legal system to the child and of the child to the legal system. She is available during the crises that inevitably occur, and her presence to some extent shields the child from the terrors of the law and the intense pressures within the family.

Lucy Berliner, one of the pioneers of victim advocacy, describes the counselor's role:

> We explain to them what can happen and what the words mean, because you can't count on lawyers to speak in language that normal people understand. A lot of time the prosecutor will ask a question and the kid will have no idea what he's talking about. It helps when there's somebody there to say, 'Do you understand what he's saying," something like that.
>
> We stick with them. We get a lot of feedback: the family's put the pressure on, they've changed their minds. It's always up and down during that time, because they tend not to know what's going on. Or, very commonly, the father will lay a big trip on them—"Oh, I'm facing twenty years in prison." When has that *ever* happened? So you have to be very involved. They have to trust you enough to call you whenever they get pressured, to learn to check it out.
>
> That's what we keep telling them: check it out. Don't accept anything that comes from him directly, because you've got to understand, he's worried about himself, not you. So check it out. Then we do a lot of liaison work. We call the detective and call

the prosecutor: "What's happening, where is the case, what are you charging, what are you recommending?"[12]

The presence of the advocate strengthens the child's position to such an extent that in most cases the father, rather than the daughter, backs down from the legal confrontation. One program reports that in 75 percent of the incest cases handled by their staff, fathers have pleaded guilty.[13] Incestuous fathers are accustomed to getting their way by intimidating their wives and daughters. When, with the help of the advocate the daughter refuses to be intimidated, the father's bluff often collapses:

> We've had cases where they wait up until the very day of the trial, seeing if the victim's going to back off. A lot of times a mother will say to me, "I'm not going to let my kid go in to trial, that's just too much." I say, "O.K., fine, but don't tell people that right now. Let's just see if by filing the charges and letting him know you're serious, see if he'll admit to it and plead guilty." And in fact very few cases go to trial, because in most cases there's a plea. Most incest offenders admit to it, on one level or another. They may minimize it or rationalize it or excuse it, but in very few cases will they go to trial. There's always a trial set, but they'll plead that morning or any time from the point they're charged to the trial date itself.[14]

The intervention of an advocate may be sufficient to reverse the balance of power between an individual father and daughter. But organized intervention on a much larger scale is necessary to overcome the institutional bias in favor of fathers within the criminal justice system. Some of this work involves changing procedures; but by far the larger part involves changing the attitudes of men who enforce the law.

Vitually an all-male club, the justice system is, by even the most charitable estimate, abysmally ignorant and careless of children. Police and prosecutors must learn how to talk and listen to children. Judges must learn to use their discretionary powers to protect child victims and control offenders. Probation officers must learn to recognize signs of recidivism. Most of all, officers of the law must give up their presumption that children lie about sexual abuse. When law enforcement officers, who are not generally known for their tender concern for the civil rights of the accused, nevertheless display such a concern toward incestuous fathers at the expense of their victims, it constitutes something close to collusion in the crime.

Given a cooperative attitude on the part of law enforcement, numerous procedural reforms could be instituted for the benefit of child victims. The primary object of such reforms is to protect the child during the months between the initial complaint and the disposition of the case. Special interviewing methods that make the process less frightening and minimize repetition and delay are essential, as are measures designed to protect the child from intimidation by the defendant.

The period of investigation can be made much less disturbing to the child if a single prosecutor is assigned for the duration of the case, so that the child becomes accustomed to one person. It is also helpful if the number and duration of interviews are limited, and if interviews are carried out in a supportive environment, such as at home instead of in the prosecutor's office. The child should be allowed to have a supportive person present during the inverview, such as her mother or an advocate. And most of all, the investigator must understand how to question a child.

Most detectives and prosecutors are not comfortable discussing sexual matters with children. This is a skill, however, that can be learned. Here, for example, are some suggestions from a training manual for criminal justice personnel, written by women at the Harborview Sexual Assault Center. Some of the instructions may seem elementary, but they are often new to law enforcement officials accustomed to a more rugged style of interrogation:

> Be sure child understands words. Be careful with words like incident, occur, prior, penetration, ejaculation, etc.
>
> Do not ask WHY questions ("Why did you go to the house? Why didn't you tell?"). They tend to sound accusatory.
>
> Be aware that the child who has been instructed or threatened not to tell by the offender (ESPECIALLY IF A PARENT) will be very reluctant and full of anxiety. The fears often need to be allayed.
>
> Never threaten or try to force a reluctant child to talk.[15]

Interrogation of the child may also be carried out by someone other than a detective or prosecutor. This method has been adopted in other countries. In Sweden and Denmark, the child is questioned by a caseworker and a policewoman working together.[16] In Israel, the child is interviewed by a "youth examiner," who is trained in both child psychology and legal investigation. The youth examiner is given broad powers in determining the course of the case. She may decide whether or not the child will be permitted to testify. She may accompany the child in court and may even present evidence in court in lieu of the victim. In order to protect the rights of the defendant, a conviction cannot be obtained on the testimony of the youth examiner alone. Corroboration is required when the youth examiner testifies in lieu of the victim.[17]

The youth examiner system as practiced in Israel cannot be applied in this country because of the constitutional protection against the introduction of hearsay evidence in court. Nevertheless, many features of the system could be adopted here. In particular, the development of a specialized corps of investigators with training in child psychology as well as law could be carried out within any police department or prosecutor's office in this country.

The tensions of the period of investigation can also be reduced by preventing fathers from harassing and intimidating their daughters. At the time of arraignment, judges have the power to set conditions limiting the defendant's activities until the trial. When a child files a criminal complaint against her father, it is reasonable to expect that the father will use his authority to influence her testimony. Therefore, for the child's protection, the father should be ordered to vacate the home and should be forbidden unsupervised contact with his daughter while the case is pending.

Reforms of the processes preceding trial are especially important because the great majority of cases never reach the courtroom. Most criminal cases are settled by negotiation between prosecutor, defense attorney, and judge. These people determine, according to informal but well-established procedures, whether the prosecutor has a strong enough case for a conviction. If not, the case is dropped; if so, the charge and sentence are negotiated through plea bargaining. With the help of an advocate, this bureaucratic process can be influenced to protect the child victim and to increase the likelihood of a guilty plea. Since all the parties involved in the case—the prosecutor and defense attorney as well as the family—are usually interested in avoiding a trial, most cases are resolved in this manner. However, in the rare instances when a case does proceed to trial, special modifications of courtroom procedure are necessary in order to make testifying less traumatic for the child. Reforms which have been proposed include limiting the child's exposure to the public, limiting the extent to which the child may be questioned, and minimizing the direct confrontation between the child and the defendant.

In some circumstances, the judge has the option to exclude the public from the courtroom or to hear the case in chambers. This is far less embarrassing and stressful to the child than a trial in open court. The Child Advocate Association of Chicago recommends that very young children be permitted to testify in chambers specially decorated and stocked with toys. A comfortable, private space should also be provided where the child can rest, play, and be with familiar people during the inevitable long waits and delays that occur in court.[18]

If a full jury trial is required, some advocates have suggested the use of a special children's courtroom, where the accused, the jury, and the public observe the trial from behind a one-way mirror or on closed-circuit television. Only the judge, prosecutor, defense attorney, and plaintiff's attorney or advocate are admitted into the room with the child. The accused and his defense attorney can communicate by means of an intercom. In this manner, the defendant's right to a public trial is protected, while the child is not forced to confront her father nor to testify before a crowd of strangers.[19]

The most controversial proposal for the protection of the child witness involves the introduction of videotaped rather than live testimony in the courtroom. Under such a system, the child's testimony, including her response to cross-examination by the defense attorney, is recorded in one session soon after the filing of charges; if the case goes to trial, the videotape is presented in court.[20] This procedure minimizes the child's exposure to repeated interrogation and protects her from confrontation with her father and the public in court. The recording of testimony soon after the initial complaint also increases the likelihood that the child will make a "good witness," since as time passes, her memory of the sexual relationship is bound to become more uncertain and confused. However, the constitutionality of such a procedure is debatable. It has not been tested.

If the case is resolved by a guilty plea or a conviction, the issue of appropriate sentencing for the father must be addressed. Although the judge is constrained by the terms of the law and the conventions of plea bargaining, he usually retains considerable discretion over sentencing. In most cases, if appropriate therapy is available, a long suspended sentence with mandatory treatment as a condition of probation is the most constructive choice. Judges must become familiar with existing treatment programs for incestuous offenders and must learn to recognize which offenders may be safely returned to the community. Because specialized treatment programs for incest offenders are still relatively few in number, fathers may have to suffer considerable inconvenience, such as long-distance travel and expense, in order to participate in a program. Most fathers will still find this preferable to a jail sentence.

Mandatory treatment is ineffective, however, unless the father's compliance is adequately enforced. Probation officers must maintain frequent contact with the family, the child, and the professionals who are responsible for treatment. On occasion, also, a probation officer must be prepared to take punitive action when the conditions of probation are violated. A prison sentence is entirely appropriate for fathers who fail to comply with the stipulations of the court.

Beyond procedural reforms, the laws themselves often need to be rewritten so that they more effectively serve the purpose of protecting children. In general, reforms should facilitate the conviction but mitigate the punishment of offenders.

Many state laws require a redefinition of coercion and consent, so that the compelling authority of a parental figure is recognized. Most laws currently stipulate an arbitrary age of consent for sexual relations, ranging from puberty to late adolescence.[21] Above this age, sexual contact is illegal only if achieved by physical threat or force, or if it falls within the narrow definition of incest as intercourse with a blood relative. But as long as a child remains a dependent under the disciplinary authority of an adult, she is incapable of consenting freely to sexual relations with that person. The use of parental power to gain sexual contact should be recognized as a criminal form of coercion, regardless of the age of the child. A few states have recently made such provisions. Ohio, for example, defines sexual battery, a felony, more broadly: "No person shall engage in sexual conduct with another when . . . the offender is the other person's natural or adoptive parent, or a stepparent, or guardian, custodian, or person in loco parentis."[22]

The requirement for corroborated testimony in cases of incest or child sexual abuse should be abolished. This requirement, which reflects an exaggerated male concern over false accusations, puts an entirely unreasonable burden of proof upon the child victim and renders the laws against sexual abuse unenforceable.

Finally, milder and more therapeutically oriented sentences should be given for offenders convicted of sexual crimes against children. The recommendation of more moderate punishment is not meant in any way to condone these crimes, but rather to remove an additional obstacle to conviction of offenders. Victims may be less reluctant to accuse, district attorneys to prosecute, juries to convict, and judges to sentence incestuous fathers if they know that their actions will not result in an unreasonably severe punishment. Except for the small minority of sadistic, violent, or grossly perverse offenders who are beyond the reach of any known modality of therapy, little social benefit is to be derived from long imprisonment.

An exception to the principle of milder sentencing should be made, however, in the case of men convicted of a second offense or those who violate the conditions of their probation or parole. Some states have recently passed legislation mandating minimum sentences for repeat offenders. New Jersey, for example, mandates a minimum five-year sentence, without the possibility of parole or probation, for men convicted a second time of sexual assault.[23]

As in the case of other crimes against women and children, for too long the power of the justice system has protected the offender. That same power can be exercised to protect the victim. But as long as the justice system remains a male preserve, it can hardly be expected to reform itself in favor of the rights of children. The initiative for those reforms that have already been carried out has come almost entirely from women; from the rape counselors, the child advocates, and the small minority of women who work within the justice system. The initiative for the much larger reforms that are needed will also undoubtedly come from women. We look forward to a time when women, who are so frequently the victims and so rarely the offenders, adjudicate the majority of domestic and sexual crimes.

11
Remedies for Victims

I know that the devastation of incest can be overcome. Hundreds of my patients have done it. I did it. So can others.
—*Susan Forward*, Betrayal of Innocence, *1978*

Most incest victims reach adulthood bearing their secrets intact. It is not known how many successfully bury their past and go on with their lives, and how many continue to suffer the effects of their victimization. There is reason to suspect that a substantial proportion, perhaps even the majority of incest victims, feel lastingly scarred by their childhood experience. The complaints of the women we have interviewed about their experiences are so similar as to suggest the existence of a syndrome common to all incest victims, a syndrome that often leads to repeated disappointments in intimate relationships in adult life.

Because the psychological effects of incest so often persist into adulthood, many victims eventually seek help from counselors in the various mental health professions. Although the proportion of incest victims who seek such help is not known, the numbers are so large that therapists who practice for any length of time are bound to see incest victims among their patients, whether they know it or not. In one outpatient clinic, for example, a random review of case records showed that four percent of the women who sought counseling, without any prompting at all, had volunteered a history of incest.[1] In our own study, the therapists we interviewed estimated that anywhere from two to twenty percent of their women patients had an incest history. Those who gave the higher estimates were those who had learned to ask routinely about sexual abuse in childhood. In one published report, a psychiatrist in private practice discovered that one third of all his women patients had an incest history. No special interviewing technique was necessary to obtain this information.

All that was needed was an awareness of the reality of incest and a willingness to ask about it.[2]

Questions about sexual abuse should be incorporated into any clinician's ordinary history-taking. The prevalence of child sexual abuse even in the general population is great enough to warrant routine questioning. In a patient population, one might expect to encounter an even higher proportion of women with histories of sexual abuse and especially of women who continue to suffer from their childhood trauma. Moreover, direct questioning can be a great boon to patients who are troubled by their incest experience but who do not dare to raise the issue themselves. Over and over we have heard the testimony of victims who longed for the opportunity to talk about their experiences with a helping person and who waited in vain to be asked. The burden of responsibility for obtaining a history of incest should lie with the therapist. There can be no therapy for the long-term sequelae of the incest trauma if the therapist never learns that the incest has taken place.

Therapists of both sexes are often resistant to the idea of raising questions about sexual abuse with their patients. Most if not all of these resistances reflect the therapists' discomfort in confronting their own feelings about the issue. The therapists' wish to shy away from the possibility of incest is often disguised as concern for the patient. They may express the fear that direct questioning will offend or frighten the patient or "put ideas into her head." Such solicitude is rarely necessary. A woman who is not troubled by a history of incest will simply answer no and go on to talk about the other things that are bothering her. Asking about incest is like asking about any other taboo subject, such as alcoholism, violence, or suicide. If the therapist is reasonably comfortable posing the question, the patient will be comfortable answering it.

If clinicians decide not to question routinely about sexual abuse, they should at least be aware of certain indications that make such questioning imperative. Women who present a history of repeated victimization, such as battering or rape, should be asked about sexual abuse in their history. So should women who are alcoholic or drug dependent, or who give a history of unusual adolescent turmoil or running away. Women whose mothers have been ill or absent or who have taken on adult caretaking responsibilities in their families from an early age should be questioned. Because these circumstances are so frequently associated with a history of childhood sexual abuse, failure to raise the question in these cases amounts to negligence on the part of the therapist.

Once the incest history is revealed, the patient and therapist have the opportunity to decide together whether it should be the focus of psychotherapy. Most women choose not to engage in ongoing therapy once they have revealed their secret. Simply having the opportunity to talk about the incest once, in the company of a therapist who believes the story and reacts in a calm, supportive manner, is sufficient for some women. For others, who feel more keenly the ways in which they are still suffering from their experiences, psychotherapy can be enormously helpful. Here is the testimony of one woman who was lucky enough to find a good therapist:

> To those of you who are incest victims I would like to say this: digging into my family experience has been (still is) one of the most depressing and painful periods of my life and I didn't start to do it *until I was ready* and really wanted to do it, feeling I had to understand myself. Through therapy I have come to see pain and fear as teachers, not as something to push down and run away from. I want to have relationships that are good for me, be able to love myself, be able to enjoy working and being creative, to see and feel the beautiful things of life more fully and be stronger and more able to fight against oppression . . . Through giving in to my pain and fear enough to clearly feel and see what's there, I'm getting to the roots of why I feel and behave the way I do. I know my pain and fears will never disappear entirely, but at least they won't control me any more . . . Only through a clear understanding of myself and also of my environment will I be able to make positive choices for myself, minimizing future suffering and maximizing satisfaction.[3]

The therapist's contribution is never mentioned in this patient's description of her successful therapy. By implication, the therapist did her job unobtrusively and well. She listened empathically to the incest history and did not get in the patient's way. She was sufficiently comfortable with her own feelings about incest so that she could tolerate the patient's feelings. She allowed and encouraged the patient to do the necessary work of therapy.

Many incest victims, unfortunately, do not have such happy experiences with their therapists. Too often, victims turn to mental health professionals who are unprepared to help them. This is not simply a problem of individual therapists. It is an institutional problem. Most therapists lack the ability to help incest victims because they have never been trained to deal with the issue. In fact, they have been trained to avoid it. Psychoanalytic tradition has created an atmosphere of denial and disbelief within the mental health professions. Within training institutions, the result has been a perpetuation of ignorance from one generation of professionals to the next.

Learning how to do psychotherapy is a complex process, much of which is transacted in the relationship between the beginning therapists and experienced supervisors. When the beginning therapists encounter problems that are beyond their range of experience, the supervisors usually assist in several ways. First, the supervisors offer an intellectual framework in which to understand the problem. References to the professional literature are often suggested. Second, the supervisors offer practical, problem-solving help with the strategies of therapy. Third and most important, the supervisors help the less experienced therapists to deal with feelings of their own that have been evoked by the patients. With the support of competent supervisors, the therapists are usually able to master their own troubled feelings and put them in perspective. This done, the therapists are better able to attend to patients with empathy, and with a confidence in their ability to offer help.

In the matter of sexual abuse, however, the tradition of institutional denial has resulted in a situation in which supervisors are no more knowledgeable than beginners. Until recently, there was little professional literature to offer the therapist intellectual support. There was no body of practical experience transmitted by oral tradition, other than the continuing tradition that questions the veracity of patients' complaints. Most important, there was no requirement for therapists to examine their own assumptions and feelings about incest. Institutional denial thus reinforced the individual therapists' tendency to deny and avoid facing their feelings.

Many therapists recall that early in their training, they inadvertently obtained an incest history from a patient. Most commonly, they hurried to their supervisors for guidance, only to learn that in this matter, their supervisors had nothing to teach them. If any advice was offered, it was usually designed to suppress the information: "I was taught in my residency and during my early years in psychiatry, as I assume most of us were, to look very skeptically upon the incestuous sexual material described by patients ... Any inclination on my part, or that of my colleagues in the training situation, to look upon these productions of the patient as having some reality basis was scoffed at and was seen as evidence of our naivete and inexperience in appraising and understanding the mysterious world of the unconscious."[4]

Thus many fully trained therapists, who handle other problems skillfully, still maintain a blind spot when it comes to incest. If confronted with a patient who insists upon talking about it, the therapists suddenly feel like novices again. Two therapists testify:

> I know I don't want to hear it. I have no idea what to do with these cases. And I don't think I'm unusual.

> When she told me about her father, I didn't know what the hell to do with her. I felt I couldn't help. My supervisor advised me not to open that can of worms.

Therapists do not like to feel helpless, any more than anyone else does. Nor do therapists enjoy exploring their own feelings about incest. Lacking the necessary training, supervision, and institutional support, too often therapists back away. Therapists of both sexes frequently fall into this error, which is often reinforced by supervisors and rationalized as concern for the "fragile" patient.

When therapists avoid the issue of incest, they are tacitly driving the patient away and discouraging her from seeking help. This response only confirms the patient's feelings of isolation and reinforces her conviction that anyone who learns her secret will shun her:

> *Rita:* The director of the institution where I was placed had been trained as a counselor. What I resent about her now is that I lived there for four years, and even though she knew what had happened to me, she never once took me aside and said, "Would you like to talk about it?" From age fourteen to eighteen I had nobody to help me work out my feelings. I cried myself to sleep every night.

At worst, when a patient's complaint of incest meets with professional denial, the patient may end up feeling that she has actually been punished for daring to reveal her secret. In one case a patient was not helped to recover and master her memories of incest but was rather made to undergo treatment aimed at obliterating those memories:

Marion: When my little sister was about twenty, she had a breakdown. She was crying and couldn't stop. Mom kept her in bed and fed her aspirin round the clock. Finally I got her into a hospital, and Mom had a fit. I don't think she's ever forgiven me for that. It all came out in our interview at the hospital. I knew Mom and Dad were scared to death. But nothing came of it. They gave her shock treatments, and today she denies she said the things about her and Dad that took place even after she was married. She's still married—lived in misery all these years, on Valium, my mother says.

In this vignette, both family and hospital staff responded to the patient's distress in a manner intended to suppress her complaint. It is not clear that the professionally prescribed treatment of electroconvulsive therapy was any more helpful to this victim than the mother's prescription of bed rest and "aspirin round the clock." Given this response, the patient concluded, not surprisingly, that human beings could offer no help and that tranquilizers offered the only possible solace for her misery.

The reactions of avoidance and denial, which are so widespread among mental health professionals, are shared equally by male and female therapists. However, there are other defensive reactions in which male and female therapists tend to differ. In institutional settings, these differences may lead to staff conflicts regarding the proper approach to a patient with a history of incest. In private therapy, these differences appear as characteristic errors made by male and female therapists.

The female therapist generally tends to identify with the victim. Her first reaction to the incest history may be a feeling of helplessness and despair. She correctly recognizes the patient's childhood feelings of betrayal and abandonment, but she may find these feelings so overwhelming that she is unable to react calmly. One woman therapist described her reaction: "When I heard about it, I felt, 'Oh God, it's more hopeless than I thought.' I was really acting out all her prophecies. I wondered why I reacted so strongly. Really, I think it's because I just can't conceptualize how a child can grow up without any protection. It made me feel so badly for her."

The patient's history may also revive the therapist's memories of seductive elements in her own relationship with her father. She may recognize for the first time the covert, or overt, incest in her own history and may relive her own childhood reactions: the excitement of being special, the fear of being overpowered, and the longing for protection:

> I had a very close—very seductive—relationship with my own father. He used to give me everything I wanted. He also used to parade around in his underwear all the time. I remember my mother once said, "She's too old for that." She was right!
>
> I don't know how much I have to get into my own feelings in order to work successfully with these people. I know I don't want to.

The female therapist who has not sufficiently mastered her feelings about incestuous elements in her own childhood is not able to listen to an incest history with the same calm curiosity with which she approaches other aspects of the patient's experience. She communicates to her patient that the incest secret is too special or too frightening to hear: "I was convinced it was an extremely powerful experience and I shied away from the details. I was not matter-of-fact about it. If I hadn't been so impressed by her 'magic,' we might have achieved more of an alliance at the beginning."

These reactions on the part of the female therapist aggravate the patient's feelings of isolation. They reinforce her sense of herself as a dangerous, contaminated person who frightens other people away. They confirm the patient's feeling that her secret is too terrible to share and that no one can help her. Often at this point the patient leaves the therapist in disappointment:

> *Christine:* The first time I told my therapist about the incest, she was entranced. She was sitting on the edge of her seat. She felt so bad for me she cried herself. But then she didn't work with it. When I told her about my sexual problems, she said she didn't think it was because of the incest. I think she missed the boat there. I'm not sure I would want to go back to her.

In this case, the patient was at first gratified that her therapist cried. She took this as a sign of the therapist's empathy and caring. But in retrospect, when the therapist avoided further exploration of the effects of the incest, the patient concluded that the therapist's crying was a sign of fear and weakness. Her perception was essentially correct. Patients who have experienced incest are aware of the feelings of horror that their stories inspire. They are extremely sensitive to any reaction of withdrawal on the part of the therapist and can detect the therapist's discomfort from even very subtle cues.

Another error that female therapists commonly make is to express anger at the offender which the patient does not share. This error also follows from too extreme identification with the victim. The therapist may find it difficult to contain her sense of outrage. She may find herself trying to persuade the patient to get angry and stand up to her father, and she may be unwilling to hear the many positive things the patient has to say about him. She may try to deflect the patient's anger away from her mother and onto her father, pointing out ways in which the mother was also a victim.

Such maneuvers almost always provoke an extremely defensive reaction. Incest victims often feel more anger toward their mothers than toward their fathers, and sometimes see their fathers as the only source of caring and affection in their lives. When the therapist expresses rage at the father, the patient may feel that the therapist is trying to rob her of a relationship which is special and precious to her. She may assume that the therapist is motivated by spite or jealousy, and this simply confirms her belief that all women are potential rivals. The relationship with the therapist then becomes hostile and competitive instead of cooperative.

Avoiding the patient's positive feelings for her father also reinforces her belief that these feelings are wicked and shameful. The therapist may unconsciously convey to the patient the sense that anger and outrage are the only acceptable, the only innocent, responses to sexual abuse. If the patient recalls other, more tender feelings, which the therapist does not want to hear about, the patient may feel judged and blamed.

Thus a female therapist is unlikely to have much success working with incest victims until she has understood and mastered her own tendency to overidentify with the victim. As long as she is overwhelmed with her own fear and sense of helplessness, she will not be able to inspire confidence in patients who already believe they cannot be helped. As long as she allows her own anger to intrude into the therapy relationship, she will not be able to understand all the complexities of the patient's feelings for her father. Once she has worked through her own counter-transference issues, however, her natural tendency to identify with the victim becomes an advantage rather than a liability. It enables her to listen empathically and hastens the formation of a successful working alliance:

Sheila: The most helpful thing about my therapist was the way she didn't shy away. She didn't push either. She was very matter-of-fact—just said the word "incest" and went on. She identified with me as a woman, and it was the first time I thought of myself as a woman, not so different from anybody else. Eventually I could entertain the idea that this had happened to me without shrinking away with horror.

The male therapist encounters a different set of problems, for his natural tendency is to identify with the offender. This leads to a different, potentially more destructive, set of common errors. The male therapist often has great difficulty permitting the patient to express anger at the offender. He may excuse or rationalize the father's behavior, either to himself or to the patient. He tends to focus on any behavior on the victim's part which might exonerate the offender, often raising inappropriate questions about the patient's complicity or enjoyment. He tends to focus on the sexual aspects of the relationship and to ignore the issues of protection and caretaking. Thus, while the female therapist often avoids eliciting sexual details, the male therapist may show early and excessive interest in them.

Here is an example of the male therapist's response to an incest victim:

This woman had had great love and respect for her father until puberty when he had made several sexual advances to her. In analysis she talked at first only of her good feelings toward him because she had blocked out the sexual episodes. When they were finally brought back into consciousness, all the fury returned which she had experienced at the age of thirteen. She felt that her father was an impotent, dirty old man who had taken advantage of her trusting youthful innocence. From some of the details which she related of her relationship with her father, it was obvious that she was not all that innocent. But she was unable emotionally to accept her own sexual involvement with him.[5]

This therapist is comfortable hearing about the patient's loving feelings for her father. But when the patient begins to express her anger, the therapist suddenly stops listening and intrudes his own opinion instead. He not only fails to offer sympathy and support which would validate her angry feelings, but attempts to deflect attention away from these feelings by raising the issue of the patient's participant role in the relationship.

The effect of these common mistakes is not simply to make the patient feel insulted or to exacerbate her guilt. They make her feel that she is reliving the incestuous situation. Once again she is involved with a powerful male in a caretaker role, and once again she is not being protected or taken care of. Once again she is told that her anger is unwarranted, and once again she is made to feel responsible for her own victimization.

The healthiest response for the patient in this situation is to become enraged with the therapist. Patients may discontinue therapy because of the therapist's inappropriate attitude. This is a sensible move under the circumstances, but it leaves the patient feeling even more hopeless than before:

> *Rita:* Three times I attempted to go to a psychiatrist. Each time I ended up with a white male. I just had bad luck with all three of them. The last one I went to for several months before I gave up on him. I talked about the incest type thing and he said, "Well, did you enjoy it?" The way I feel, if I enjoyed it, I would not recognize it as a problem. If I didn't recognize it as a problem, I wouldn't have brought it up. So I thought it was a ridiculous question.

The patient who is less able to protect herself may feel more guilty than ever because of her therapist's reaction. She may continue in a fruitless and unrewarding therapy relationship which recapitulates past disappointments, and she may take upon herself the blame for the therapeutic failure.

The male therapist, because of his tendency to identify with the offender, also runs the risk of becoming sexually involved with the patient, either in fantasy or in reality. Like other men, the therapist may find himself becoming excited by the victim's narrative of forbidden sexual activity. These feelings are almost always detected by the patient, even if the therapist conscientiously does his best to suppress them:

> *Estelle:* When I began trying to find help, it was the beginning of a bitter education in human failings. As I went from therapist to therapist, it became terribly clear that the supposedly dispassionate professionals seemed just as titillated by my story of incestuous involvement with my father as my father had been excited by the actual experience with me.[6]

The male therapist's sexual response evokes in the patient all her original feelings of shame, guilt, and disappointment, even when the therapist
is careful not to act upon his feelings. When the therapist does choose to
eroticize the relationship, the result is a calamitous repetition of the original incest.

Unfortunately, this is not an uncommon event. Several surveys of
mental health professionals indicate that a substantial minority of therapists indulge in sexual relations with their patients or condone this behavior in others. In one study, 5 percent of male psychologists, but only
0.6 percent of female psychologists, reported having intercourse with
patients.[7] In another, 10 percent of male psychiatrists admitted that they
had engaged in erotic relationships with patients.[8] In yet another survey,
20 percent of male therapists said they thought there were "exceptions"
to the prohibition against sexual relations with patients, and 70 percent
said they knew of colleagues who engaged in such activities.[9]

The incest victim who encounters such a therapist may be particularly
at risk for seduction. Like other men, the therapist may consider the incest victim "fair game." Since she has engaged in forbidden sexual relations, he may see her as already corrupted and therefore may imagine
that he cannot do her any further harm. The patient, for her part, may
display a kind of ritualized erotic behavior which excites the therapist
and permits him to believe that she really wants to be seduced. After all,
she has been trained to stimulate and please men, and she often knows
how to do this very well. She may indeed believe that any man can be
seduced, and that no man can possibly care for her without a sexual relationship. Since she often has a very low opinion of herself, she will not
consider sexual involvement too high a price to have to pay for the
therapist's attention. In short, the same traits that render the incest victim susceptible to repeated abuse by other men also render her particularly vulnerable to seduction by a male therapist.

Once entrapped in a sexual relationship with a therapist, the patient
relives the betrayal and disappointment that she first experienced with
her father. The outcome can only be a disaster for her. To add insult to
injury, the therapist usually rationalizes the sexual relationship as an attempt to help the patient with her problems, thus requiring her to feel
grateful:

> *Sheila:* There was one relationship I got tangled into that sort of
> made things worse. It was with a priest who decided he was going

to try and help me. I knew him as a teacher, and after I made a suicide attempt, I decided I really should confess that I had tried to kill myself. So he came in to hear my confession, and then he decided he wanted to get involved and undo some of the damage. He was a very warm affectionate person and he was trying to make me see that sex was not bad, that it was all right. But unfortunately things got worse, because on the one hand he was a priest and I very much saw him as a priest, and on the other hand I definitely wanted it—a sexual relationship—you wouldn't believe the mess that that made! For a while I rationalized it in my head, because he said it was all right. But I think there was a part of me that knew all along that it wasn't all right at all. It probably did more harm than good. In the end he left the priesthood. He disappeared for a while and then he came back and announced that he had gotten married. But he still wanted to continue seeing me. I landed in the hospital then and I haven't seen him since. When he was ill, he asked me to come visit him and I refused. I do feel guilty for that. He did try very hard to help me.

A male therapist who finds himself becoming sexually excited by his female patients should immediately raise the problem in his own supervision or psychotherapy. If the problem cannot be quickly resolved, the therapist should refer the patient elsewhere for treatment.

Once the male therapist has sufficiently worked through his tendency to identify with the offender, he may be in a position to identify with the victim. He then experiences the same set of reactions found in female therapists. Only after these feelings, too, are overcome is the therapist ready to form an empathic relationship with the patient. One therapist who had mastered his personal reactions to the extent that he was able to work successfully with several incest victims testified:

I think one of the countertransference issues is everybody's repugnance to being enslaved. I don't mean just in a political sense. I mean becoming a love slave. Everybody is susceptible to it, and it's a very scary thing. There's a way men experience the same danger, sometimes from a father and sometimes from a mother, that allows me to identify with the victim; otherwise I don't think that I'd be able to get very far. You know how angry therapists are always getting at "enveloping mothers," as if they are causing all the harm in the world? Well, I think that particular rage gets

directed at mothers—usually fathers aren't mentioned—because
of a fear of love slavery. I have found a lot to identify with [in incest victims], and that's how we begin to get a sense of contact.

The patient lucky enough to find such a therapist has the opportunity
to undergo a corrective emotional experience. In the process of therapy
she may learn that not every man is corrupt, and that it is possible for a
man to understand and care for her without exploiting her.

Although the countertransference reactions of therapists, both male
and female, present the major obstacles to successful therapy with incest
victims, they are not the only obstacles. The patient, for her part, may
have to overcome resistances to therapy which result from her experience of incest. It is the therapist's task to recognize these resistances
early and to explain them to the patient in a manner that the patient can
understand and accept.

The major obstacles to forming a good working alliance are the same
problems that often lead the patient to seek help in the first place: her
feelings of shame and hopelessness and her fear of betrayal in intimate
relationships. The incest victim's feelings of shame are often so intense
that once she has revealed her secret, she has a strong impulse to flee
from the therapist and finds it difficult to return. This inclination to run
away and hide can be moderated, however, by a calm, accepting attitude
on the part of the therapist. The therapist should communicate to the
patient that she has heard about incest before and knows that many people have had the same experience. She should make it clear that, while
she understands that the patient may feel guilty and ashamed, she, the
therapist, does not blame or scorn her. Finally, she should convey a confident and hopeful attitude about the possibility of resolving the patient's
residual problems through therapy. It is important to communicate to
the patient the idea that, while the incest may have had some very trou-
blesome and lasting effects in her life, the damage need not be permanent. Such an attitude helps alleviate the patient's feeling of being indeli-
bly "marked" and eternally barred from normal social intercourse.

The patient's shame is usually the first obstacle that the therapist encounters. If this obstacle is successfully overcome, the patient may feel
relieved and grateful. Here, the second obstacle usually presents itself,
for once the patient experiences such feelings, she may also feel endan-
gered. The more she longs to trust and confide in her therapist, the more
her suspicion is aroused. Since the legacy of her childhood is a feeling of
profound betrayal by both parents, she fears a repetition of this experi-

ence in all intimate relationships, including the relationship with the therapist. She fears that the therapist will dominate and exploit her, as her father did, or neglect and abandon her, as her mother did. She has little faith in any other possibility. If this fear is not clarified and understood, the patient may act on it, just as everything seems to be progressing well. In one case the therapist was initially caught off guard by his patient's mistrust, but he understood it in time to prevent a serious disruption of therapy:

> Under a facade of compliance there was an incredible amount of wariness and mistrust. At first she seemed like such a "good" patient, and then all of a sudden I didn't know what the hell was happening, what I'd done wrong. It took me a long time to figure out that the anger and suspicion I ran into was a necessary defense. She felt, "You're getting to know me too well, you're getting too close. I really have to watch out for you." She protected herself from getting into my orbit, from feeling in the position she was in with her father. The fear of surrender is very basic.

Forming a successful working alliance is often furthered by clarifying the issue of trust early in therapy. It usually helps the patient to understand, first, that she has difficulty in intimate relationships; second, that this difficulty stems in large part from her inability to feel trust when trust is appropriate and, conversely, to protect herself when trust is not appropriate; and third, that this problem is almost certainly related to her history of having been abused and neglected by her parents. Formulating the problem in this way helps the patient anticipate some of her reactions to the therapist and makes it possible for the patient and therapist to examine these reactions together as they arise. Another advantage of formulating the problem in this way is that it tends to defuse the whole issue of complicity and blame. The therapist makes it clear to the patient that regardless of her behavior, the fact that she was involved in incest as a child means that she could not have been properly cared for. The focus of therapy then becomes the patient's problem in intimate relationships which she suffers as a consequence of this improper care.

Once the patient and therapist have reached this shared understanding of the problem, a good working alliance is usually established. The patient will then proceed to ventilate her feelings about her parents, especially feelings of hurt, anger, and betrayal. Often, initially, she feels anger toward only one parent, most commonly the mother, while the other parent, most commonly the father, is idealized. Though her anger may be absurdly one-sided, it is a mistake to try to redirect it or to mobilize anger at the idealized parent. The therapist's task is to permit the patient to express her anger and to understand it as a reaction to her disappointed longing for care. In time, anger gives way to a more direct expression of grief and loss. The patient often recovers poignant memories of her childhood wish for a strong and competent mother, and of her terror and dismay at her mother's failure to protect her. If the mother was obviously ill or handicapped, the patient may feel, consciously or not, that she was to blame for her mother's disability, as if the rage and hatred she felt toward her mother had magically resulted in harm. This fantasy often persists into adult life and contributes to the patient's feeling that she is too evil or dangerous to be intimately involved with other people, for she maintains an exaggerated fear of her own destructive potential. The therapist must help the patient to clarify the fact that, whereas her rage is no doubt terrifying to her and can be expressed in very destructive ways, it is not responsible for whatever misfortunes befell her mother. As the patient develops a new perspective on her angry feelings toward her mother, she often feels less guilty and begins to give up her magical, negative identity.

This process can be enhanced if, at the same time, the therapist fosters the development of a new and more positive image of womanhood with which the patient can identify. The patient should be encouraged to recover memories of helpful female figures in her childhood—an aunt, a teacher, a friend's mother—anyone who offered a model of competence and self-respect. If the therapist is a woman, she herself becomes a model for the patient. Finally, when the patient has reached the point where she can see her mother realistically, she may even rediscover some admirable traits in her. As this process unfolds, the patient may find herself forming closer female friendships and gradually developing a better opinion of herself.

At this point, anger at the father and at other abusive men usually surfaces spontaneously. Once the patient feels more positive about herself and about other women, she is able to see her relationship with her father in a new light. When she no longer feels that she must submit to exploitation in order to deserve any sort of care, her resentment at being mistreated becomes much more lively. As one patient put it:

> *Lynn:* I used to feel that, in spite of everything, no matter what happened, at least my father would always be there for me. But I

finally realized that it was just the other way around; I was always there for him. I was meeting his needs; he wasn't meeting mine.

With this changed perspective, the patient is also able to come to a more realistic appreciation of the specialness of the incestuous relationship. She comes to understand that the favors, the excitement, the privileges she may have enjoyed were poor compensations for the childhood which was stolen from her. With this insight, she often feels quite sad, but at the same time she feels much less guilty about whatever part she played in the incestuous relationship. At this point in therapy, patients who have been involved with abusive husbands or lovers often muster the courage to extricate themselves from these relationships. Patients who have fearfully avoided becoming involved with lovers often feel freer to do so.

Therapy by this time is already well advanced. When the patient has worked through many of her feelings about both parents and come to a new perspective on her family, she may wish to discuss the incest openly with a family member for the first time. She may want to find out if other sisters, or brothers, were also molested. She may want to warn the parents of other children in the extended family who might still be at risk. Or most commonly, she may simply want to confront her parents.

Such confrontations have the potential for great benefit to the patient, and also for some harm. By confronting her family, the patient repudiates her role as the family's secret-bearer. She serves notice that she will no longer accept the burden of responsibility for her parents' behavior. Regardless of the family's response, many women are satisfied simply by making such a declaration:

> *Sheila:* My sister was very much against it: "You can't tell Ma, you'll hurt her." But I had to do it for myself, even if it did hurt her. I had protected her long enough. I finally had to stand up and say, "You have to look at me." All I wanted was for her to acknowledge that it happened, not to deny it or pretend it didn't happen or smooth it over. Taking the chance on telling her had a lot to do with setting me free, to the extent that I am free.

The major disadvantage of such confrontations is that the patient rarely gets the response she is looking for. Unless she is well prepared for her parents' possible reactions, she is almost certain to come away disappointed. The patient generally hopes that her parents will admit that the incest occurred and that it did her harm. She wants her parents to accept responsibility, her father for abuse and her mother for neglect. She wants an apology, and she wants her parents to show some regret and some desire to make amends for the wrong done to her.

Although these wishes might seem just and reasonable, they are rarely, if ever, fulfilled. The patient may have changed a great deal as a result of her therapy, but the family usually has not changed. When the patient tries to expose the incest secret, she usually provokes a great deal of fear and hostility in other family members. She may meet with steadfast denial, or she may get some of the responses she wishes for, followed by retraction or retaliation:

> *Janet:* Last year my father came to visit. I told him he could come, because I had in mind that we would see my therapist and have a family meeting. Which was very hard for me to do, but I did it. I started out by telling him that I didn't trust him, and I didn't want him to touch my daughter, and that he had hurt me a great deal. He said that he hadn't known, but now he could see that he did hurt me. He admitted it because the therapist asked him to do it. The way he did it was very backhanded—he wanted to get it over with real quick and have me forgive him right away. He also lied about what he did; he didn't admit the full extent of it. He said, "Well, I just touched her breasts a few times," and that's *not* all he did, but I didn't confront him at the time, because I was surprised to hear anything at all. It was very helpful to hear him admit it. When we left the interview, he spent the day with me and he cried a little and said he was sorry, it was real evil what he'd done. Then a week later he took it all back. I got a letter saying that there was something wrong with *me,* that I was sick, that I should just get over this little problem of mine, and blah blah blah.

Patients should not be encouraged to proceed with a confrontation until they have thoroughly explored their own motives and goals, and until they have anticipated and prepared themselves emotionally for the reactions they may provoke. This anticipatory work can be done without the benefit of any special techniques, though some therapists use role-playing or psychodrama to rehearse for the confrontation or even to substitute for it.[10] Once adequate preparation has been done, the confrontation can be an important milestone in the patient's mastery of the incest trauma. It becomes a kind of rite, in which the patient sheds her identity as witch, bitch, or whore and casts off her role as the guardian of the family secret. She does not expect her family to absolve her of guilt; rather, she absolves herself in their presence. If family members respond with denial, panic, hostility, or threats, she is encouraged to observe these reactions and to judge from them how powerful the family pressures upon her must have been when she was a child.

Instead of confronting family members, the patient may choose to talk about the incest with another person who is important to her. Generally the issue cannot be considered fully resolved until the patient is able to talk about it with another person besides the therapist. As long as the secret is confined to the consulting room, the therapy relationship takes on some of the magical specialness of the incestuous dyad. When the patient is able to exercise choice about sharing her secret, so that she neither hides from everyone nor talks about it compulsively, this is often a sign that the necessary work of therapy has been accomplished.

Individual psychotherapy is itself not necessarily the best form of treatment for all incest victims. For many patients, group therapy may be preferable to individual treatment. At least one therapist who specializes in the treatment of adults with problems related to incest considers group therapy the treatment of choice.[11] Time-limited groups focusing on a common history of incest are also an invaluable supplement to individual therapy, offering much more rapid and complete results than are possible with individual therapy alone.

Group therapy, first of all, offers patients the opportunity for a fuller resolution of the issue of secrecy. Within the group, the special, almost conspiratorial dyadic relationship of patient and therapist is not recreated, for the patient shares her secret with others as well as the therapist. To be sure, this is still a very special and privileged audience, since the rule of confidentiality is energetically laid down at the outset, and since all group members are also incest victims. But sharing a secret with a select group of the initiated offers the chance for a feeling of belonging, and it does far more than any therapist can do to break down the victim's feeling of isolation.

Group therapy also offers a fuller opportunity for the resolution of feelings of shame and guilt. If the therapist is able to create an atmosphere of safety and mutual acceptance, the group members will be able to grant each other absolution, in a way that no therapist can. For while each woman fully believes herself to be a terrible sinner, she generally does not feel the same way about the others in the group. She is better able to identify ways in which the others were coerced and victimized. As one member of a group commented: "I heard what happened to all those women. They didn't do anything wrong." Sooner or later, each participant is able to apply the group's more tolerant judgment to herself.

Patients who have already done considerable work in individual therapy may find a group helpful when they have reached the point of confronting family members. Within the group, patients can clarify their goals, anticipate reactions, and learn from each other's experiences. As a result, when confrontations do occur, they are more creatively planned and better handled by both patients and their families. Some of the most successful confrontations have come about after they were carefully thought through and rehearsed in a group.

Finally, group therapy diminishes the humiliation of the patient role, for group members give to each other and become each other's therapists. Being in a helping role for at least a part of each session enables incest victims, who generally feel so undeserving, to accept attention and care from others more readily.

Although the literature on therapy for incest victims is sparse, the existing sources are unanimous in their enthusiasm for groups. The most thorough study to date documents the outcome of a series of ten time-limited groups, each lasting for only four sessions, with one follow-up meeting after two or three months. Members were recruited by advertisement and were placed in groups without any formal prior screening. The groups were led by male and female co-therapists and had four to six members each. Responding to a questionnaire six months after the group ended, most patients said they thought their group had been very beneficial. They reported feeling less guilty, more self-accepting, and more positive about their present mates. The most helpful aspect of the experience had been the opportunity to share feelings about sexual abuse with other women. One patient wrote: "I'm so excited that I'm comfortable with saying I was molested. It's a way of showing that I'm over my shame and guilt. I didn't do anything to be ashamed of—it was done to me."[12]

These results testify to the extraordinary potential that victims have for helping one another. Therapists who are in a position to bring incest victims together should make every attempt to do so, even if the therapists themselves are relatively inexperienced with groups.

At the completion of successful therapy, some women may choose to put the incest experience behind them and simply get on with their lives. Others may feel so exhilarated at having overcome the effects of the incest trauma in their own lives that they are moved to share their success with other victims. Many women who have worked through their own issues sufficiently to reach out to others may choose to work in rape crisis centers, runaway shelters, battered women's shelters, and other settings where they are likely to encounter other victims. A few find a real vocation in the struggle to raise public consciousness about sexual abuse and in the creation of self-help services for victims of incest.

The decision to speak out publicly or to become an organizer requires courage. No matter how thoroughly the issue has been worked through in therapy, the victim still makes herself vulnerable by exposing her secret. Such daring is contagious, however: the example of one woman speaking out is inspiring to others. A victim reported her own illumination on hearing another victim publicly identify herself: "In 1972 a group of courageous women in Northampton, Mass. held a Rape Speakout, and only after listening to a participant recount her similar experience did it dawn on me for the first time that I was, number one, a *victim*, of, number two, statutory rape. My father had committed statutory rape. I was an educated person. I knew what statutory rape was. But I had never made the mental connection that I was a victim, because I had the identity of an offender. That Rape Speakout was the beginning for me of recovering from childhood."[13]

After initial therapy, this same woman took upon herself the task of progressive public disclosure. She first revealed her secret anonymously, using a pseudonym, in testimony before professional audiences. The response encouraged her, for she felt that her audience listened with respect and appreciated the importance of the information. She next agreed to be interviewed on television, first in silhouette. She described the stress and the rewards of this stage of self-disclosure:

> I had come to believe that a rape or child sexual assault victim should be unafraid, unashamed, and as unstigmatized by others as a mugging victim. Nevertheless, it took a one-hour beforehand discussion with my counselor to quell enough fear so that I was able to be interviewed. There were the interviewer, a camera person, and several strangers present to whom I was identified as an incest victim. I proceeded based on my reasoning that if I was really not to blame, and if my ex-father was really the offender, then I should have nothing to fear from talking about it (albeit an anonymous shadow did the talking). Luckily, this reasoning

worked. Over time, I experienced a decrease in the feeling of stigma.[14]

Facing the camera was her next important milestone in self-disclosure. Following this television appearance, she began to reveal her secret to close friends and to family members who were still unaware of it. The final step in this process was the assumption of an organizer's role in forming self-help groups for other victims. Because she had publicly identified herself as an incest victim, other women began to look to her for leadership. Some of her self-help groups organized others in turn. She also wrote an instruction manual for women who wish to form their own groups.[15] Thus she returned to others the gift that she had first received, years before, from the stranger at the rape speakout.

A self-help group is any gathering of people who share a problem and who meet to give each other mutual support. In the past decade, such groups have been widely developed within the women's liberation movement, both as a method of general consciousness-raising and as a means of approaching particular issues. In the atmosphere of safety and trust developed within these small groups, many women's secrets previously regarded as shameful have been shared. Women have spoken out about abortion, rape, beatings, and sexuality, and have found that their pain is recognized and understood.

The advantages of self-help groups for incest victims are numerous. First of all, most self-help groups are free and therefore available to many more people than psychotherapy is. Second, such groups foster a sense of health and competence, because participants do not identify themselves as patients in need of treatment. Third, since incest victims run such a high risk of insensitive or destructive treatment in the traditional mental health system, a self-help group may offer a safer and more therapeutic environment than the available professional services. The victim may find more comfort, understanding, and emotional support with her peers than in a therapist's office. Finally, self-help groups, in contrast to psychotherapy, develop a social analysis of personal problems, and sometimes offer the opportunity of collective action. Self-help groups have campaigned actively to increase public awareness of sexual abuse and to reform public institutions. In some areas these efforts have had tangible results: a conference or speakout, a discussion of sexual abuse in a fifth-grade classroom, an advocacy program in a district court, a shelter for adolescent victims who cannot remain at home. The woman who becomes involved in such projects gradually sheds her identity as a passive victim. For the first time in her life, perhaps, she feels powerful, not as the concubine of a powerful man, but as a woman fighting on her own behalf, in alliance with others.

Self-help groups also have limits and potential disadvantages. They are not generally appropriate for women in extreme distress, such as those who are actively suicidal, alcohol or drug dependent, or unable to cope with the routine tasks of daily living. Establishment of a safe, nurturing atmosphere in a group necessitates some degree of prior screening, so that women who cannot benefit from the group do not disrupt it. Self-help groups also present the danger, inherent in any small group process, that the necessary atmosphere of cooperation and mutual support may be jeopardized by suspicion and conflict among their members. A successful self-help group does not form spontaneously; it requires as careful organization and structuring as a therapy group.

The most common vehicle for self-help is the small group of three to ten women. But self-help can be organized either more or less formally. Any time one victim identifies herself to another, some degree of self-help occurs. One woman put up a sign, "Were you molested as a child?" on a supermarket bulletin board, giving her first name and a phone number. Another woman responded, and the two met and shared their experiences. After several months of meetings, they agreed to travel together to each other's home towns in order to confront the offenders. Both found the trip a success. This kind of intimate involvement in each other's lives would not have been possible in a larger, more formal group.

At the other end of the spectrum are elaborately structured self-help programs organized by and for victims. The most highly developed of these is Christopher Street in Minneapolis, Minnesota. Its staff, most of whom publicly identify themselves as incest victims, have created a highly effective program.

The project is fueled by a militant feminism. Men are entirely excluded. The reasoning is that men cannot work with victims, and that victims always feel unsafe in the presence of men and cannot possibly reveal to men the extent of their hurt.

Written in black ink on the door as one enters Christopher Street is a sign: "I DON'T KNOW" IS UNACCEPTABLE. Self-knowledge and self-confrontation are the basic tenets of the program. Victims are encouraged to share their stories, to relive their childhood feelings in all their original intensity, to recognize and understand their own self-destructive behavior, and finally, to put their victimization experiences behind them.

There is ample recognition, however, that such a process is difficult, and that not every woman is ready for it. Two requirements of the program are made clear at the outset: participants must not be drug or alcohol dependent, and they must agree that suicide is not an out. If a woman is drug dependent, she is first referred to an affiliated program for her addiction.

A victim who is accepted into the program is initially placed in a "holding group," led by a counselor who is usually herself an incest victim. This first phase of the program parallels early sessions in psychotherapy. While the victim is developing some comfort in talking about her experiences, the group leader assesses her psychological functioning and defenses. The new group member may stay in the "holding group" as long as she wishes, and she is not encouraged to proceed to the second stage of the program until both she and the leader are confident that she can handle the stress of reliving her childhood trauma.

The second stage of the program is the "learning lab." In small, supportive groups, victims re-enact their experiences with their fathers and re-experience their childhood feelings. Many techniques are used to evoke intense feeling, especially techniques from the active therapies, such as gestalt or psychodrama. Victims act out how they felt at the moment that the abuse happened, dramatizing their fears and their extreme anger. Victims are allowed to act "crazy" and are accepted by the group.

Because the learning labs actively encourage victims to regress into childhood feeling states, the labs must be highly structured. A firm set of rules and limits protects the participants at a time when their own internal controls and defenses may be temporarily weakened. Group members are required to attend four three-hour meetings per week. They must not drink or be sexually active with each other. They are encouraged to seek protection and support either from women's shelters or from people in the "concerned persons program," which includes former victims who have already completed the program or others who have volunteered in the project. Thus the environment created during the learning lab is almost equivalent to a day hospital or semiresidential program. The duration of the learning lab is fixed at the outset and does not exceed two months.

The program is educational as well as therapeutic. Group leaders deliver lectures on aspects of the victims' lives, such as their relationships, sexuality, and self-image. In these lectures, victims are told that they are in some way destroying and blaming themselves. As the program director explains: "I know that they are destroying themselves and I ask them how they are doing it. Often it is hard for them to look at the abuse they are presently subjecting themselves to, because they so need someone to love them. 70–80% of victims have also been raped—most often they feel they deserved it. We try to turn this kind of thinking around."[16]

This didactic approach differs sharply from traditional psychotherapy. Not all of the victim's feelings are tolerantly accepted; rather, victims are taught that certain attitudes are erroneous. For example, they are not allowed to make excuses for their fathers or to blame their mothers: "We tell them that you can be mad at mom but don't blame her. Blame doesn't allow for anger. We try to get at who told you Mom was to blame. We try to convey more understanding for mothers than for fathers."

There are some drawbacks to this approach. Although fathers and not mothers are entirely to blame, victims must be permitted to express the depth of their anger at both parents. The victim who is not permitted to express her anger at her mother or her tender feelings for her father will not be able to transcend these feelings or put them in a new perspective.

The third and final part of the program is "aftercare." Here participants are encouraged to put the past behind them. Having now accepted the fact that they were damaged by incest, they re-examine their present lives, identifying self-destructive patterns that they wish to change and seeking ways to restore themselves. To aid in the process of coming to terms with the past, two exercises are suggested. In the first, all group members are asked to identify one thing, however small, that was positive about their families. Recalling even one pleasant memory makes it easier for group members symbolically to say goodbye to their families. In the second exercise, group members are asked to consider confronting their fathers in person. If they decide to do so, the counselors are available to accompany them.

The counselors see themselves not as impartial observers but as advocates. They disclaim the role of the traditional therapist who attempts to see all sides of the picture. They are there to support and defend the victim. As one counselor put it: "Look, these women need support and they also need protection. Some have been abused since birth. The covert rules of the family may be not to talk about anger, but I encourage the victims to tell their fathers how angry they are. I tell the victim I am here to help *her*—he's been helped all his life."

A participant is judged to have completed the program successfully when she has changed her present way of living so that she no longer subjects herself to abuse. Participants may remain in aftercare as long as they feel is necessary; after completing the program, they may maintain some connection by staying in touch with someone in the concerned persons program or by volunteering in the program themselves, thus completing the cycle of self-help by caring for others. The stages in this self-help program in many ways parallel the stages of psychotherapy. An initial alliance is formed in the holding group; childhood feelings are re-evoked and worked through in the learning lab, and a new and more successful adult adaptation is reached in aftercare.

Like most traditional therapy programs, Christopher Street and other, less highly organized self-help groups do not collect outcome data. On the basis of individual testimony, however, it is clear that many women find in self-help a means to take possession of themselves and transform their lives. As one woman who had participated in the program put it: "We go from being victims to being survivors. It never really goes away, but it just doesn't bother you or control you as much any more."

12

Preventing Sexual Abuse

If the little girl were brought up from the first with the same demands and rewards, the same severity and the same freedom, as her brothers ... promised the same future, surrounded with women and men who seemed to her undoubted equals, the meanings of the castration complex and of the Oedipus complex would be profoundly modified. Assuming on the same basis as the father the material and moral responsibility of the couple, the mother would enjoy the same lasting prestige; the child would perceive around her an androgynous world and not a masculine world. Were she emotionally more attached to her father— which is not even sure—her love for him would be tinged with a will to emulation and not a feeling of powerlessness.
>   —Simone de Beauvoir, The Second Sex, 1949

The sexual abuse of children is as old as patriarchy itself. Fathers have had sexual relations with their children from time immemorial, and they are likely to continue to do so for a long time to come. As long as fathers dominate their families, they will have the power to make sexual use of their children. Most fathers will choose not to exercise this power; but as long as the prerogative is implicitly granted to all men, some men will use it.

If incestuous abuse is indeed an inevitable result of patriarchal family structure, then preventing sexual abuse will ultimately require a radical transformation of the family. The rule of the father will have to yield to the cooperative rule of both parents, and the sexual division of labor will have to be altered so that fathers and mothers share equally in the care of children. These ambitious, even visionary changes will not be the work of one lifetime.

Before the arrival of the millennium, however, there are some more immediate things that can be done. In the short run, consciousness raising among potential victims probably represents the best hope of preventing sexual abuse. This means sex education for children, an idea that much of society still finds controversial. In particular, the idea of sex education seems to be anathema in highly traditional, devout, authoritarian, and male-dominated families—that is, in families where children are most at risk for sexual abuse. This should not be surprising, since incestuous fathers, after all, have been carrying on their own brand of "sex education" for centuries. They have the most to lose if their children receive information from sources outside the family.

Women who have been victimized, however, are unanimous in their enthusiasm for consciousness raising among children. As one victim recalled: "If there were some knowledge as a child, nine, ten years old, that fathers were not like that, were not sexual with their daughters . . . I was ignorant, and I did not know whether fathers were really like that or not. And if I could have gotten some information when I was younger, I think that would have helped." Another victim added: "I think if there was a big billboard out there when I was eight years old that said, 'If your father's bothering you call this number,' you know, I probably would have done it."[1]

Since most sexual abuse begins well before puberty, preventive education, if it is to have any effect at all, should begin early in grade school. Ideally, information on sexual abuse should be integrated into a general curriculum of sex education. In those communities where the experiment has been tried, it has been shown conclusively that children can learn what they most need to know about sexual abuse, without becoming unduly frightened or developing generally negative sexual attitudes. In Minneapolis, Minnesota, for example, the Hennepin County Attorney's office developed an education program on sexual assault for elementary school children. The program was presented to all age groups in four different schools, some eight hundred children in all. The presentation opened with a performance by a children's theater group, illustrating the difference between affectionate touching, and exploitative touching. The children's responses to the skits indicated that they understood the distinction very well indeed. Following the presentation, about one child in six disclosed a sexual experience with an adult, ranging from an encounter with an exhibitionist to involvement in incest. Most of the children, both boys and girls, had not told anyone prior to the classroom discussion.[2]

In addition to basic information on sexual relations and sexual assault, children need to know that they have the right to their own bodily integrity. As Sandra Butler put it in a "letter to a young victim": "Nobody, not even your parents, has the right to do anything to your mind or body that makes you feel bad or uncomfortable. And you are right to want to put an end to it. It is your body, and you can say no without feeling guilty."[3] This idea of the child's right to her own body is a radical one. In the traditional patriarchal family, there is no such concept. The child is the legal property of the father. Only in the last century have reforms in law and custom recognized the *mother's* custodial rights to her child.[4] The concept that the child too might have some individual rights or interests not represented by either parent is even more recent.

Finally, children need to know the recourse that is available to them outside their families if they are being abused. Rather than awaiting the crisis that leads to reporting, child protective workers might go out to the children and talk about what they have to offer. In Tacoma, Washington, for example, workers from Pierce County Rape Relief make regular presentations in elementary school classrooms. The workers explain what incest is and what can be done about it. Children participate in role playing, in which they act out what it would be like to be a victim, to keep the abuse a secret, and to report it. The disruptive consequences of reporting are not glossed over. Children take part in an exercise in which they imagine the possible results of reporting and rank them according to those they would find the hardest to face. Of all the unpleasant consequences of reporting, the children find the idea of being taken out of their homes and placed in foster care the most objectionable. In spite of the fact that the situations they are being asked to discuss are very upsetting, the children seem both relieved to be able to express their feelings on the subject of incest, and reassured to know that there are concerned adults outside their families to whom they can turn if necessary.[5]

As in the case of sex education generally, parents are often as much in need as their children. Parents who want to warn their children about the possibility of sexual abuse need, first, to be well informed about the problem themselves; second, to feel comfortable talking about it; and third, to learn appropriate ways to impart the necessary information to young children. Many parents feel so uncomfortable giving children any sort of information related to sex that whatever warnings are given are vague and confusing. Preventive education for parents, therefore, should focus on relieving parental anxiety and on teaching parents how to discuss sexual matters with their children. To the extent that communication between parents and children is established, the likelihood that a child would feel obliged to maintain secrecy about a sexual overture is diminished. As social worker Linda Sanford put it in a guide for parents to the prevention of sexual abuse:

> It is crucial to warn children about the potential danger of entering into a secret pact with an adult . . . An almost sure-fire way to prevent incest is to include the father or stepfather in these preventive discussions. If the father tells the child in a calm, guiding way, "Never let an adult put his hands down your pants, and please don't keep secrets about that sort of thing from us," the father has eliminated any chance he ever had of successfully victimizing his children . . . If the mother alone warns the children, the warning might not clearly extend to adults who are part of the family.[6]

Many parents initially feel anxious and threatened by a discussion of incest. Often, they are somewhat aware of their own incestuous feelings toward their children and react as if accused or judged when the subject is raised. Conscientious parents often wonder where to draw the line between affectionate intimacy and inappropriate sexual conduct with children. The single most helpful guideline is the criterion of secrecy. If incest is defined as any physical contact between parent and child that has to be kept a secret, the parents can judge for themselves if their behavior is becoming overly eroticized. If they are beginning to feel the impulse to hide what they are doing, then it is probably inappropriate. If they are comfortable expressing affectionate feelings in the presence of others, there is probably no need to worry. This guideline is not infallible. There are extreme situations in which an incestuous relationship is carried on with the full knowledge of other family members. But when the situation has deteriorated to this point, the family is already beyond the reach of preventive education in any case.

If an educational campaign for children and parents were carried out on a national scale, it would probably result in some degree of prevention. Some fathers might be discouraged from initiating an incestuous relationship if they could not assume that their wives and children were entirely naive. More important, some children might be able to deter their fathers' advances by immediate reporting, or might be able to put a stop to an incestuous relationship more quickly once it had begun. Older children might be able to intervene more successfully to protect their younger siblings if they knew what resources were available to them. Thus, one could expect to see a decrease in the incidence of incest, and perhaps an even greater decrease in the average duration of incestuous relationships. But this reform alone can never be sufficient for the primary prevention of child sexual abuse. For the locus of the problem is ultimately in the structure of the family. As long as fathers rule but do not nurture, as long as mothers nurture but do not rule, the conditions favoring the development of father-daughter incest will prevail. Only a basic change in the power relations of mothers and fathers can prevent the sexual exploitation of children.

Changes in the power structure of the family are in fact occurring. They are being brought about in part by the organized efforts of women. Some feminists, appalled by the seemingly endless history of female victimization within the family, have envisioned abolishing the family altogether.[7] But most seek rather a new and regenerated form of family life established on the basis of equality. If the basic demands of the women's liberation movement were fulfilled, if civil equality, reproductive freedom, economic security, and physical safety were guaranteed to all women, it might be possible for men and women, parents and children, to love one another without coercion or exploitation.

Although the women's liberation movement is often perceived as hostile to maternity and child rearing, the welfare of children has always been a central concern of feminists, and struggles for child protection are historically linked to struggles for women's rights. For example, the earliest struggles to abolish child labor were advanced by a coalition of labor unions and women's organizations, including the Women's Christian Temperance Union, the League of Women Voters, and the YWCA. Conversely, the major opposition to restricting child labor was organized by the National Association of Manufacturers and antisuffrage groups.[8]

Every gain in the general status of women also improves the status of mothers and children. And every improvement in the condition of motherhood potentially strengthens the mother-child bond. For example, the establishment of legal guardianship rights to the child's primary caretaker, regardless of her relationship to a man, ensures that the mother-child bond is not disrupted by male claims of ownership or legitimacy. Reproductive freedom strengthens the mother-child bond by ensuring that every child born is chosen and wanted. Economic security for women and the socialization of child care ensure that mothers have adequate means to support and care for their children. Physical security ensures that the bond between mother and child is not disrupted by paternal violence of all sorts, including sexual abuse.

In particular, any improvement in the social status of mothers creates a better climate for mother-daughter relationships. The painful hostility between mother and daughter so frequently observed in incestuous families is only an exaggeration of a common generational pattern among women. When mothers are powerless, their daughters are inevitably alienated from them. At present, too many girls learn by observation that oppression is their destiny and that to love a man is to be enslaved. If daughters are to be protected, they must learn from their mothers' example that they have the ability to fight and the right to defend themselves. When daughters see in their mothers an image of dignity and self-respect, they can more easily find in themselves the courage to resist abuse. Just as healing in incestuous families begins with the restoration of the mother-daughter bond, prevention of incest ultimately depends on strengthtening that relationship to the point where the daughter would never feel the need to preserve the incest secret.

At first glance, a proposal for radical change in the status of women may seem too general, too theoretical, and too remote a solution for the specific problem of incest. But every time sexual abuse occurs, it implicitly raises the most fundamental issues of women's status. A case history illustrates how one woman's struggle to put a stop to her husband's incestuous behavior linked her to the struggle for the liberation of all women:

> Lorraine and Robert met while she was working as a secretary and he as a salesman in an insurance company. They were married, and Lorraine immediately became pregnant. Both agreed that Lorraine should quit her job and stay home with the children; both looked forward to raising a large family. Within three years three daughters were born.
>
> Shortly after the birth of their first child, Robert began drinking heavily and occasionally beat Lorraine. This behavior worsened with each subsequent pregnancy. Lorraine began to reconsider her initial plan to raise a large family; after the birth of the third child she suggested waiting before having any more children. Robert disagreed; he was opposed to the use of birth control, and besides, he wanted a son. Lorraine therefore attempted to avoid pregnancy by avoiding sexual intercourse. Robert blamed her "coldness" for his increasing use of alcohol.
>
> The fourth child born to Lorraine and Robert was a son. After the birth of this child, Lorraine was advised not to become pregnant again. However, her medical problems precluded the use of oral contraceptives or an intrauterine device. Other methods such

as the diaphragm or condom remained impractical because of Robert's continued objection to birth control. When Lorraine became pregnant for a fifth time, she considered abortion. She finally rejected this possibility because of strongly ingrained religious prohibitions which made her feel too guilty to proceed. However, after the birth of her fifth child, Lorraine chose to undergo sterilization. Robert was opposed to this decision and was incensed when he learned that his consent was not legally required.

The marriage continued to deteriorate, and Lorraine found herself considering separation. She rejected the idea as impractical, however. She could not imagine how she would support herself with five small children. At least Robert was a faithful provider. By this time he was making quite a good income and had bought a house.

Feeling increasingly desperate, Lorraine finally confided in a friend, whose husband, she knew, also had a drinking problem. The friend persuaded her to attend meetings of Al-Anon, a self-help group for spouses of alcoholics. She kept her attendance at these meetings secret, because Robert was becoming increasingly jealous and suspicious of her whenever she left the house.

When the oldest child was twelve and the youngest four, Lorraine's daughters came to her and told her that all three had been molested by their father. The sexual abuse was most extensive with the oldest daughter, having gone on for five years. Lorraine immediately confronted Robert. An argument ensued, and Robert attacked Lorraine. The oldest daughter called the police.

The police arrived after forty minutes. In spite of the pleas of Lorraine and the children, they refused to make an arrest. They did agree to take Robert for a "walk around the block." While they were gone, Lorraine called her friend from Al-Anon, who told her about a shelter for battered women. Before Robert came back, Lorraine and all five children had fled to the shelter.

At the shelter, Lorraine consulted a feminist lawyer who specialized in domestic relations. The next day she went to court to file charges of assault. She obtained a court order requiring her husband to vacate the house and restraining him from any contact with her or the children. Armed with the court order and escorted by her lawyer and a worker from the shelter, she returned home to confront her husband. Robert made no further threats once he had seen the court order. He immediately moved out of the house. He warned his wife that she could not get along without him and that sooner or later she would beg him to come back.

Lorraine applied for welfare. She was shocked to discover that the allotment for herself and five dependents would be approximately one third of her husband's salary. After two months of trying to survive in this manner, Lorraine considered allowing Robert to return home. She was dissuaded by her children, her friends, and her counselor at the women's shelter, all of whom pointed out that Robert had given no indication of a desire to change. They encouraged Lorraine instead to go back to work.

Lorraine had been out of the paid labor force for twelve years. She had little confidence in her ability to hold a full-time job, earn an adequate income, and still provide what she considered the proper care for her children. At the urging of her children and her women friends, however, she assessed the job market and evaluated the available child care resources. The results of her search confirmed many of her fears; child care was so inaccessible and so expensive, and the available jobs paid so little, that she concluded she could not afford to work full time. She eventually went to work part time for a temporary office help agency. Out of her earnings she paid a neighbor to look after her youngest child for six hours a day. Her earnings, after deducting the expense of child care, equaled approximately one half of her husband's salary.

Six months after the initial separation, Robert called and proposed a trial reconciliation. Lorraine agreed to meet and talk it over. As they parted, Robert handed Lorraine two hundred dollars.

Eight months after the initial separation, Lorraine agreed to have Robert return home. She gave three conditions for the reconciliation: no more drinking, no more violence, and no more sexual abuse. She also insisted upon marital counseling. Robert agreed. The week he moved back home, Lorraine quit her job and returned to full-time child care.

Robert and Lorraine sought counseling at a local mental health center. They saw a male therapist who accepted Robert's assertion that his alcoholism and incestuous behavior were no longer serious problems and who focused in the therapy sessions on the couple's sexual adjustment, particularly on Robert's complaints of his wife's frigidity. After ten sessions, Robert refused to continue, maintaining that the counseling was a waste of time because Lorraine had not become more compliant in bed.

Lorraine resigned herself to the fact that no serious personality change could be expected from Robert. She began to focus her attention increasingly on her children's psychological development. She sought to impart to her sons and daughters a new image of motherhood, which included competence and self-respect, and a new image of fatherhood, which included caretaking and tenderness. Since the separation, her children had gained respect for her as a woman and had lost some of their fear of their father, causing Robert to complain that the children were "undisciplined." But they still had no concrete image of a nurturant father. There were no such men in their social environment.

One year after the initial separation, Robert had begun to drink again, but there had been no violent incidents and overt incest. The girls complained, however, that Robert continued to make suggestive remarks in their presence and to peep at them while they were undressing. On the oldest daughter's thirteenth birthday, Robert bought her two dozen long-stemmed roses.

On his wedding anniversary, Robert went out drinking.

At every stage of Lorraine's history, her ability to act as a strong, competent, and protective mother was directly related to her status as a woman. Her successes in defending herself and her children reflected the achievements of the women's liberation movement; her failures reflected its limitations. Lorraine was partially successful in determining the number of children she would bear, because she had legal access to the one form of birth control, sterilization, that was appropriate for her. She was denied other, more flexible methods of birth control, however, because of unacceptable medical risks or because of religious and social barriers to their use. Lorraine's inability to limit the size of her family as she wished prolonged her dependency upon Robert, and deepened her involvement in her marriage at the same time that it contributed to the marriage's deterioration. Her success in finally gaining reproductive control was a precondition for her eventual success in protecting her daughters.

During the crisis of disclosure, Lorraine was able to establish physical security for herself and her children largely because of the help she received from women friends, organized feminist groups, and other self-help organizations, such as Al-Anon and the women's shelter. She received only partial support from the legal system, in the form of restraining and vacate orders and the award of child custody, and very little help from the local police. The degree to which each institution was helpful to her in the crisis reflects the degree to which it was influenced or controlled by women.

Lorraine's attempt to provide economic security for herself and her children collapsed after eight months. Although the support provided by the state, in the form of welfare, did offer an immediate alternative to financial dependence on her husband during the crisis, it was inadequate as a long-term solution. The support offered by private industry, in the form of jobs accessible to women, was only marginally better. The resources available for child care were so inadequate that they further limited Lorraine's capacity to earn a living. Exposure to the segregated and discriminatory world of work convinced Lorraine of the economic necessity of preserving her marriage. Her individual failure reflects the more general failure of the women's movement to overcome economic discrimination.

Lorraine's effort to control her husband's abusiveness was more successful than her attempt to change his basic attitudes. Robert's behavior changed to some extent, but his concept of manhood and fatherhood did not. Manhood, for Robert, meant the ability not only to provide his family with a good material environment, but also to impose his will upon his family, to command sex from his wife, and to father sons. Reared in a traditional patriarchal family, Robert had no concept whatsoever that marriage involved mutuality or partnership. The traditional mental health system, represented by the marriage counselor, supported and reinforced Robert's sexist attitudes instead of fostering a psychological change in him. A treatment resource that might have enlarged the psychological possibilities for Robert, and ultimately for the whole family, was unavailable.

Lorraine's struggle to protect her children was only partially successful. She did prevent a recurrence of overt incest, a gain that should not be minimized. Nevertheless, this change fell far short of establishing an acceptable marriage or family. Robert's abusiveness was curtailed, but his sexist attitudes remained unchanged. The balance of power in the family was altered in Lorraine's favor, but it was far from equalized. Lorraine's gain in power was sufficient to change Robert from an incestuous to a seductive father. It was not sufficient to develop his capacity to become an affectionate father. With the exquisite sensitivity to the realities of power so characteristic of incestuous fathers, Robert changed only as much as he had to.

Many mothers, like Lorraine, have made the unhappy discovery that in their fight to protect their children, their strongest weapon is the power to exclude fathers from their families. Although some mothers would prefer to raise their children alone or in the company of other women, many are driven to this choice reluctantly, as a last resort. Most women, if given the choice, would prefer to share the tasks of child rearing with men, if only the men could be induced to behave like responsible, affectionate parents. But an increase in the relative power of mothers is not enough, in itself, to foster the development of nurturant capacities in men. In fact, as the relative power of mothers increases further, fathers may respond by abandoning their families altogether. If men are no longer allowed to dominate their families, they may simply withdraw in a pique. The final result of a change in the balance of power in the family, without a corresponding change in the sexual division of labor, could be the establishment of the one-parent, mother-child family as the social norm.

Any long-term hope for changing the psychology of men, and women, rests on shared responsibility for the care of children. The fact that women are the primary caretakers of young children creates the psychological conditions for reproducing male dominance in each succeeding generation. In girls, the identification with the mother forms the basis for a secure sexual identity and for the development of the capacity to nurture. In boys, adult sexual identity is achieved only by repudiating the primary identification with the mother. In this process, all the qualities associated with mothering—tenderness, emotional responsiveness, and nurturance—are ruthlessly suppressed. The result is the formation of a male psychology in which sexual identity is forever open to question, dominance and sexuality are confused, and the capacity for caretaking is atrophied. Such a psychology makes it inevitable that some men will abuse children.

If the primary responsibility for child care were shared by men and women, the entire basis for the psychology of male dominance and female submission might be abolished. Boys might be able to establish the same kind of secure gender identity that girls do, based on a primary identification with a nurturing father. Girls might be able to establish a sense of autonomy and self-respect based upon identification with a mother who is not perceived as inferior. For children of both sexes, the internalization of the incest taboo would not require repudiation of the mother or submission to the rule of the father, and the sexual asymmetry in the application of the taboo would no longer exist. The "rule of the gift" would apply to both sexes without distinction. Children raised by parents of both sexes presumably would not reach adult life expecting nurturance, sacrifice, and service only from women. The capacities for caretaking would be developed in both boys and girls, making it possible for grown men and women to share in the rearing of the next generation.[9]

But the idea of integrating men into the world of children, simple as it sounds, is profoundly radical. Even within the long tradition of human liberation struggles, this idea is in its infancy. Neither the socialist world nor the utopian experiments throughout history have made any serious attempt to involve men in the work of child care. The possiblity of transcending a biologically determined sexual division of labor is a very recent development, whose implications are not yet fully understood. Nothing in present society reflects this possibility. The rigid segregation of adult men from women and children, and the resultant absence of fathers from the home, have been a constant theme in recent history. Many of the causes that women have supported most passionately in the last century—temperance, animal rescue, the suppression of vice—can best be understood as attempts to get men out of the barroom, the game pit, the whore house, and into the home.[10] Only in the last decade have feminists dared to suggest, not only that men come home, but that they engage in the work that is done there: housework and child care.

In reality, adult men are totally absent from an increasing proportion of families. About 17 percent of all American families now consist of a mother raising her children alone.[11] In the remainder of families, fathers may be nominally present and may contribute to the financial maintenance of the family, but they generally do not participate in the care of their children in any meaningful way. One recent study of white middle-class families in the Boston area determined that only 25 percent of the fathers had any regular child care responsibilities at all, and only seven percent were attempting to share equally in the work of caring for children.[12] Other studies, based on direct observation or parental reports, estimate that fathers spend, on the average, something on the order of fifteen minutes a day in direct interaction with their young children.[13] In one study, fathers were observed to spend an average of 37.7 seconds per day talking to their infants.[14] What little time men do spend with their children, they prefer to spend with their sons.[15] The only predictable way that fathers show interest in their daughters is in an early and strong insistence that their girls conform to rigid stereotypes of femininity.[16]

Traditionally, although the literal absence of the father from the family has been viewed as deviant, the father's lack of involvement with his children has not been considered a social problem. In the past few decades, however, the increase in the number of female-headed households has generated a paternalistic worry about the effects of the father's absence on young children, especially among minorities and the poor. Out of this concern has grown an increasing volume of academic research, all of which leads to the inescapable conclusion that, if paternal neglect is a problem, then most children suffer from it.[17] Studies of the effects of fathers on child development document rather commonplace ideas, familiar to anyone who deals with children, that children form strong attachments to their fathers when they are even the least bit available, that children thrive on the attention of affectionate and competent fathers, and that children suffer from paternal abandonment, indifference, or hostility.[18] The sum of this large and growing body of work seems to be a recognition that fathers have much to contribute to the emotional development of their children, if only they could be persuaded to do so.[19]

The potential rewards to men for sharing the work of child care are great. They are the same rewards that have made motherhood a joy for countless women, even in its present degraded condition. Rearing children is far more interesting and creative than most work in the paid labor force. To be loved and trusted by a small child is a profound pleasure, one that has sustained women through many sorrows. These rewards, however, are purely subjective. Against them, men must weigh the force of an economic system that offers virtually no material reward for the work of child care, and an entrenched ideology that despises child care as women's work and defends men's privilege to be excused from it. Integrating men into the world of children would therefore require a transformation both of production and of consciousness.

The transformation of production means far more than the massive entry of women into the paid labor force. This process, which in traditional socialist thinking holds the key to abolishing sexual inequality, has been occurring in capitalist America at an accelerated pace in the past three decades and shows no sign of abating. It has not, however, resulted in desegregation, either in the paid labor force or in the home. Rather, it has increased the stress on working mothers, who must in effect perform two jobs at once, and on children, for whom no reliable alternative source of care is available. It has forced mothers out of the home and away from their children, without bringing fathers and children any closer together.

In order to permit men to take on the work of child care, the conditions of work in the paid labor force have to be modified so as to provide for the needs of parents. Such reforms as flexible working hours, paid maternity and paternity leaves, and child care facilities at the workplace are beginning steps. Historically, these goals have not been given priority by an organized labor force that is predominantly male. It remains for women workers to organize and lead the struggle to free parenthood from the tyranny of the workplace.

One of the most successful projects of the feminist movement in the past decade has been the naming of women's oppression. "Consciousness raising," originated by radical feminists, has become both an analytical and an organizing method; it has given women a voice and a sense of community.[20] Patriarchal assumptions about sexuality, motherhood, and child care have been challenged and put on the defensive. Much of the male reaction to feminist ideas has been intractably hostile, since men benefit from the exploitation of women, and stand to lose their privileges if equality is established. Nevertheless, there have been some promising responses. Many men as well as women understand that the continued oppression of women, and the endless battle of the sexes which results, ultimately deform and impoverish everyone; men as well as women are capable of a dream of human liberation and equality that reconciles the sexes and the generations.

The feminist critique of the sexual division of labor has provoked a re-valuation of received ideas on the family and child care, both among radical theorists and among liberal and establishment experts.[21] One significant accommodation appeared in the latest edition of Benjamin Spock's *Baby and Child Care,* a book that holds a unique place in American popular culture. Revised in response to severe feminist criticism, this basic manual of "enlightened" parenthood now embraces the doctrine of equal parental responsibility for child care and looks forward to a time when the ideal might become a reality:

> It will be a great day when fathers:
> Consider the care of their children to be as important *to them* as their jobs and careers.
> Seek out jobs and work schedules that will allow them ample time to be with their wives and children.
> Will let it be known at their work places that they take their parental responsibilities very seriously and may have to take time off when their children need them—just as working mothers have always done.

Will try to get other fathers in their work places to take the same stands.[22]

Further glimmerings of male interest in parenthood have begun to appear. The inclusion of fathers in prenatal education and attendance of fathers at births has grown from a marginal social experiment to a commonplace event. The idea that men as well as women can care for children is now a part of popular consciousness, though not a part of popular practice. At least a small minority of fathers have committed themselves to the attempt to share equally in the care of their children. In so doing, they have often braved fierce hostility from their peers, who sense correctly that the example of some men doing "women's work" will encourage women to demand the same from all men.

Unfortunately, the new male interest in fatherhood often tends to focus more on paternal rights than on paternal obligations. One result has been an attack upon women's recently won guardianship rights and on the institutions of child support and alimony. Two psychologists, for example, in a manual for parents called *Father Power*, object to the custom of awarding child custody to mothers in divorce cases. They consider this "discrimination" against fathers, even though they acknowledge that mothers are almost always the children's primary caretakers. They also suggest that alimony is an "anachronism," because of the "greater opportunities for women in the working world today."[23] This argument, which women can expect to hear with increasing frequency, essentially uses the very limited gains of the women's movement as a pretext for enlarging the scope of male prerogative.

The integration of fathers into families cannot be carried out under the banner of "father power." Women have had quite enough of that. If it comes about, it will be as a result of the organized and self-conscious struggle of women to win for child care the dignity and respect that any essential human activity deserves. It will also have to be carried out gradually and with a certain amount of caution. Men cannot be expected to overcome their abusive tendencies or to develop their nurturant capacities overnight, and it makes no sense to expose children to the unsupervised care of men whose interest in them may be ambivalent at best, and perverse at worst. Women are going to have to be the teachers and the protectors for some time to come.

One way this process might begin is described by a mother, Nora Harlow, who reported on the evolution of feminist awareness and political sophistication in a group of mothers. They began by sharing the care of their small children in their homes, went on to organize a cooperative day care center, and finally challenged their own mates to become involved. It is probably no coincidence that these women felt justified in making demands on their spouses only after they had formed a strong and cohesive group, which had affirmed the value of caretaking as work, which had overcome its own internal race and class divisions, and which had successfully weathered struggles with a church, a university, and a state bureaucracy. Far less visible and apparently less formidable than those institutions, the sexual division of labor was the last and the most difficult institution the mothers confronted.

The mothers' effort to involve fathers in child care began as a charitable gesture toward boys with absent fathers. It progressed as the mothers came to realize how profoundly all of their children, especially the girls, were neglected:

> We reassessed our situation. Each woman was asked to add up the time her child was cared for by his father.
>
> There was no time to add up. The fathers did not have the responsibility of nurturing their children for even one hour a week . . . We were determined to put these children firmly in the middle of a two-sex world. So we continued with the only means we saw to get men for all eighteen of our children—direct social pressure.[24]

The fathers' resistances, and the mothers' strategies to overcome them, are recounted with considerable good humor. The fathers said that much as they would like to spend time taking care of their children, they could not possibly do it because they had jobs. The mothers replied that they, too, had jobs for the most part, but that nevertheless they managed to be available for their child care duties. The mothers reviewed the fathers' work schedules and pointed out specific times that the fathers might work at the center. The fathers countered that their work was more important, and anyway child care was women's work. The mothers said they understood this had always been the case in the past, but they were determined it would not be so in the future, and they made participation by fathers a condition of admission to the center for new families.

As fathers were slowly recruited into the classroom, the mothers had to learn to work with them. Some fathers tried passive resistance: calling a mother to pick up a crying child, clean up a mess, change a diaper, or break up a fight. The mothers insisted that the fathers learn to handle these problems themselves. Little by little, the fathers began to speak of their sense of inadequacy and helplessness in the face of little children. The mothers acknowledged that they had felt the same way many times. The fathers began to invent their own ways of taking care of the children, drawing on their own childhood memories and fantasies, and using a forgotten part of their imagination. Finally, some fathers began to enjoy and look forward to their time at the daycare center. The story ends with almost all the fathers integrated into the daycare center for one half day per week, some still grudging and resentful, but many others discovering for the first time the pleasure and excitement of relationships with children. "Our children," Harlow reports, "were growing up with a very different image of a father. The biggest part of that image was formed by the men who came to the children's school to spend time with them, to teach them, to care for them."[25]

In this "very different image of a father" lies the best hope, not only for ending sexual abuse, but for reconciling fathers with mothers and children. Incest is only one of the abuses that inevitably result from a patriarchal family structure. As long as mothers and children are subordinated to the rule of fathers, such abuses will continue. In the short term, mothers who seek to protect their children may have no choice but to fight to banish abusive fathers from the family. In the long run, most mothers would not wish for single parenthood, but would prefer to raise their children in partnership with fathers who have learned to understand the needs of children, who can distinguish between sexuality and affection, and who recognize the appropriate limits of parental love. If a mother's immediate defense rests on her power to exclude an incestuous father from the family, her ultimate hope lies in the possibility of transforming fatherhood so that such a defense would never become necessary.

As long as fathers retain their authoritarian role, they cannot take part in the tasks or the rewards of parenthood. They can never know what it means to share a work of love on the basis of equality, or what it means to nurture the life of a new generation. When men no longer rule their families, they may learn for the first time what it means to belong to one.

Afterword, 2000: Understanding Incest Twenty Years Later

This book, like so many feminist writings, began with two women talking. Our simple acts of speaking and listening joined us to a world-wide liberation movement. In the "free space" we created in our intimate dialogues with our patients and with each other, we joined with numerous other women who were uncovering the secret crimes at the heart of patriarchal order.[1] When Lisa Hirschman and I began our study in the mid-1970s, incest was publicly invisible, yet the private confidences of numerous victims led us and a number of other feminist writers to suspect that sexual exploitation of women and children was endemic in our society.[2] Against the evidence of our patients' personal testimony, we encountered a suffocating array of denials, rationalizations, and excuses that passed for authoritative wisdom in literature, social science, medicine, and law. At the time it was generally held that sexual offenses were rare in reality but rampant in the overactive imaginations of women and children. The opposite turned out to be true.

In the past two decades, the original premises of our incest study have been amply confirmed. It is now widely understood that father-daughter incest is not an aberration but rather a common and predictable abuse of patriarchal power. It is also a means of perpetuating the power of fathers, one of the many private crimes (rape, sexual trafficking, domestic battery) by which male dominance and female subordination are enforced.[3] Perhaps those who grasp the importance of incest most fully are practical businessmen who profit from the sale of women's bodies. A pimp explains to a naive student what he looks for in a prostitute:

Beauty, yes. Sexual expertise, somewhat. That can be taught easier than you think. What is important above all is obedience. And how do you get obedience? You get obedience if you get women who have had sex with their fathers, their uncles, their brothers—you know, someone they love and fear to lose so that they do not dare to defy.[4]

While conceding that incest is much more common than previously thought, some commentators have attempted to understand the problem apart from the context of male dominance. They point out, quite rightly, that not all perpetrators are men (only some 90 percent of them),[5] and not all victims are girls (boys are also sexually abused in significant numbers, mostly by older boys and men).[6] Nevertheless, a feminist analysis remains the only one capable of explaining how such widespread abuses visited mainly by one sex upon the other could be so long denied or condoned. Only a feminist analysis explains why incest perpetrators look like the ordinary men they are—indeed, why so many are men of power and respect. Only a feminist analysis explains why women have always been the most committed advocates for abused children and adult survivors. And only a feminist analysis explains why such bitter conflict arises any time a serious effort is made to hold incest perpetrators accountable for their crimes.

Global and National Consciousness-Raising

Twenty years is a short time in the long history of the women's movement. In that time the pandemic violence against women and children has become more visible, both in this country and in many other parts of the world. "The Progress of Nations," a 1997 UNICEF report on issues affecting the health, welfare, and rights of children, concluded that violence against women and girls is the most pervasive form of human rights abuse in the world.[7] In some countries, consciousness-raising of the sort that took place in the United States twenty to thirty years ago is just beginning. Wherever a little "free space" opens up, incest survivors come forward to disclose their secrets.[8] At a speakout in Osaka or Istanbul, the familiar stories are all too recognizable, transcending the particularities of language and culture.

In many parts of the world, clinicians are among the first to hear incest survivors' stories. Inevitably, those who publish their findings encounter stubborn prejudice among their peers, who uniformly prefer to believe that

"it doesn't happen here." Yet reports in the psychiatric literature now starting to emerge from Asia and the Middle East turn out to be virtually indistinguishable from those documenting abuses in Europe and North America.[9] Because epidemiological studies have not been conducted in most
countries, it is not possible to compare the prevalence of incest in North
America with that in most other parts of the world, but wherever comparable research has been done, the findings are strikingly similar.[10]

In North America, the problem of incest has received widespread public
attention in the past twenty years. Leading authors of contemporary fiction
have taken up the subject,[11] as have leading figures of daytime television.
Many survivors, including well-known celebrities, have disclosed their own
experiences. For example, the widely beloved talk-show host Oprah Winfrey
has identified herself as a survivor in the interest of public education. A self-
help movement of incest survivors has also grown out of a larger movement
exposing the secrets of "dysfunctional" families. *The Courage to Heal*, a self-
help manual for survivors, became a national best-seller upon its publication
in 1988.[12] An annual speakout, "To Tell the Truth," encourages survivors all
over the country to disobey their families' rule of silence. And a traveling art
exhibit, "The Clothesline Project," offered survivors of sexual and domestic
violence the opportunity to paint their messages on t-shirts and display them
in public, breaking the taboo on hanging out their families' "dirty laundry."
As general awareness of sexual and domestic violence has increased, grass-
roots victim-service organizations have also proliferated. Thanks to pioneer-
ing feminists, rape crisis centers and battered women's shelters can now
be found throughout the United States and Canada, offering information,
counseling, practical help, and legal advice to victims.

The movement to right the wrongs of abused women and children has
also inspired a wealth of new legislation and social programs. The passage
of the Victims of Crime Act (VOCA) and the establishment of the National Organization of Victim Assistance (1986) were a landmark in official
recognition of victims' rights. This innovative legislation establishes a policy of reparation, by mandating that offenders convicted of certain crimes
must pay into a fund for organizations such as rape crisis centers, battered
women's shelters, counseling services, and courtroom advocacy programs.
Funds are also available to compensate individual victims directly for medical expenses, counseling, and lost earnings. Victim representatives and advocates serve on the state advisory boards that control the distribution of
funds. In the 1998 fiscal year, 324 million dollars was collected for the
VOCA fund. Those of us who have dedicated our lives to serving victims

find a certain satisfaction in the knowledge that offenders have been compelled to contribute to our work.

Legislation establishing a federal agency to address the problem of child maltreatment, the Child Abuse Prevention and Treatment Act, first passed the U.S. Congress in 1974. Since that time, three national studies of the incidence of child abuse and neglect have been conducted. In addition to confirmed reports from state child protective agencies, these studies collect data from a large representative sample of "sentinels," professionals such as teachers, doctors, social workers, and police whose work frequently brings them into contact with abused and neglected children. The most recent survey, conducted in 1996, arrived at a conservative estimate that 217,000 children were sexually abused in that year. Roughly half of these children were abused by their fathers, stepfathers, or other father figures. These estimates represented an increase of 83 percent from the previous study, conducted only a decade earlier, in 1986. The authors of the study attributed the increase in large part to the improved reporting of professional sentinels, who had become more skilled at detecting child abuse. In little less than ten years, recognized incidences of child maltreatment had doubled in law enforcement, more than tripled among hospital staff, and quadrupled in mental health agencies.[13]

Unfortunately, the capacity of state authorities to intervene on behalf of abused children has not kept pace with the professional capacity to identify children at risk. As reporting has soared, the number of case investigations has remained static, resulting in a declining percentage of investigated cases. By 1996, only 28 percent of the cases identified by sentinels were officially investigated, even when the children had serious physical injuries. Social workers on the front lines, overwhelmed by their case loads, have had to "triage" the reports they receive, reserving their limited resources for those children in the most obvious and immediate danger, and hoping that one of their cases will not end up on the front pages of the newspaper when the child is found dead. In these circumstances, suspected sexual abuse cases are often among those "screened out."

The child protective agencies that exist today are simply not designed to respond to problems of this magnitude. By 1990, the National Advisory Board on Child Abuse and Neglect was describing the situation in child protection as a "national emergency."[14] Since then, matters appear to have gotten worse. A review of social policy in child protection concluded in 1994: "Rather than moving forward toward more comprehensive services for maltreated children, we appear to be falling further behind."[15] This crisis in child protective services is but one example of a larger conflict between public concern about the welfare of children and reluctance to intervene or to commit resources on a scale that might realistically be necessary to provide all children with adequate care and protection.

In spite of increased public awareness, undoubtedly most incest cases still escape detection. The best estimates of the true prevalence of incest can be found, not in studies that rely on "sentinels," like the National Incidence Survey, but in studies that gather information directly from adult survivors. Large-scale surveys conducted in the last two decades have made it clear that my 1981 estimate of the prevalence of incest was too low. In a survey of 930 randomly selected women in California, the sociologist Diana Russell found that 16 percent reported having been sexually abused by a relative before age eighteen, and 4.5 percent reported sexual abuse by a father or stepfather.[16] Similar results were obtained in a smaller community study, also conducted in California, by the sociologist Gail Wyatt.[17] These two studies in many ways represent the gold standard of survey methodology, because of the care that was taken to establish a relationship of trust and confidentiality with the informants. In-depth interviews were conducted in person, usually in the informant's home, and in the informant's native language. Several other studies have reached larger groups of people across the country, using more impersonal telephone interviews. Their prevalence figures are somewhat lower, but still above my original estimate.[18]

Russell's findings also confirmed many of the observations of our small clinical study. Incest appeared to be as common in middle-class and wealthy families as in poor families, and its prevalence varied little among ethnic groups. One finding that we did not anticipate was the risk of abuse from stepfathers. Russell found that one in six of all women who had spent any part of their childhood living with a stepfather had been abused. She speculates that men with an active sexual interest in children may intentionally seek out vulnerable single mothers in order to gain access to their daughters, as in the archetypal scenario of *Lolita*.

Of the forty-four women who disclosed their histories of incest to Russell's interviewers, only three had reported the abuse at the time. These data confirm what experienced workers in the field have long suspected: reported cases represent less than 10 percent of the true prevalence of incest. Most child victims still keep their secrets. If they tell at all, it is much later, when they are grown, when they have escaped from their fathers' direct control, and when they are no longer intimidated by their fathers' continued demands for loyalty and silence. Some do not acknowledge, even to themselves, that their fathers abused them. Sometimes it is easier not to know, easier to accept denial than to face the depths of betrayal and loss. Sometimes it is easier to forget.

Understanding Survivors

At the time of our original study, in the mid-1970s, there was virtually no scientific literature on the psychological impact of incest. Our study helped to open up this previously neglected area of investigation. The problem was noticed first by psychotherapists like ourselves because so many of the people who sought psychiatric treatment turned out to be survivors of childhood abuse. Once therapists took the trouble to ask, many patients disclosed histories of abuse within their families. In the 1980s, when the matter was studied more systematically, clinical researchers consistently found that approximately 50–60 percent of patients in psychiatric hospitals and 40–60 percent of outpatients in clinics and private psychotherapy reported childhood experiences of physical and/or sexual abuse.[19]

Some of the most severe and bewildering cases that clinicians encountered turned out to be related to previously undisclosed childhood trauma. Moreover, many patients began to get better when the source of their trouble was finally recognized. These discoveries led to an explosion of new research documenting the long-term effects of childhood abuse. By the mid-1990s, studies relating childhood sexual abuse to adult psychiatric problems had become so numerous, and the amassed data so compelling, that the leading U.S. psychiatric journal, the *American Journal of Psychiatry,* deemed it wise to remind its readers (reasonably enough) that not *every* psychiatric problem could be laid at the door of the "abusive father."[20]

Most of the clinical observations that Lisa Hirschman and I reported in our original study of forty incest survivors have now been replicated in numerous studies by investigators in this country and in other parts of the world.[21] It is clear from the testimony of numerous accomplished women who have disclosed their personal histories that survivors display astonishing strength and resiliency; a history of incest does not determine a single life path. It is also clear, however, that survivors are at high risk for a wide range of problems. Most ominously, exploitation in childhood seems to render survivors highly vulnerable to repeated exploitation in adult life. The data on this point are compelling. In Russell's study, for example, incest survivors suffered rape, domestic violence, sexual harassment, and recruitment for prostitution and pornography *twice* as frequently as women who had not been abused in childhood. These horrible statistics led Russell to speculate that "the incest experience itself could have stripped away some of the victims' potential ability to protect themselves . . . Men appear to be selecting previously victimized females for further . . . victimization."[22] The street wisdom of the pimp has thus been confirmed by the rigorous methods of modern social science.

Incest also appears to heighten survivors' risk of experiencing a wide range of adult psychiatric problems, most commonly depression, anxiety disorders, eating disorders, and substance abuse.[23] Along with other forms of childhood abuse, incest is common in the histories of patients who attempt suicide or intentionally cut, burn, or mutilate themselves.[24] It appears to be particularly common in those patients, mostly women, whose rapid mood swings and intense unstable relationships earn them the reputation of being "difficult" and the diagnosis of "borderline personality disorder."[25] And it has been strongly implicated in the pathogenesis of the strange and troubling conditions known as dissociative disorders.[26]

Research in this area has been advanced by the growth of the field of traumatic stress studies, for it turns out that the effects of incest have much in common with the consequences of exposure to other forms of severe, prolonged, and repeated trauma. Survivors of sexual and domestic abuse often resemble people who have endured captivity and torture as hostages, cult members, or political prisoners. They suffer not only from a wide range of symptoms, but also from a profound damage to their sense of self and their capacity for relationships with others. These surprising similarities among traumatized people led me to formulate the concept of "complex post-traumatic stress disorder."[27] This concept has now been incorporated into the DSM-IV, the official diagnostic manual of the American Psychiatric Association.[28]

The accumulated research and clinical experience of the past two decades have led to some discoveries that we did not anticipate in our original study. We did not fully appreciate the profound effects of incest on the developing child's mind and body; nor did we understand the complex range of adaptations to an environment of fear, secrecy, and betrayal.[29] Our initial study and others that followed in the 1980s were also limited by the fact that our information came from the retrospective reports of adult survivors. In the last few years, however, it has become possible to conduct more sophisticated prospective studies, following children with known histories of abuse as they grow up. A new generation of researchers is now tracking the development of children whose abuse came to the attention of child protective agencies five to ten years ago.[30] These studies promise to deepen even further our understanding of the impact of incest and other forms of child abuse.

Our initial study did not lead us to suspect that childhood sexual abuse would affect survivors' physical health. More recent research has made it clear, however, that survivors are as likely to end up in the office of a primary care physician as in a mental health clinic.[31] In one study, survivors were more likely than others to make frequent office visits with multiple medical complaints, especially headaches and gastrointestinal problems.[32] In another study, childhood abuse was associated with chronic pelvic pain.[33] Although chronic health problems appear to be the lot of trauma survivors in general,[34] traumatized children may be particularly vulnerable to traumatic disruptions in their maturing biological regulatory systems.[35] Researchers following the development of sexually abused children are now reporting abnormalities in the central nervous system regulation of adrenal, thyroid, and reproductive hormones.[36] These neurobiological abnormalities appear to persist long after the abuse has presumably come to an end.[37] The implications of this growing body of evidence are quite disturbing, for it would appear that childhood trauma may have permanent effects on the developing brain.[38]

Another discovery that we did not anticipate twenty years ago was the link between trauma and altered states of consciousness. Although the phenomenon of dissociation has in fact been documented by clinical observers for more than a century, only recently has the connection between psychological trauma and dissociation been fully appreciated.[39] Studies conducted in many different parts of the world, with survivors of accidents, natural disasters, wars, rape, and domestic violence, report extraordinarily consistent findings: in situations of helpless terror, some people spontaneously enter an altered state of consciousness. In this "dream-like" state of numbness and detachment, people feel disconnected from their own sensations, emotions, or awareness of what is happening to them. Perceptions are altered, time is slowed, and the traumatic events are observed from a distance, as though they are happening to someone else. Though this response might seem adaptive at a moment when no escape is possible, it comes at a heavy cost. Many studies show that people who enter a dissociative state at the time of the trauma are among those most likely to develop post-traumatic stress disorders.[40]

It also appears that the more severe and prolonged the traumatic exposure, and the earlier its onset in childhood, the greater the likelihood that dissociative mental processes will develop. In a prospective study of sexually abused girls conducted at the National Institute of Mental Health, the psychiatrist Frank Putnam and his colleagues have been observing the ominous progression of dissociative symptoms over the past ten years, as the girls have grown up. Dissociation at the time of the trauma was one of the most powerful predictors of later troubles of all sorts, including physical health, psychiatric, and social problems. Anxiety disorders, depression, self-injury, suicide attempts, difficulties at school, peer conflicts, and early sexual involvement in adolescence all appeared to be strongly linked to the severity of dissociative symptoms in childhood.[41]

Another, related finding that we did not anticipate in our original incest study was the phenomenon of traumatic amnesia. In the early 1980s, as I gained experience in running psychotherapy groups for incest survivors with my colleague Emily Schatzow, we began to notice that some of our patients complained of puzzling gaps in memory. Even more puzzling was the phenomenon of delayed recall. The first time a patient spontaneously recovered previously inaccessible traumatic memories in a group, we were astonished. Rather than searching for a childhood memory, we had been focusing on a discussion of the patient's current interactions with her father. We were quite unprepared for the moment when the patient became extremely agitated, began to speak in a pleading, childlike voice, and appeared to be re-experiencing an assault by her father as though it were happening in the present. Other therapists who witnessed the return of traumatic memories similarly reported being taken by surprise. In 1987, we published a report on recovery and verification of traumatic memories in fifty-three patients whom we had treated in our groups. We noted that the severity of memory disturbance seemed to be related to the early age of onset and the degree of violence of the reported abuse. We also found that the majority of our patients, both those with continuous memory and those who reported a period of amnesia, were able to obtain external corroboration for their memories.[42] Since that early report, numerous investigators have confirmed the observation of memory disturbances in some, but not all, survivors of childhood sexual abuse.[43]

Survivors themselves have written descriptions of their experiences of amnesia and recall. The concert pianist Linda Cutting emphasizes the role of terror and coercion in the alteration of memory: "Survivors don't only forget because of the trauma, although that in itself would be enough. They forget because they were told to forget. Whether by threat ('if you tell, I'll kill you') or by edict ('this did not happen') reality gets reshaped."[44] She also describes the profound life crisis that can attend the return of traumatic memory: "There are three kinds of memory slips, I tell my students. One, when memory slips but you find your way back without losing a beat. Two, when you don't find your way back until the downbeat. Three, when you don't find your way back in time and must stop and restart the music. I don't tell them about a fourth possibility, when one memory slips, another intrudes, and you don't find your way back for a very long time."[45]

These disturbances of memory are by no means unique to incest survivors; indeed, they are common in people who have survived many kinds of traumatic events. Amnesia, in fact, is one of the diagnostic symptoms of post-traumatic stress disorder.[46] Traumatic memory disturbances are among the most perplexing phenomena that clinicians and researchers encounter. They offer a window into the nature of consciousness, the formation of identity, and the links between body and mind.[47] Current neurobiological studies have begun to delineate the impact of psychological trauma on the memory systems of the brain.[48] In the process of investigating traumatic memory, these studies also promise to deepen our understanding of normal memory. Understanding these phenomena represents the next frontier of scientific investigation.

While the accumulated evidence linking incest to a host of psychological disorders is now very powerful, one cannot reason backwards to presume that incest is the causative factor in any particular case. The fact that many or even most patients with a particular psychiatric problem have an incest history does not imply that all patients do. Although a constellation of symptoms commonly associated with incest should raise the index of suspicion, it should not lead clinicians to infer that any particular patient *must be* an incest survivor, whether or not she remembers the abuse. Similarly, it is important to remember that incest occurs in a context of disturbed family relationships that may be as destructive as the incest itself.[49] Many investigators have pointed out that being physically abused, neglected, abandoned, or exposed to domestic violence may be just as traumatic to children and may cause as much long-term damage as sexual abuse. By contrast, a strong relationship with one caring and protective person—a sibling, a grandparent, a concerned teacher—can sometimes mitigate the destructive impact of even the bleakest childhood. Recognizing the full gravity of incest does not imply that nothing else in the survivor's life matters.

Because incest was so long overlooked in the mental health professions, patients often encountered denial when they attempted to disclose their secrets. As one of the first researchers to offer treatment guidelines for clinicians, I found that the main obstacle to overcome was clinicians' avoidance of the topic: when this book was first published, it hardly seemed necessary to warn against falling into the opposite error. As awareness of incest increased, however, some clinicians appear to have pursued the possibility of childhood abuse too aggressively, as though the surfacing of traumatic memories in and of itself would effect a cure. The subject of incest arouses such strong emotions that clinicians can sometimes be swayed in either direction from their basic professional stance of empathic and open-minded curiosity.

Fortunately, in the last decade a reasonable consensus on the standard of care for incest survivors has emerged, thanks to the contributions of many thoughtful and experienced clinicians.[50] The treatment of incest survivors follows the guidelines for treating traumatized people in general. The purpose of treatment is not to pursue recollection of the past for its own sake, but rather to help the survivor integrate and make meaning of her experience, so that her life is no longer held hostage to the past. Most experienced clinicians recognize that recovery unfolds in stages, beginning always with careful attention to the survivor's present life circumstances and goals, proceeding gradually through a period of reflection on formative past events, and ending with a fuller engagement in the present. I have elaborated on this approach to treatment more fully in my book *Trauma and Recovery*.[51]

Understanding Incest Perpetrators

Because survivors have been willing to tell what they know, to participate in formal studies, and, indeed, to become researchers themselves, our understanding of the impact of incest has deepened immeasurably in the past two decades. By contrast, because perpetrators have remained committed to silence and secrecy, we do not understand them very much better than we did twenty years ago. Research on offenders has made comparatively little progress because the vast majority of perpetrators continue to escape detection. Those who do not get caught do not generally volunteer to be subjects of research, and the few who do get caught do not seem particularly interested in telling the truth; they are more likely to tell investigators whatever they think the investigators might want to hear.

In spite of these obstacles, some dedicated and persistent investigators have managed to get to know incest perpetrators in some depth. The consensus that emerges from their studies confirms the general accuracy of the descriptions given by survivors. Despite persistent searching, no one has been able to come up with a psychological "profile" that might identify incest offenders, because they look too normal. Careful psychiatric evaluations fail to uncover signs of mental illness; indeed, the majority do not qualify for any psychiatric diagnosis.[52] Gene Abel, a psychiatrist with extensive experience studying unreported offenders in the community, offers this impression: "These paraphiliacs are not strange people. They are people who have one slice of their behavior that is very disruptive to them and to others . . . But the other aspects of their lives can be pretty stable. We have executives, computer operators, insurance salesmen . . . and people in a variety of occupations in our program. They are just like everyone else, except they can not control one aspect of their behavior."[53]

Rather than obvious psychopathology, what seems to characterize offenders is their obsessive involvement in sexual fantasy and their compulsive behavior, which I and many other observers have compared to an addiction.[54] A clinical study of 373 incest perpetrators identified in prisons, mental health centers, and community treatment centers reported that while common "personality factors" proved "elusive," the men displayed many signs of sexual obsession and compulsivity. Eighty percent fed their incest fantasies with pornography.[55]

Many other investigators have also discovered pornography to be the royal road to the inner world of sex offenders. This finding has been so often and reliably replicated that it has now become a generally accepted basis for psychological assessment of offenders. Standard forensic evaluation now includes measuring an offender's sexual arousal while he views a variety of pornographic scenes in a private booth.[56] Although this variant of the polygraph (known colloquially as the "peter meter") is no more infallible than any other "lie detector," it does seem to be an effective method of encouraging offenders to acknowledge their sexual preoccupations. Using this method, one group of investigators found that most of the incest offenders they studied were pedophiles whose sexual interest was not limited to their own children. Indeed, almost half (44 percent) of these incestuous fathers admitted that they had also abused other children outside their families.[57]

In order to protect their sexual compulsions, offenders typically develop an elaborate intellectual system to deny, minimize, and justify their behavior. Like other addicts, they are often adept at recruiting loyal supporters, including family members, who share their attitudes or accept their excuses. The Canadian psychologists Howard Barbaree and William Marshall conclude on the basis of their many years of experience: "Denial of the offense and minimization of the offender's responsibility and the harm he has done is so common . . . as to be regarded as a defining characteristic of this population . . . The offender will present his denial at every opportunity, often in a compulsive manner, and his arguments are almost always plausible and convincing."[58]

Offenders' arguments have apparently changed little over the past two decades. Investigators who study offenders consistently encounter the same standard repertoire of rationalizations and excuses. Incestuous fathers seem to persist in their beliefs that children are or should be free to consent to sex with adults, that children are not harmed and may in fact benefit from such experiences, or that if any harm does occur, it must be someone else's fault. Many offenders seem to consider themselves part of a privileged elite exempt from the moral rules of ordinary people. What might perhaps be a crime for lesser beings becomes for them an entitlement, governed by a higher law. Thus the Nicaraguan head of state Daniel Ortega, according to the testimony of his stepdaughter Zoilamerica Narvaez Murrillo, justified the sexual abuse that began when she was eleven years old by explaining that "someone as busy as he was needed regular sexual release—and that through her sacrifice she was helping the Sandinista cause."[59] Those of a more conservative persuasion may invoke a higher Authority, as Linda Cutting, a minister's daughter, testifies:

> For every Saturday our father beat us, we were given the chance to ask his and God's forgiveness the very next day. For God, the Father, and our father seemed to be one. At the very least, our father, from up high in his pulpit, in his black velvet robes with the purple satin vestments, projected the image of God to us. We hungrily accepted Christ into our hearts and our mouths. Communion was a problem because when my father said "This is my body which is given for you," and put the bread in his mouth and commanded us to "Eat ye all of it," I felt so sick and confused, not remembering all those times he'd forced his body into my mouth.[60]

Clinicians who attempt to treat offenders quickly learn to respect the tenacity of their resistance to change. Most agree that treatment must be mandated by some outside authority to have even a remote chance of success, because the majority of offenders lack any reliable inner motivation to stop their abusive behavior. Even with mandated treatment, however, results have not been very encouraging. Reviewing the state of the art, Barbaree and Marshall acknowledge the limits of an approach that conceptualizes sexual exploitation as a problem of individual psychology:

> In a sense it is inaccurate to call our interventions "treatment," as we do not construe our patients as having a "disorder" that can be

"cured." Rather, we see them as having learned certain unacceptable behaviors to obtain rewards and satisfactions . . . Because these . . . acts have produced strong, immediate rewards in the past, and because thoughts of deviant acts have been frequently associated with the enjoyment of strong sexual arousal, we expect deviant tendencies to retain some degree of strength even after the very best treatment program.[61]

Whereas offenders appear fiercely committed to the defense of their own predilections, they display an almost uniform indifference to the feelings of their victims. Indeed, the few who pay close attention appear to be sadists who derive pleasure from their victims' suffering.[62] In the majority of cases, observers are struck by the perpetrators' apparent lack of empathy or concern for their victims. In one study, for example, only 14 percent of offenders expressed regret or remorse for their actions.[63]

In contrast, many victims express a strong and generally unrequited desire to know and understand their perpetrators. In the absence of any real dialogue, victims often attempt to project themselves into the perpetrators' emotional world. The author Sylvia Fraser writes of her father:

I can't even imagine the loneliness of such an existence. I can't imagine the frustration that caused him to do what he did or the agony that must have resulted. Did he pretend I was a willing victim? Did he do to me what had been done to him? Did he know that I couldn't remember what we did in secret? Was he as profoundly split as I? Was there a Daddy Who Knew and a Daddy Who Did Not Know?[64]

Many private family confrontations are fueled by the adult survivor's desire finally to understand the perpetrator, and to be understood by him. In spite of all the callous treatment they have endured, many survivors simply refuse to give up on their fathers. Punishment of the offender seems to be a surprisingly low priority for most survivors. Perhaps they have already seen enough of punishment. In confronting their fathers, they are often driven by the hope of reconciliation.[65] What survivors want most is an acknowledgment of the truth. Beyond this, incest survivors, like other crime victims, want the perpetrator to put an end to his abusive behavior and to make some effort at restitution. They want an acknowledgment of the harm that has been done to them, an apology, and if such a thing is possible, an explanation. The author Sue William Silverman addresses the following questions to her dying father, knowing he is no longer capable of giving an answer, if indeed he ever was:

> Father, I want to ask you, what do you remember? I want to ask you: What do you know? How did you first decide to open the door to enter my bedroom? What was your desultory, internal passage through time and space that brought you to my body? . . . Did you love me, hate me, or think you merely owned me? . . . My body/your possession. What did my skin say to you? Did my skin shudder like the curtains, or was it still, shocked to silence?[66]

I noted twenty years ago that perpetrators rarely respond to these simple and reasonable requests. What I failed to appreciate at the time was the ferocity of resistance that perpetrators would mount when confronted in increasing numbers by their victims. It appears that most perpetrators prefer to fight to the bitter end rather than acknowledge their crimes. Incapable of compassion for their daughters, many also seem to be incapable of recognizing their daughters' compassion for them. They seem to imagine, rather, that their victims will exact revenge with the same cruelty they were taught at home. When accused, perpetrators are apt to portray themselves as the persecuted victims of vengeful women.

Accountability

The increase in child abuse reporting in the 1980s brought attention to incest cases, not only from social workers, but also from law enforcement. Many jurisdictions saw an increase in criminal prosecution of child abuse cases, and some developed child abuse units, with staff skilled in working with child victims. At the same time, some adult survivors also began to seek civil damages for the crimes committed against them in childhood. In order to have their day in court, adult survivors first had to overcome the statutes of limitations that narrowly restricted the time frame in which a complaint could be filed. They argued that the nature of the injury itself prevented them from taking action until many years after the fact, either because they had no memory of the abuse for a period of time, or because they did not understand the connection between their abuse in childhood and their resulting psychological problems. Extending the statutes of limitations, they argued, would allow them a reasonable chance to seek justice. These arguments, based on the concept of "delayed discovery," proved persuasive to many courts and state legislatures. As of 1997, thirty-seven states had provided some time extension for adult survivors of childhood abuse to institute legal proceedings against their abusers.[67]

A number of women's advocacy organizations also entered the arena of the civil courts on behalf of survivors' claims, arguing that it was time for society to end the era of impunity for perpetrators. As Sally Goldfarb, a senior staff attorney at the National Organization for Women's Legal Defense and Education Fund in New York, argued: "Basically, the message that the courts have traditionally given men in our society is that it's OK to abuse your child, because there's no way she can get legal redress. We need to turn that on its head and tell men that any act of abuse will be punished."[68]

In fact, the goal of holding all or even most perpetrators publicly accountable is still far out of reach. But the serious prospect of legal action against even a minority of perpetrators set off considerable alarm in some quarters. Indeed, if the ordinary citizens who have long felt entitled to abuse women and children were to be held accountable, our society might well be "turned on its head." Many highly publicized trials of the last decade have illustrated the dilemmas of a society attempting to come to terms with the common crimes of sexual and domestic violence. Like countries emerging from dictatorship, our country is faced with a record of widespread human rights violations that once were ignored or condoned. The prospect of justice is highly unsettling when so many people have participated or colluded in the crimes of rape, domestic battery, or child abuse. The claims of victims necessarily conflict with the general desire for social harmony, especially in family relationships.

Moreover, just as in newly emerging democracies, those who have been accustomed to abusing power tend to become more belligerent when threatened with exposure or accountability.[69] And indeed, the prospect of an end to impunity has led to the formation of highly aggressive advocacy organizations for accused and convicted perpetrators. Victims of Child Abuse Laws (VOCAL) in the 1980s was followed by the False Memory Syndrome Foundation (FMSF) in the 1990s. On behalf of accused offenders, these organizations mobilized the resources of defense attorneys, professionals who testified regularly as expert witnesses for the defense, and some academics. With a flamboyant cast of characters, including some females in lead roles, these organizations mounted a furious campaign in the courts and the media, advancing some ingenious new variations on very old arguments.

One of the founding fathers of the FMSF was the psychologist and theologian Ralph Underwager. By the time he helped to form this organization, in 1992, Underwager was already a seasoned defense witness, having testified on behalf of accused perpetrators in some two hundred civil and criminal cases. While under oath, Underwager was apt to defend accused pedophiles in the name of medical science; in more candid moments he defended them in the name of God. Interviewed in the Dutch publication *Paidika: The Journal of Pedophilia,* Underwager offered an old-fashioned libertine argument with a novel admixture of piety:

> Paedophiles can boldly and courageously affirm what they choose. They can say that what they want is to find the best way to love . . . As a theologian, I believe it is God's will that there be closeness and intimacy, unity of the flesh, between people . . . I do believe that God's will is that we have absolute freedom. No conditions, no contingencies. When the blessed apostle Paul says, "All things are lawful for me," he says it not once, but four times. "All things are lawful for me."[70]

This unusual interpretation of Scripture proved to be too much of an embarrassment for the organization he had helped to create, and Underwager resigned from the FMSF board in 1993.[71] Others came forward, however, to defend the accused in the name of traditional family values. FMSF Executive Director Pamela Freyd helped to found the organization after a private family confrontation in which her husband, Peter, was accused of incest by their grown daughter. Faced with the classic conflict of loyalty, Freyd unquestioningly chose her husband's side. Though their daughter had not taken any legal action, and indeed had asked only to be left alone, the Freyds embarked on a public campaign to prove they had been wronged. They soon found that they had company. Other parents, outraged by similar accusations, were willing to join or contribute money to an organization formed to combat the grass-roots incest-survivor movement. As calls to the FMSF increased, Freyd began to tally the numbers as evidence of an "epidemic" of false complaints.

Freyd acknowledged, when pressed, that her organization could not demonstrate that the complaints were false. Lacking the capability to determine the facts of any particular case, the organization simply accepted the denials of accused parents as an article of faith. But the absence of facts did nothing to dampen Freyd's conviction. Most of the incest complaints she heard about *could not* be true, she reasoned, because the accused parents were respectable, middle-class people like themselves. In one of the organization's first newsletters, Freyd took on the question, "How do we know we are not representing pedophiles?"

> We are a good looking bunch of people: graying hair, well-dressed, healthy, smiling. The similarity of the stories is astounding, so script-like and formulaic that doubts dissolve after chats with a few families. Just about every person who has attended is someone you would likely find interesting and want to count as a friend.[72]

The FMSF maintained, moreover, that it had discovered the source of the false complaints: psychotherapists. Unable to imagine that their grown children could be acting on their own initiative, many accused parents became convinced that some subversive agent must have literally put ideas in their heads. Their sons and daughters had been led astray by feminists bent on destruction of the family. The archvillain's role in this imaginary drama was played by the "recovered memory therapist," a creature thought to have remarkable suggestive powers. As one accused parent complained, "By the use of guided imagery and dream interpretation, therapists have caused thousands of adults to believe that those they formerly trusted and loved are, in fact, guilty of the worst possible crimes."[73]

The empirical evidence supporting this claim was also rather scanty. It was not clear, for example, how many of the accusing sons and daughters had ever seen a therapist at all, much less how many might have been swayed by improper suggestion. But sensational anecdote, speculation, and the vehement opinions of a small group of professional "experts" more than compensated for the lack of data. Though the FMSF was unable to document its "epidemic" according to any of the accepted rules of science, the organization met with great success in inspiring media excitement. The *New York Times Book Review* admonished its readers to "Beware the Incest-Survivor Machine."[74] In the *New York Review of Books*, the English professor Frederick Crews sounded dire warnings about the "revenge of the repressed":

> Throughout the past decade or so, a shock wave has been sweeping across North American psychotherapy and in the process causing major repercussions within our families . . . A single diagnosis—that of unconsciously repressed sexual abuse in childhood—has grown in this brief span from virtual nonexistence to epidemic frequency . . . It is hard to form even a rough idea of the number of persuaded cli-

ents . . . but a conservative guess would be a million persons since 1988 alone. The number *affected* is of course vastly higher, since . . . virtually every case sows dissension and sorrow throughout a family.[75]

Alarms about the destruction of the family have been a standard reaction to the feminist movement for more than a century.[76] The public speech of incest survivors, in particular, poses a direct challenge to the traditional authority of the father: it also calls into question cherished images of family harmony. Like other grass-roots movements that expose the secrets of "dysfunctional" families, the incest-survivor movement poses a particular threat to those "pillars of the community" who have so much invested in their public image as successful patriarchs. The rule of the father dies hard.

The press seemed particularly responsive to the arguments of the FMSF in cases where respectable men found themselves facing civil or criminal charges in court. The cry of "witch hunt" was raised, invoking the image of packs of irrational females bent on the destruction of upstanding citizens. Journalists seemed quite susceptible to the appeal of "false memory" stories, which offered them an exciting role as crusaders against a miscarriage of justice. Stories frankly sympathetic to accused or convicted perpetrators became increasingly common in the mass media in the mid-1990s.[77]

The need to safeguard against conviction of an innocent person is a cornerstone of our justice system. For this reason our Constitution rightly provides strong protections for defendants and requires high standards of proof in criminal cases. False complaints do occur for sexual abuse, just as they do for all other crimes. Studies of thoroughly investigated child sexual abuse cases document the frequency of false complaints at between 2 and 7 percent.[78] Moreover, it is clear that some suggestible children and adults can be persuaded to make false allegations. It takes repeated drill, persistent pressure, or conscious manipulation, but it can be done.[79] Occasionally this kind of coercive behavior can be found among child protective workers, police, prosecutors, and therapists. It is quite appropriate, therefore, for defense attorneys and the press to raise questions about the proper conduct of child abuse investigations in order to protect against such abuses of power.

Coercive manipulation, however, is also characteristic of abusive fathers, and victims can be bullied into retracting true allegations. Experienced child protective workers understand that abused children are likely to make contradictory or inconsistent statements because they are so vulnerable to intimidation. Adult survivors, though they are better able to defend themselves, are still subject to intense pressure from their parents. Loyalty and desire for family acceptance, guilt for disrupting the family, and fear of retaliation represent powerful motives to recant.[80] For this reason, each case needs to be evaluated thoroughly and carefully. This is a task that requires patience, balance, and compassion rather than zealous advocacy of a single point of view.

Zealous advocacy is the task of defense attorneys. In our adversarial system of justice, the defense must attempt to impeach the credibility of anyone who comes forward to make an accusation. If the authority of "science" can be invoked to discredit the accuser, so much the better. Enter the expert witness. The psychologist Elizabeth Loftus, a member of the FMSF advisory board, has been among the most tireless defense witnesses for many years. At the International Tribunal in The Hague, where she testified in 1998 on behalf of a concentration camp guard accused (and subsequently convicted) of rape and torture, Loftus estimated that since 1975 she had testified as an expert witness in 220 to 230 trials, and only once on the side of the prosecution. A laboratory researcher, she studies "people's memories for crimes and accidents, and also . . . the malleability . . . or distortion of memory that occurs through suggestive influences."[81]

Loftus's basic argument is that memory is subject to error and influence. To demonstrate this rather obvious point, she has designed numerous ingenious laboratory studies in which volunteer subjects are asked to describe their recollection of a filmed incident such as an accident or a crime. She finds that many subjects can be tricked into making mistakes, especially in matters of detail. These laboratory experiments, generalized to apply to real-life situations, can be used in court to cast doubt on any eyewitness testimony.

With the advent of claims based on delayed discovery, Loftus extended her research to demonstrate not only that people could be influenced to make mistakes, but also that they could be induced to "remember" fictitious stories about their own childhood experiences. She found that it was possible to convince some volunteer subjects that they "remembered" plausible childhood experiences such as being lost in a shopping mall. As it turned out, however, only a minority of her subjects could be so persuaded, and then only if family members cooperated in the deception by insisting that they had been present at the time and remembered the event themselves.

Although these studies might be interpreted to mean that most people are fairly resistant to suggestion, or that some people are susceptible to family mythmaking, Loftus bypassed these straightforward conclusions in favor of bolder speculative leaps. In her academic writings and courtroom testimony, she cited her studies as the basis for supposing that therapists would be likely to implant fabricated "memories" of childhood abuse in suggestible patients.[82] Ranging even further from her scientific base, Loftus sometimes contended that amnesia for traumatic events was simply a myth.[83] Any complaint based on delayed recall could therefore be dismissed out of hand.

These arguments, presented in the guise of expert scientific testimony, have been used to prevent some women from having their day in court.[84] Although this strategy has succeeded in some cases, it is unlikely to prevail in the long run, for it is based on selective presentation of data and convoluted inferences that clearly misrepresent the scientific consensus of the field.[85] Numerous studies (including one by Loftus herself)[86] have documented the phenomena of traumatic amnesia and delayed recall. Moreover, in many studies, adult survivors' recovered memories of childhood abuse are corroborated by other sources.[87] The consensus recognizing the possibility of traumatic amnesia is clearly expressed in the DSM-IV and in the official position papers of professional organizations, including the American Psychiatric Association, the American Psychological Association, and the American Medical Association.[88] Even Loftus will concede this point on cross-examination, under oath.[89]

Once it is established that traumatic amnesia and delayed recall can indeed occur, the question remains whether memories recovered after a period of amnesia should be viewed with particular skepticism. At present, no scientific evidence suggests that recovered memories are less reliable than any other memories. On the contrary, well-designed follow-up studies of documented cases indicate that survivors who recall their abuse after a period of amnesia remember about as accurately as those who never forgot.[90] Furthermore, no scientific evidence indicates that either children or adults who claim to have been sexually abused are particularly suggestible or prone to confabulation. If memory is fallible and subject to distortion, then skepticism should apply equally to all parties in a dispute. The majority of courts have recognized that claims brought on the basis of delayed recall must be heard and evaluated, like all other claims, on their individual merits.

Advocacy for accused perpetrators has not been limited to an aggressive defense in the courts or in the media. On the theory that the best defense is a good offense, FMSF has promoted attacks on the "sentinels," the child protective workers, police, prosecutors, victim advocates, and therapists who encounter victims of child abuse. Legal challenges have taken the form of professional licensure, malpractice, and civil rights complaints. Frontline workers in child protection have had to become accustomed to working in a highly contentious atmosphere.[91]

In a recent, closely watched decision in the state of Washington, a jury supported the authorities who had investigated an organized sex ring in a small rural town. In this case, twenty-eight adults were charged with child sexual abuse; fourteen pleaded guilty, five were convicted at trial, three were acquitted, and charges against six others were dismissed. The three who were acquitted sued the investigators, claiming that their civil rights had been violated. After the jury found that the authorities had not acted improperly, County Sheriff Dan LaRoche expressed relief that his department would be able to continue investigating reports of child abuse without fear of reprisals: "When your livelihood is threatened for doing your job, and your family's jeopardized," he said, "that's pretty hard to take."[92]

Psychotherapists who work with adult survivors have also found themselves under attack. Psychotherapy represents a threat to perpetrators precisely because it creates a "free space" in which survivors can reveal their secrets. Although psychotherapists do not perform an investigative role, they do bear witness to their patients' stories and help them take charge of their lives. Some accused perpetrators, reasoning that their daughters would never have dared to accuse them without a therapist's support, have tried to sue the therapists for malpractice. In one notorious case, an accused father was able to prevail in this strategy, over his adult daughter's vehement objections.[93] Although this case was highly publicized, it is unlikely to set a precedent, for it opens the door to all sorts of interference by third parties in the therapist-patient relationship. By extension of this logic, any family member displeased by a relative's opinions or life choices might seek damages from that person's therapist. Allowing such intrusion by third parties would completely undermine the basic principle of confidentiality.[94]

Members of FMSF have also attempted to silence professionals who disagree with their position by suing them for libel. The psychologist Anna Salter found herself slapped with a lawsuit when she wrote a scholarly critique of the works of Ralph Underwager and his wife, Hollida Wakefield. In an exhaustive, point-by-point examination of their published writings and court testimony, Salter argued that Underwager and Wakefield had systematically misrepresented the scientific literature.[95] They sued. Their case was dismissed. They appealed. In a scathing opinion, the Seventh Circuit Court of Appeals upheld the summary judgment of the lower court, finding that Salter was protected by guarantees of free speech:

> A person who concludes that a public figure is a knave may shout that conclusion from the mountain tops. Salter . . . came to believe that Underwager is a hired gun who makes a living by deceiving judges about the state of medical knowledge and thus assisting child molesters to evade punishment. Persons who hold such opinions

cannot be expected to look kindly on their subjects, and the law certainly does not insist that they shut up as soon as they are challenged . . . Underwager and Wakefield cannot, simply by filing suit . . . silence those who hold divergent views . . . Scientific controversies must be settled by the methods of science rather than by the methods of litigation.[96]

When neither legal defense nor legal attack prevails, the only strategy left is direct confrontation. A number of therapists noted for their work with survivors have been subject to threats, picketing, stalking, and other forms of physical harassment.[97] While not explicitly endorsing violence, FMSF has expressed its sympathy for members of the organization who might feel moved to take extreme measures. "If somebody came into your house and shot your child, it would probably be justifiable homicide if you did something, and that's how these parents feel," says Pamela Freyd. "When you get between parents and children, you can expect things to happen."[98]

Like other reactionary groups formed in opposition to the women's liberation movement, the FMSF appeals to people who long to return to a better time, when fathers ruled and daughters were obedient. Despite their zeal, they cannot ultimately prevail in the realms of science, public opinion, or law. In their attacks on victim support services, FMSF activists have followed the same strategies as grass-roots organizations opposed to reproductive choice. Because opponents of abortion rights have lost the battle in principle, they have attempted to win it in practice by obstructing women's access to medical services, and by intimidating service providers and advocates. The more it has become apparent that they cannot achieve their goals by lawful methods, the more they have resorted to violence.

There is no doubt that these methods have been partly successful. Access to abortion has been curtailed in many parts of the country, and training in basic techniques has declined in teaching hospitals. Bullying usually works, at least for a while. Similarly, advocacy groups like FMSF may be partly successful in their efforts to intimidate the professionals who serve as "sentinels" for child abuse. Many professionals may shy away from the high-conflict arena of child protection, just as many therapists may seek to preserve their own safety by avoiding engagement with adult survivors.

But the rule of the father cannot be re-established simply by making it more difficult for victims of abuse to get help or redress. After all the violence women have endured, we are not about to be prevented from speaking out against rape, battery, and incest, just as we will not be deterred from making our own reproductive choices. The abuses have gone on for too long. Too many survivors have disclosed their secrets. It is too late now to go back to silence.

Notes

1. Pamela Allen, *Free Space: A Perspective on the Small Group in Women's Liberation* (Washington, N.J.: Times Change Press, 1970).

2. Other feminist thinkers who investigated this issue at the same time were Florence Rush, *The Best Kept Secret: Sexual Abuse of Children* (Englewood Cliffs, N.J.: Prentice Hall, 1980); Louise Armstrong, *Kiss Daddy Goodnight: A Speak-Out on Incest* (New York: Hawthorne, 1978); Sandra Butler, *Conspiracy of Silence: The Trauma of Incest* (San Francisco: Glide, 1978); and Jean Goodwin, *Sexual Abuse, Incest Victims and Their Families* (Boston: John Wright, 1982).

3. Susan Brownmiller, *Against Our Will: Men, Women and Rape* (New York: Simon and Schuster, 1975); Catherine MacKinnon, *Feminism Unmodified: Discourses on Life and Law* (Cambridge, Mass.: Harvard University Press, 1987).

4. Richard Kluft, "On the Apparent Invisibility of Incest," in Richard Kluft, ed., *Incest-Related Syndromes of Adult Psychopathology* (Washington, D.C.: American Psychiatric Press, 1990), p. 25.

5. Diana Russell, *The Secret Trauma: Incest in the Lives of Girls and Women* (New York: Basic Books, 1986).

6. D. Finkelhor, G. Hotaling, I. A. Lewis, and C. Smith, "Sexual Abuse in a National Survey of Adult Men and Women: Prevalence, Characteristics, and Risk Factors," *Child Abuse and Neglect* (1990), 14:19–28.

7. "UN Details Widespread Violence against Women," *Boston Globe*, Wednesday, July 23, 1997, p. A4.

8. Diana Russell, *Behind Closed Doors in South Africa: Incest Survivors Tell Their Stories* (London: Macmillan, 1998).

9. Hamdi Tutkun, Vedat Sar, L. Ilhan Yargic, Tuga Ozpulat, Madaim Yanik, and Emre Kiziltan, "Frequency of Childhood Abuse among Psychiatric Inpatients in Turkey." Paper presented at the 13th Annual Meeting of the International Society for Traumatic Stress Studies (Montreal, Quebec, November 6–10, 1997); Hamdi Tutkun, Vedat Sar, L. Ilhan Yargic, Tuba Ozpulat, Madaim Yanit, and Emre Kiziltan, "Frequency of Dissociative Disorders among Psychiatric Patients in a Turkish University Clinic," *American Journal of Psychiatry* (1998), 155:800–806; Isin Baral, Kaan Kora, Sahika Yuksel, and Ufuk Sezgin, "Self-Mutilating Behavior of Sexually Abused Female Adults in Turkey," *Journal of Interpersonal Violence* (1998), 13:427–437; Saturo Saito, "Childhood Sexual Abuse and Dissociation in Japan: A Clinical Overview from an Outpatient Clinic Standpoint," *Psychiatry and Clinical Neurosciences* (1998), 52:S151–S155; Takako Konishi, "Study on Victimization and Crime: The Trauma of Crime Victims in Japan," *Psychiatry and Clinical Neurosciences* (1998), 52:S139–S144.

10. Nel Draijer, *Sexual Abuse of Girls by Relatives: A Nation-Wide Survey of*

the Nature, Emotional Signs, and Psychological and Psychosomatic Sequelae (Den Haag: Ministerie van Sociale Zaken en Verkgelegenheid, 1990); R. J. Goldman and J. D. G. Goldman, "The Prevalence and Nature of Child Sexual Abuse in Australia," *Australian Journal of Sex, Marriage and Family* (1988), 9:94–106; P. Mullen, J. Martin, I. Anderson, S. Romans, and G. Herbison, "Childhood Sexual Abuse and Mental Health in Adult Life," *British Journal of Psychiatry* (1993), 163:721–732.

11. Jane Smiley, *A Thousand Acres* (New York: Knopf, 1991); Alice Walker, *The Color Purple* (New York: Harcourt, Brace, Jovanovich, 1982); Toni Morrison, *The Bluest Eye* (New York: Pocket Books, 1972).

12. Ellen Bass and Laura Davis, *The Courage to Heal: A Guide for Women Survivors of Child Sexual Abuse* (New York: HarperCollins, 1988; third ed., 1996).

13. Andrea J. Sedlak and Dianne D. Broadhurst, "Executive Summary of the Third National Incidence Study of Child Abuse and Neglect" (Washington, D.C.: US DHHS, 1996).

14. U.S. Advisory Board on Child Abuse and Neglect (ABCAN), "Child Abuse and Neglect: Critical First Steps in Response to a National Emergency" (Washington, D.C.: DHHS, 1990).

15. Sheree L. Toth and Dante Ciccetti, "Child Maltreatment: Where Do We Go from Here in Our Treatment of Victims?" in Dante Ciccetti and Sheree L. Toth, eds., *Child Abuse, Child Development, and Social Policy* (Norwood, N.J.: Ablex, 1994), pp. 399–430, quote p. 425.

16. Russell, *The Secret Trauma*.

17. Gail E. Wyatt, "The Sexual Abuse of Afro-American and White Women in Childhood," *Child Abuse and Neglect* (1985), 9:507–519.

18. Finkelhor et al., "Sexual Abuse"; D. G. Kilpatrick and H. S. Resnick, "Posttraumatic Stress Disorder Associated with Exposure to Criminal Victimization in Clinical and Community Populations," in J. R. Davidson and E. B. Foa, eds., *Posttraumatic Stress Disorder: DSM-IV and Beyond* (Washington, D.C.: American Psychiatric Press, 1993), pp. 113–143.

19. A. Jacobson and B. Richardson, "Assault Experiences of 100 Psychiatric Inpatients: Evidence of the Need for Routine Inquiry," *American Journal of Psychiatry* (1987), 144:908–913.; J. B. Bryer, B. A. Nelson, J. B. Miller, and P. A. Kroll, "Childhood Sexual and Physical Abuse as Factors in Adult Psychiatric Illness," *American Journal of Psychiatry* (1987), 144:1426–1430; A. Jacobson, "Physical and Sexual Assault Histories among Psychiatric Outpatients," *American Journal of Psychiatry* (1989), 146:755–758; J. Briere and L. Y. Zaidi, "Sexual Abuse Histories and Sequelae in Female Psychiatric Emergency Room Patients," *American Journal of Psychiatry* (1989), 146:1602–1606.

20. Aaron H. Esman, "Sexual Abuse, Pathogenesis, and Enlightened Skepticism," *American Journal of Psychiatry* (1994), 151:1101–1103.

21. K. Kendall-Tackett, L. M. Williams, and D. Finkelhor, "Impact of Sexual Abuse on Children: A Review and Synthesis of Recent Empirical Studies," *Psychology Bulletin* (1993), 113:164–180; P. E. Mullen, J. L. Martin, J. C. Ander-

son, S. E. Romans, and G. P. Herbison, "Childhood Sexual Abuse and Mental Health in Adult Life," *British Journal of Psychiatry* (1993), 163:721–732; Bernardine J. Ensink, *Confusing Realities: A Study on Child Sexual Abuse and Psychiatric Symptoms* (Amsterdam: VU University Press, 1992).

22. Russell, *The Secret Trauma*, pp. 172–173.

23. John Briere, "The Long-Term Clinical Correlates of Childhood Sexual Victimization," *Annals of the New York Academy of Sciences* (1988), 5528:327–334; A. B. Rowan and D. W. Foy, "Posttraumatic Stress Disorder in Child Sexual Abuse Survivors: A Literature Review," *Journal of Traumatic Stress* (1993), 6:3–20.

24. Bessel A. van der Kolk, J. Christopher Perry, and Judith L. Herman, "Childhood Origins of Self-Destructive Behavior," *American Journal of Psychiatry* (1991), 148:1665–1671.

25. Judith L. Herman, J. Christopher Perry, and Bessel A. van der Kolk, "Childhood Trauma in Borderline Personality Disorder," *American Journal of Psychiatry* (1989), 146:490–495; J. G. Johnson, P. Cohen, J. Brown, E. M. Smails, and D. P. Bernstein, "Childhood Maltreatment Increases Risk for Personality Disorders during Early Adulthood," *Archives of General Psychiatry* (1999), 56:600–606.

26. Frank W. Putnam, *Diagnosis and Treatment of Multiple Personality Disorder* (New York: Guilford, 1989).

27. Judith L. Herman, "Complex PTSD: A Syndrome in Survivors of Prolonged and Repeated Trauma," *Journal of Traumatic Stress* (1992), 5:377–391.

28. American Psychiatric Association, *Diagnostic and Statistical Manual of Mental Disorders, Fourth Edition* (Washington, D.C.: American Psychiatric Press, 1994), p. 425.

29. B. A. van der Kolk, D. Pelcovitz, S. Roth, F. S Mandel, A. McFarlane, and J. L. Herman, "Dissociation, Somatization and Affect Dysregulation: The Complexity of Adaptation to Trauma," *American Journal of Psychiatry* (1996), 153:7 (Festscrift Supplement), 83–93.

30. Catherine S. Widom, "Posttraumatic Stress Disorder in Abused and Neglected Children Grown Up," *American Journal of Psychiatry* (1999), 156:1223–1229.

31. Richard J. Loewenstein, "Somatoform Disorders in Victims of Incest and Child Abuse," In Kluft, *Incest-Related Syndromes*, pp. 75–112.

32. Vincent J. Felitti, "Long-Term Medical Consequences of Incest, Rape, and Molestation," *Southern Medical Journal* (1991), 84:328–331.

33. E. A. Walker, W. J. Katonn, K. Neraas, R. P. Jemelka, and D. Massoth, "Dissociation in Women with Chronic Pelvic Pain," *American Journal of Psychiatry* (1992), 149:534–537.

34. Matthew J. Friedman and Paula Schnurr, "The Relationship between Trauma, PTSD, and Physical Health," in M. J. Friedman, D. S. Charney, and A. Y. Deutch, eds., *Neurobiological and Clinical Consequences of Stress: From Normal Adaptation to Post-Traumatic Stress Disorder* (Philadelphia: Lippincott-Raven, 1995); V. J. Felitti et al., "The Relationship of Childhood

Abuse and Household Dysfunction to Many of the Leading Causes of Death in Adults: The Adverse Childhood Experiences (ACE) Study," *American Journal of Preventive Medicine* (1998), 14:245–258.

35. D. L. Lipschitz, A. M. Rasmusson, and S. M. Southwick, "Childhood Posttraumatic Stress Disorder: A Review of Neurobiologic Sequelae," *Psychiatric Annals* (1998), 28:452–460.

36. M. D. De Bellis, G. P. Chrousos, L. D. Dorn, L. Burke, K. Helmers, M. A. Kling, R. Trickett, and F. Putnam, "Hypothaiamic-Pituitary-Adrenal Axis Dysregulation in Sexually Abused Girls," *Journal of Clinical Endocrinology and Metabolism* (1994), 78:249–255.

37. E. L. Weiss, J. G. Longhurst, and C. M. Mazure, "Childhood Sexual Abuse as a Risk Factor for Depression in Women: Psychosocial and Neurobiological Correlates," *American Journal of Psychiatry* (1999), 156:816–828.

38. Charles B. Nemeroff, "The Emerging and Disheartening Picture of the Consequences of Child Abuse and Neglect: Implications for Psychiatric Morbidity," *CNS Spectrums* (1997), 2:68.

39. Bessel A. van der Kolk, Onno van der Hart, and Charles R. Marmar, "Dissociation and Information Processing in Posttraumatic Stress Disorder," in Bessel A. van der Kolk, Alexander C. MacFarlane, and Lars Weisaeth, eds., *Traumatic Stress: The Effects of Overwhelming Experience on Mind, Body and Society* (New York: Guilford, 1996), pp. 303–327.

40. E. Cardena and D. Spiegel, "Dissociative Reactions to the Bay Area Earthquake," *American Journal of Psychiatry* (1993), 150:474–478; C. Koopman, C. Classen, and D. Spiegel, "Predictors of Posttraumatic Stress Symptoms among Survivors of the Oakland/Berkeley, California, Firestorm," *American Journal of Psychiatry* (1994), 151:888–894; C. R. Marmar, D. S. Weiss, W. E. Schlenger, J. A. Fairbank, K. Jordan, R. A. Kulka, and R. L. Hough, "Peritraumatic Dissociation and Posttraumatic Stress in Male Vietnam Theater Veterans," *American Journal of Psychiatry* (1994), 151:902–907; A. Shalev, T. Peri, L. Caneti, and S. Schreiber, "Predictors of Posttraumatic Stress Disorder in Injured Trauma Survivors," *American Journal of Psychiatry* (1996), 153:219–225.

41. Frank W. Putnam, "Clinical Implications of Longitudinal Research on Childhood Sexual Abuse." Paper presented at the Annual Meeting of the International Society for Traumatic Stress Studies (Montreal, Quebec, November 8, 1997).

42. Judith L. Herman and Emily Schatzow, "Recovery and Verification of Memories of Childhood Sexual Trauma," *Psychoanalytic Psychology* (1987), 4:1–14.

43. Daniel Brown, Alan W. Scheflin, and D. Corydon Hammond, *Memory, Trauma Treatment and the Law* (New York: Norton, 1997); Kenneth S. Pope and Laura S. Brown, *Recovered Memories of Abuse: Assessment, Therapy, Forensics* (Washington, D.C.: American Psychological Association Press, 1996).

44. Linda Katherine Cutting, *Memory Slips: A Memoir of Music and Healing* (New York: HarperCollins, 1997), p. 6.

45. Ibid., p. 2.

46. *DSM-IV*, p. 428.

47. Bessel A. van der Kolk, "The Body Keeps Score: Memory and the Evolving Psychobiology of Posttraumatic Stress," *Harvard Review of Psychiatry* (1994), 1:253–265.

48. L. Shin, R. J. McNally, S. M. Kosslyn, W. L. Thompson, S. L. Rauch, N. M. Alpert, L. J. Metzger, N. B. Lasko, S. P. Orr, and R. K. Pitman, "Regional Cerebral Blood Flow during Script-Driven Imagery in Childhood Sexual Abuse–Related PTSD: A PET Investigation, *American Journal of Psychiatry* (1999), 156:575–584; S. L. Rauch, B. A. van der Kolk, R. Fisler, N. M. Alpert, S. P. Orr, C. R. Savage, A. J. Fischman, M. A. Jenike, and R. K. Pitman, "A Symptom Provocation Study of Posttraumatic Stress Disorder Using Positron Emission Tomography and Script-Driven Imagery," *Archives of General Psychiatry* (1996), 53:380–387.

49. Frank W. Putnam and Penelope Trickett, "Child Sexual Abuse: A Model of Chronic Trauma," *Psychiatry* (1993), 56:82–95; Jennifer Freyd, *Betrayal Trauma: The Logic of Forgetting Childhood Abuse* (Cambridge, Mass.: Harvard University Press, 1996).

50. James Chu, *Rebuilding Shattered Lives: The Responsible Treatment of Complex Post-Traumatic and Dissociative Disorders* (New York: Wiley, 1998); Christine Courtois, *Healing the Incest Wound: Adult Survivors in Therapy* (New York: Norton, 1988); John Briere, *Child Abuse Trauma: Theory and Treatment of the Lasting Effects* (Newbury Park, Calif.: Sage, 1992); Catherine Classen and I. D. Yalom, eds., *Treating Women Molested in Childhood* (San Francisco: Jossey-Bass, 1995); Anna Salter, *Transforming Trauma: A Guide to Understanding and Treating Adult Survivors of Child Sexual Abuse* (Thousand Oaks, Calif., Sage, 1995); Susan Roth and Ronald Batson, *Naming the Shadows: A New Approach to Individual and Group Psychotherapy for Adult Survivors of Childhood Incest* (New York: Free Press, 1997).

51. Judith L. Herman, *Trauma and Recovery* (New York: Basic Books, 1992, 1997).

52. G. G. Abel, M. S. Mittelman, and J. Becker, "Sex Offenders: Results of Assessment and Recommendations for Treatment," in M. H. Ben-Aron, S. J. Hucker, and C. D. Webster, eds., *Clinical Criminology: The Assessment and Treatment of Criminal Behavior* (Toronto: M and M Graphics, 1985), pp. 207–220.

53. Quoted in Faye Honey Knopp, *Retraining Adult Sex Offenders: Methods and Models* (Syracuse, N.Y.: Safer Society Press, 1984), p. 9.

54. Judith L. Herman, "Considering Sex Offenders: A Model of Addiction," *Signs: Journal of Women in Culture and Society* (1988), 13:695–724.

55. David T. Ballard, Gary D. Blair, Sterling Devereaux, Logan K. Valentine, Anne L. Horton, and Barry L. Johnson, "A Comparative Profile of the Incest Perpetrator," in Anne L. Horton, Barry L. Johnson, Lynn M. Roundy, and Doran Williams, eds., *The Incest Perpetrator: A Family Member No One Wants to Treat* (Newbury Park. Calif.: Sage, 1990), pp. 43–64.

56. For a review of the state of the art in assessment, see H. E. Barbaree and W. L. Marshall, "Treatment of the Sexual Offender," in Robert M. Wettstein, ed., *Treatment of Offenders with Mental Disorders* (New York: Guilford, 1998), pp. 265–328.

57. G. G. Abel, M. S. Mittleman, and J. Becker, "The Characteristics of Men Who Molest Young Children." Paper presented at the World Congress of Behavior Therapy (Washington, D.C., 1983).

58. Barbaree and Marshall, "Treatment of the Sexual Offender," p. 294.

59. Francisco Goldman, "The Autumn of the Revolutionary," *New York Times Magazine*, August 23, 1998, p. 38.

60. Cutting, *Memory Slips*, pp. 133–134.

61. Barbaree and Marshall, "Treatment of the Sexual Offender," p. 308.

62. Jean M. Goodwin, "Human Vectors of Trauma: Illustrations from the Marquis de Sade," in Jean M. Goodwin, ed., *Rediscovering Childhood Trauma: Historical Casebook and Clinical Applications* (Washington, D.C.: American Psychiatric Press, 1993), pp. 95–112.

63. J. Wormith, "A Survey of Incarcerated Sexual Offenders," *Canadian Journal of Criminology* (1983), 25:370–390.

64. Sylvia Fraser, *My Father's House* (New York: Harper and Row, 1987), p. 240.

65. Emily Schatzow and Judith Herman, "Breaking Secrecy: Adult Survivors Disclose to Their Families," *Psychiatric Clinics of North America* (1989), 12:337–349.

66. Sue William Silverman, *Because I Remember Terror, Father, I Remember You* (Athens, Ga.: University of Georgia Press, 1996), pp. 249–250.

67. Brown, Scheflin, and Hammond, *Memory, Trauma Treatment and the Law*, p. 591.

68. Quoted in Carol Lynn Mithers, "Incest and the Law," *New York Times Magazine*, October 21, 1990, p. 58.

69. Tina Rosenberg, *The Haunted Land: Facing Europe's Ghosts after Communism* (New York: Vintage, 1995).

70. Joseph Geraci, "Interview: Hollida Wakefield and Ralph Underwager," *Paidika: The Journal of Pedophilia* (Winter, 1993), p. 4.

71. Stephanie J. Dallam, "Unsilent Witness: Ralph Underwager and the FMSF," *Treating Abuse Today* (1997), 7:31–39.

72. *FMSF Newsletter*, February 29, 1992.

73. Irene L. Miller, "Letter to the Editor," *The Sun* (August 1998), p. 3.

74. Carol Tavris, "Beware the Incest-Survivor Machine," *New York Times Book Review*, January 3, 1993.

75. Frederick Crews, "The Revenge of the Repressed," *New York Review of Books*, November 17, 1994.

76. Susan Faludi, *Backlash: The Undeclared War against American Women* (New York: Doubleday, 1991); Eleanor Flexner, *Century of Struggle: The Woman's Rights Movement in the United States* (Cambridge, Mass.: Harvard University Press, 1959).

77. Judith L. Herman, "Presuming to Know the Truth," *Nieman Reports* (1994), 48:43–45; Mike Stanton, "U-turn on Memory Lane," *Columbia Journalism Review* (July/August 1997), 44–49.

78. D. Jones and J. M. McGraw, "Reliable and Fictitious Accounts of Sexual Abuse to Children," *Journal of Interpersonal Violence* (1987), 2:27–45.

79. G. S. Goodman, J. A. Quas, J. M. Batterman-Faunce, M. M. Riddleberger, and J. Kuhn, "Predictors of Accurate and Inaccurate Memories of Traumatic Events Experienced in Childhood," *Consciousness and Cognition* (1994), 3:269–294; K. Pezdek and C. Roe, "Memory for Childhood Events: How Suggestible Is It?" *Consciousness and Cognition* (1994), 3:374–387.

80. J. M. Goodwin, D. Sahd, and R. T. Rada, "False Accusations and False Denials of Incest," in Goodwin, *Sexual Abuse* (1982), pp. 17–26.

81. *Prosecutor v. Anto Furundzija*, United Nations International Criminal Tribunal for the Former Yugoslavia, The Hague, The Netherlands, June 22, 1998, p. 595.

82. *People v. Franklin* (1993), San Mateo (California) Superior Court, No. C-24395; *Burgus v. Braun* (1997), Cook County (Illinois) Circuit Court, County Department, Law Division, No. 93 L 14050; *Rodriguez et al. v. Perez et al.* (1998), Chelan County (Washington) Superior Court, No. 96-2-00704-2; E. F. Loftus, "The Reality of Repressed Memories," *American Psychologist* (1993), 48:518–537.

83. E. F. Loftus and K. Ketcham, *The Myth of Repressed Memory: False Memories and Allegations of Sexual Abuse* (New York: St. Martin's Press, 1994).

84. *New Hampshire v. Hungerford* (1997), WL 358620.

85. Brown, Scheflin, and Hammond, *Memory, Trauma Treatment and the Law*, chap. 12.

86. E. F. Loftus, S. Polonsky, and M. T. Fullilove, "Memories of Childhood Sexual Abuse: Remembering and Repressing," *Psychology of Women Quarterly* (1994), 18:67–84.

87. A. W. Burgess, C. Hartman, and T. Baker, "Memory Presentations of Childhood Sexual Abuse," *Journal of Psychosocial Nursing* (1995), 33:9—16; S. Feldman-Summers and K. Pope, "The Experience of 'Forgetting' Childhood Abuse: A National Survey of Psychologists," *Journal of Consulting and Clinical Psychology* (1994), 62:636–639; Herman and Schatzow, "Recovery and Verification"; C. M. Roe and M. F. Schwartz, "Characteristics of Previously Forgotten Memories of Sexual Abuse: A Descriptive Study," *Journal of Psychiatry and Law* (1995), 24:189–206; B. A. van der Kolk and R. Fisler, "Dissociation and the Fragmentary Nature of Traumatic Memories: Overview and Exploratory Study," *Journal of Traumatic Stress* (1995), 8:505–525; P. M. Coons, "Confirmation of Childhood Abuse in Child and Adolescent Cases of Multiple Personality, and Dissociative Disorder Not Otherwise Specified," *Journal of Nervous and Mental Diseases* (1994), 182:461–464; J. L. Herman and M. R. Harvey, "Adult Memories of Childhood Trauma: A Naturalistic Clinical Study," *Journal of Traumatic Stress* (1997), 10:557–571; L. M. Williams, "Recovered Memories of Abuse in Women with Documented Child Sexual Victimization

Histories," *Journal of Traumatic Stress* (1995), 8:649–673; C. S. Widom and S. Morris, "Accuracy of Adult Recollections of Childhood Victimization: Part 2: Childhood Sexual Abuse," *Psychological Assessment* (1997), 8:412–421.

88. For a comparative analysis of the position papers of the various professional organizations, see Brown, Scheflin, and Hammond, *Memory, Trauma Treatment and the Law*, pp. 50–55.

89. *Seignious v. Fair* (1998), Fulton County (Georgia) Superior Court No. 9E-56169; *New Hampshire v. Walters* (1995), No. 93-S-2111–2112.

90. Williams, "Recovered Memories of Abuse"; Widom and Morris, "Accuracy of Adult Recollections of Childhood Victimization."

91. John E. B. Myers, ed., *The Backlash: Child Protection under Fire* (Thousand Oaks, Calif.: Sage, 1994).

92. Aviva L. Brandt. "Jury Rejects Claims of Official Misconduct in Sex Ring Case," Associated Press, June 29, 1998.

93. *Ramona v. Ramona* (1994), Napa County (California), Case No. C61898.

94. C. G. Bowman and E. Mertz, "A Dangerous Direction: Legal Intervention in Sexual Abuse Survivor Therapy," *Harvard Law Review* (1996), 109:549–639; P. Appelbaum and R. Zoltek-Jick, "Psychotherapists' Duties to Third Parties: *Ramona* and Beyond," *American Journal of Psychiatry* (1996), 153:457–465.

95. Anna Salter, "Accuracy of Expert Testimony in Child Sexual Abuse Cases: A Case Study of Ralph Underwager and Hollida Wakefield," unpublished ms. prepared for New England Commissioners of Child Welfare Agencies, 1991.

96. U.S. Court of Appeals, Seventh Circuit, No. 93-2422, April 25, 1994.

97. David L. Calof, "Notes from a Practice under Siege: Harassment, Defamation, Intimidation in the Name of Science," *Ethics and Behavior* (1998), 8:161–187.

98. Katy Butler, "Caught in the Crossfire," *Networker* (April 1995), pp. 68–79, quote p. 75.

Appendix

Notes

Index

The Incest Statutes

Leigh B. Bienen

For their continued support, the author would like to thank the New Jersey Department of the Public Advocate, Commissioner Stanley C. Van Ness, Assistant Commissioner Marcia Richman, Assistant Public Defender John M. Cannel, and especially Francine A. Lee. Research was supported in part by New Jersey State Law Enforcement and Planning Agency Special Projects Grant No. A-C:10-18-79 (Oct. 12, 1979–Nov. 28, 1980). For a detailed state-by-state breakdown of the laws defining sex offenses, see Leigh B. Bienen, "Rape III" and "Rape IV," *Women's Rights Law Reporter* 6, no. 3 and Supplement (Rutgers-Newark School of Law, 1981), or Hubert S. Feild and Leigh B. Bienen, *Jurors and Rape: A Study in Psychology and the Law* (Lexington, Mass.: Lexington Books, 1980).

State	Incest Statute	Parallel Statutory Provisions
Alabama	Ala. Code Tit. 13A-13-3 *Incest* (1977): Marries or engages in sexual intercourse with a person known to be legitimately or illegitimately an ancestor or descendant by blood or adoption, brother or sister of the whole or half blood, or stepchild or stepparent, while the marriage exists, aunt, uncle, nephew or niece of the whole or half blood; statutory corroboration requirement (enacted 1977); Class C felony: one year and one day to 10 years, §13A-5-6. *Prohibited Marriages,* §30-1-1.	*1st Degree Rape:* Sexual intercourse by male 16 or older with female under 12, §61(a) (3) and (b); Class A felony: 10–99 years of life, §13A-5-6. *2nd Degree Rape:* Sexual intercourse by male 16 or older with female under 16 and over 12, if actor 2 years older, Class C felony, §62(a) (1) and (b). Offense could also come under 1st or 2nd degree sodomy, 1st or 2nd degree sexual abuse, or sexual misconduct.

Copyright © 1981 by Leigh Bienen.

State	Incest Statute	Parallel Statutory Provisions
Alaska	Alaska Stat. §11.41.450 *Incest* (1978): Sexual penetration with an ancestor or descendant or brother or sister (whole or half blood), or uncle, aunt, nephew or niece by blood (enacted 1978); Class C felony: maximum 5 years, presumptive term of 2 years for second offense, 3 years for third offense, §12.55.-125(d).	*1st Degree Sexual Assault:* Sexual penetration (expanded definition) without consent, sexual penetration with person under 13, or sexual penetration with person under 18 who is entrusted to his care by an authority of law, or his son or daughter, whether adopted, illegitimate, or stepchild, §11.41.-410; Class A felony: maximum 20 years, presumptive term of 6 years for first felony, 10 years for 2nd felony, 15 years for 3rd felony, §12.55.125(c). *Sexual Abuse of a Minor:* Sexual penetration with person under 16 and over 13 or sexual contact with person under 13, Class C felony, §11.41.440.
Arizona	Ariz. Rev. Stat. Ann. §13-3608 *Incest; Classification* (1978): Persons within prohibited degrees of consanguinity who intermarry, or commit fornication or adultery; Class 4 fel-	*Sexual Conduct with a Minor:* Sexual intercourse or oral sexual contact with person under 18; Class 2 felony if minor under 15; Class 6 felony if minor over 15, §13-1405;

State	Incest Statute	Parallel Statutory Provisions
Arizona (cont.)	ony: 4 years, §13-701B(3).	Class 2 felony: 7 years, §13-701; Class 6 felony: 1½ years, §13-701.
		Molestation of a Child: Fondling, touching or playing with private parts of child under 15, Class 2 felony without eligibility for suspended sentence, commutation, etc. until ⅔ or a minimum of 5 years served, §13-1410.
Arkansas	Ark. Stat. Ann. §41-2403 *Incest* (1977): A person (over 16) who purports to marry, has sexual intercourse with or engages in sexual intercourse with a person he knows to be an ancestor or descendant, a stepchild or adopted child; a brother or sister of the whole or half blood; or an uncle, aunt, nephew or niece, including illegitimates; Class C felony: minimum 2 years, maximum 10 years, §41-901. *Degrees of Consanguinity,* §55-103.	*Rape:* Sexual intercourse or deviate sexual activity (expanded definition) with person under 11, §41-1803; Class A felony: minimum 5 years, maximum 50 years or life, §41-901. *1st Degree Carnal Abuse:* Person over 18 who engages in sexual intercourse or deviate sexual activity with person under 14, Class C Felony, §41-1804. *1st Degree Sexual Abuse:* Sexual contact with person under 14, §41-1808; Class D felony: maximum 5 years, §41-901.

State	Incest Statute	Parallel Statutory Provisions
Arkansas (cont.)		Several other offenses are defined as misdemeanors.
California	Cal. Penal Code §285 *Incest* (1970): Persons within the prohibited degrees of consanguinity who intermarry, commit fornication or adultery are punishable by imprisonment in the state prison (specification of penalty removed in 1977); (enacted 1872). *Prohibited Marriages,* Cal. Civil Code §4400.	*Unlawful Sexual Intercourse with Female under 18:* Sexual intercourse with female under 18, §261.5; Penalty: one year in county jail or state prison, §264. *Lewd and Lascivious Acts with a Child under 14:* Lewd or lascivious acts with intent or by force, §288; Penalty: 3, 5, or 7 years, §264.1. *Oral Copulation:* Acts of oral copulation under circumstances defined by age of participants and use of force, §288a; Penalty: one year, or 3, 6 or 8 years or more if aggravating circumstances, §288a.
Colorado	Colo. Rev. Stat. Ann. tit. 18-6-301 *Incest* (1978 Repl.): Any person who knowingly marries or has sexual intercourse with an ancestor or descen-	*2nd Degree Sexual Assault:* Sexual penetration (expanded definition) or sexual intrusion (penetration by an object or digital penetration) with victim under

State	Incest Statute	Parallel Statutory Provisions
Colorado (cont.)	dant, a brother or sister of the whole or half blood, or an uncle, aunt, nephew or niece; Class 5 felony: 1–2 years, plus one year on parole, §18-1-105. Colo. Rev. Stat. Ann. tit. 18-6-302 *Aggravated Incest* (1978 Repl.): Any person who knowingly has sexual intercourse with his child (including stepchildren and adopted children) unless legally married to the stepchild or child by adoption; "child" means person under 21; Class 4 felony: minimum one day, maximum 10 years, §18-1-105.	15 by actor 4 years older or when victim is less than 18 and actor is victim's guardian or is responsible for the general supervision of victim's welfare; Class 4 felony unless by force, then Class 3 felony §18-3-403; Class 3 felony: minimum 5 years, maximum 40 years, §18-1-105. *3rd Degree Sexual Assault:* Sexual contact with victim under 18 by actor who is guardian, etc.; Class 1 misdemeanor; if forcible, Class 4 felony, §18-3-404. *Sexual Assault on Child:* Sexual contact with victim under 15 by actor 6 years older; Class 4 felony; if forcible, Class 3 felony, §18-3-405.
Connecticut	Conn. Gen. Stat. Ann. §53a-191 *Incest: Class D Felony* (1972): A person who marries or engages in sexual intercourse with a person he knows to be related	*2nd Degree Sexual Assault:* Sexual intercourse with person under 15, or with person under 18 if actor is person's guardian or responsible for person's

State	Incest Statute	Parallel Statutory Provisions
Connecticut (cont.)	to him within the prohibited degrees; Class D felony: up to 5 years, §53a-35. *Incestuous Marriages Void*, §46-1.	supervision, §53a-71; Class C felony: up to 10 years, §53a-35. *4th Degree Sexual Assault:* Intentional sexual contact under circumstances of 2nd degree, §53a-73; Class A misdemeanor: up to one year, §53a-36.
Delaware	Del. Code Ann. tit. 11§771 *Incest; Class A Misdemeanor* (1978 Supp.): A person who engages in sexual intercourse with persons within the prohibited degrees of relationship, including relations of adoption and illegitimacy; Incest a Class A misdemeanor within the exclusive jurisdiction of the family court; prohibited relationships specified; Class A misdemeanor: up to 2 years or fine, tit. 11 §4206.	*2nd Degree Rape:* Sexual intercourse with female less than 16, §763; Class B felony: 3–30 years, tit. 11§4205. *1st Degree Sodomy:* Deviate sexual intercourse with person under 16, Class B felony, §766. *Sexual Assault:* Sexual contact when defendant knows victim is less than 16 and defendant 4 years older, Class A misdemeanor, §761. *Sexual Misconduct:* Sexual intercourse or deviate sexual intercourse with person under 16 when defendant 4 years older,

State	Incest Statute	Parallel Statutory Provisions
Delaware (cont.)		§762; Class E felony: maximum 7 years or fine, tit. 11§4205.
District of Columbia	D.C. Code Ann. §22-1901 *Definition and Penalty* (1973): Any person within the 4th degree of consanguinity, shall marry or cohabit or have sexual intercourse, knowing of such relationship, shall be punished by imprisonment for not more than 12 years (enacted 1901).	*Carnal Knowledge and Abuse of a Female Child under 16:* Carnal knowledge (penetration offense) of female under 16; Penalty: any term of years or life, §22-2801. *Sodomy:* Defined to include male/female oral genital acts; Penalty: fine of $1000 or maximum 10 years, or if victim under 16, maximum 20 years, §22-3502.
Florida	Fla. Stat. Ann. §826.04 *Incest* (1976): Knowingly marries or has sexual intercourse with a person related by lineal consanguinity, or brother or sister, uncle, aunt, nephew or niece; penetration required; 3rd degee felony: maximum 5 years, §775.082(3)(d).	*Sexual Battery:* Person over 18 who commits sexual battery (expanded definition of sexual penetration) or injures the sexual organ of person 11 or under in an attempt; Capital felony: life with 25 years before parole or death; but see *Coker* v. *Georgia*, 433 U.S. 584 (1977) re constitutionality of death penalty for rape.

State	Incest Statute	Parallel Statutory Provisions
Florida (cont.)		*Sexual Battery:* Sexual battery upon person over 11 and under 18 when offender in position of familial authority, §794.011(4); 1st degree felony: maximum 30 years or life, §775.082(3)(b).
Georgia	Ga. Code Ann. Ch. §26-2006 *Incest* (1978): Person who engages in sexual intercourse with a known relative, by blood or marriage; father, daughter or stepdaughter, mother, son or stepson; brother and sister of the whole or half blood; grandparent and grandchild; aunt and nephew, uncle or niece; Penalty: minimum one year, maximum 20 years.	*Statutory Rape:* Sexual intercourse with female under 14; Penalty: minimum one year, maximum 20 years (statutory corroboration requirement), §26-2018. *Child Molestation:* Any immoral or indecent act to or in the presence of child under 14; Penalty: 1–20 years, §26-2019.
Hawaii	Hawaii Rev. Stat. Tit. 37, Hawaii Penal Code §707-741, *Incest* (1976 Repl.) (L. 1972): Sexual intercourse with another within the degree of consanguinity or affinity within which marriage is prohibited;	*Rape 1st Degree:* Sexual intercourse with person less than 14 and serious bodily injury, §707-730(1)(b); Class A felony: minimum 20 years, §707-660. *Rape 2nd Degree:* Sexual intercourse with

State	Incest Statute	Parallel Statutory Provisions
Hawaii (cont.)	Class C felony: maximum 5 years, §707-660. *Prohibited Marriage,* Hawaii Rev. Stat. §572-1.	person less than 14, §707-731; Class B felony: maximum 10 years, §707-660. *Sexual Abuse 1st Degree:* Sexual contact with person less than 14, §707-736(1)(b); Class C felony. *Sexual Abuse 2nd Degree:* Sexual contact with person 14 or 15 when actor 4 years older, §707-737; Misdemeanor: maximum one year, §707-663.
Idaho	Idaho Code §18-6602 *Incest* (1979). Persons within the degrees of consanguinity within which marriages are declared by law to be incestuous and void who intermarry or commit fornication or adultery are punishable by a maximum period of imprisonment of up to 10 years. *Degrees of Consanguinity Defined,* §932-205.	*Rape:* Sexual intercourse with female under 18 when actor is over 14, §18-6101(1); Penalty: minimum one year, maximum life, §18-6104.
Illinois	Ill. Ann. Stat. Ch. 38 §11-10 *Aggravated In-*	*Indecent Liberties with a Child:* Sexual inter-

State	Incest Statute	Parallel Statutory Provisions
Illinois (cont.)	*cest* (Smith-Hurd 1979): Sexual intercourse or act of deviate sexual conduct with daughter or son, including illegitimates, stepchildren, and adopted children under 18; Class 2 felony: minimum 3 years, maximum 7 years, Ch. 38 §1005-8-1(a)(5). Ill. Ann. Stat. Ch. 38 §11-11, *Incest* (Smith-Hurd 1979): Sexual intercourse or act of deviate sexual conduct with brother or sister, whole, half blood; Class 3 felony: 2-5 years, Ch. 38 §1005-8-1. *Incestuous Marriages,* Ill. Ann. Stat. Ch. 40 §212 (Smith-Hurd 1979).	course or deviate sexual intercourse or lewd touching of child under 16 by person over 17, Ill. Ann. Stat. Ch. 38 §11-4 (Smith-Hurd 1979); Class 1 felony: minimum 4 years, maximum 15 years, Ch. 38 §1005-8-1(a)(4).
Indiana	Ind. Ann. Stat. §35-46-1-3 *Incest* (1977 Cum. Supp.) (Burns): A person over 18 who engages in sexual intercourse or deviate sexual conduct with another person, who knows the other person	*Child Molesting:* Sexual intercourse or deviate sexual conduct with child under 12 or between 12 and 16, if actor is over 16, §35-42-4-3; Class B felony if child under 12; Class C felony for sexual con-

State	Incest Statute	Parallel Statutory Provisions
Indiana (cont.)	is parent, stepparent, child, stepchild, grandparent, grandchild, sibling, aunt, uncle, niece or nephew; Class D felony: fixed term of 2 years or court may sentence for a misdemeanor, §35-50-2-7.	tact offense, §35-42-4-3; increased penalties if forcible or offender armed; Class B felony: 10 years, §35-50-2-5; Class C felony: 5 years, §35-50-2-6.
Iowa	Iowa Code Ann. §726.2 *Incest* (1979 Pamph.): A person who has sexual intercourse with any person whom he or she knows to be related, either legitimately or illegitimately, as an ancestor, descendant, brother, sister of whole or half blood, aunt, uncle, niece or nephew; Class D felony: maximum five years, §902.9. *Degrees of Relationship,* §702.5.	*3rd Degree Sexual Abuse:* Any sex act, except between cohabiting spouses, when one participant is 14 or 15 and a member of the same household or related by blood or affinity to the 4th degree, or person is in position of authority; or any sex act when the other person is a child (under 14), §709.4(3) and (4); Class C felony: maximum 10 years, §902.9.
Kansas	Kan. Stat. Ann. §21-3603 *Aggravated Incest* (1974): Sexual intercourse or unlawful sexual act by a parent with a person he knows is his child, including adoptive and stepparents, grandparents, and relations of illegiti-	*Reform Provision:* Protection from Abuse Act (L. 1979 Ch. 92): Civil remedies for sexual abuse among family members or persons who reside together; statute allows for civil complaint, emergency relief, hearing and civil

State	Incest Statute	Parallel Statutory Provisions
Kansas (cont.)	macy; Class D felony: minimum 1–3 years, maximum 5–10 years, §21-4501(d).	remedies including the requirement of counseling and other civil orders of restraint.
	Kan. Stat. Ann. §21-3602 *Incest* (1974): Marriage or sexual intercourse with a person known to be a brother or sister, one half as well as of the whole blood, uncle, aunt, nephew or niece; Class E felony: minimum 1 year, maximum 2–5 years, §21-4501(e).	*Indecent Liberties with a Child:* Acts of sexual intercourse or lewdness with child under 16, §21-3503; Class C felony: minimum 1–3 years, maximum 10–20 years, §21-4501(c).
Kentucky	Ky. Rev. Stat. §530.020 *Incest* (1975 Repl.): Sexual intercourse with a person known to be an ancestor, descendant, brother or sister, including whole and half blood, illegitimate, adopted, and stepchildren; Class C felony: minimum 5 years, maximum 10 years, §532.060.	*Rape 1st Degree:* Sexual intercourse with person under 12, §510.040(1)(b)(2); Class B felony: minimum 10 years, maximum 20 years, §532.060. *Rape 2nd Degree:* Sexual intercourse by person over 18 with person under 14, Class C felony, §510.050(1). *Rape 3rd Degree:* Sexual intercourse by person over 21 with person under 16, §510.060; Class D felony: minimum one year, maximum five years, §532.060.

State	Incest Statute	Parallel Statutory Provisions
Kentucky (cont.)		*Sexual Abuse in the 1st, 2nd and 3rd Degree,* §510.110 to §510.130; 1st degree, Class D felony; all others misdemeanors: maximum one year.
Louisiana	La. Rev. Stat. §14.78 *Incest* (1974): Marriage or cohabitation with any ascendant or descendant, brother or sister, uncle or niece, aunt or nephew, including illegitimates, but relationship must be by consanguinity; Penalty: If between ascendant and descendant or brother and sister, maximum 15 years; if between uncle and niece, or between aunt and nephew, maximum fine of $1000 or maximum 5 years or both.	*Aggravated Rape:* Anal or vaginal sexual intercourse with a victim under 12; Penalty: life, §14:42. *Carnal Knowledge of a Juvenile:* Male over 17 with female over 12 and under 17 (with consent) when age difference of over 2 years; Penalty: maximum 10 years, §14.80. *Sexual Battery:* Genital acts short of intercourse and oral genital acts under compulsion; Penalty: maximum 10 years, §14.32.1.
Maine	Me. Rev. Stat. Ann. tit. 17-A §556 *Incest* (1979 Pamph.): A person over 18 who has sexual intercourse with another person as to whom he knows he is related within the second degree of consan-	*Rape:* Sexual intercourse with person under 14, Class A or Class B crime, if person within exception for voluntary social companion, §252; Class A crime: definite term, maximum 20 years,

State	Incest Statute	Parallel Statutory Provisions
Maine (cont.)	guinity, legal marriage a defense; Class D crime: definite term less than one year, §1252 (enacted 1975).	§1252; Class B crime: definite term, maximum 10 years, §1252. *Gross Sexual Misconduct:* Sexual act with person under 14, Class A crime or Class B crime, as above, §253. *Sexual Abuse of Minors:* Sexual intercourse or sexual act by person over 19 with person over 14 and under 16, Class D crime, §254. *Unlawful Sexual Contact:* Sexual contact with person under 14 and actor 3 years older, Class C or Class D crime, §255; Class C crime: maximum 5 years, §1252.
Maryland	Md. Code Ann. Art. 27 §335 *Carnal Knowledge of Another Within Degrees of Consanguinity Within Which Marriages Prohibited* (1976 Repl.): Knowingly have carnal knowledge of another person within the prohibited degrees of consanguinity; Penalty: minimum one year,	*2nd Degree Rape:* Vaginal intercourse with person under 14 when other person is at least 4 years older; Penalty: maximum 20 years, §463. *2nd Degree Sexual Offense:* Sexual act with person under 14 when other person 4 years older; Penalty: maxi-

State	Incest Statute	Parallel Statutory Provisions
Maryland (cont.)	maximum 10 years (enacted 1884). *Prohibited Marriages,* Art. 62, §2.	mum 20 years, §464A. *3rd Degree Sexual Offense:* Sexual contact with person under 14 and other person 4 years older; Penalty: maximum 10 years, §464B. *4th Degree Sexual Offense:* Sexual act or vaginal intercourse with person 14 or 15 and other person 4 years older; Penalty: maximum one year and/or $1000 fine, §464C.
Massachusetts	Mass. Gen. Laws Ch. 272 §17 *Incestuous Marriage or Intercourse* (1970): Persons within the degree of consanguinity within which marriages are void who intermarry or have sexual intercourse; Penalty: maximum 20 years in state prison or 2½ years in county jail (enacted 1965). *Marriages between Relatives,* Ch. 207, §2.	*Reform Provision* (1978) creates civil remedies for family abuse, including payment for compensation, ordering defendant to vacate house, awarding of custody, and restraint orders; abuse includes causing another to engage involuntarily in sexual relations by force, threat of force or duress, Ch. 209A§1-6 (1979 Supp.). *Rape and Abuse of a Child:* Sexual intercourse or unnatural sexual intercourse and

State	Incest Statute	Parallel Statutory Provisions
Massachusetts (cont.)		abuse of child under 16, Ch. 265 §23 (1979).
		Rape of a Child; Use of Force: Sexual intercourse by force of child under 16, Ch. 265 §22A (1979); Penalty: life or any term of years, mandatory 5-year term for second conviction for both offenses, §22A;§23.
Michigan	Former traditional incest statute repealed in 1974 when Michigan enacted rape reform legislation incorporating some categories of incest within the sex neutral definitions of criminal sexual conduct.	*1st Degree Criminal Sexual Conduct:* Sexual penetration (expanded definition) with person under 13, or when a person is over 13 and under 16 and actor is a member of the household, relative, or in a position of authority; Penalty: life or any term of years, Mich. Comp. Laws Ann. §750.520(b) (1979–80 Supp.).
		3rd Degree Criminal Sexual Conduct: Sexual contact under the circumstances of 1st degree criminal sexual conduct; Penalty: maximum 15 years, Mich. Comp. Laws Ann. §750.520(d)

State	Incest Statute	Parallel Statutory Provisions
Michigan (cont.)		(1979–80 Supp); mandatory 5-year term for second conviction of 1st or 3rd degree criminal sexual conduct, Mich. Comp. Laws Ann. §750.250(f) (1979–80 Supp.).
Minnesota	Minn. Stat. Ann. §609.365 *Incest* (1980 Supp.): Whoever has sexual intercourse with another, nearer of kin than first cousins, whether of the half or whole blood, with knowledge, is guilty of incest; Penalty: maximum 10 years. *Prohibited Marriages,* §517.03.	*New Domestic Abuse Act* includes criminal sexual conduct by family members against minors, §518B.01. *1st Degree Criminal Sexual Conduct:* Sexual penetration (expanded definition) when complainant is under 13 and when actor is 3 years older or when complainant is over 13 and under 16 when actor is in a position of authority and 4 years older; Penalty: maximum 20 years, §609.342. *2nd Degree Criminal Sexual Conduct:* Sexual contact under the circumstances of 1st degree criminal sexual conduct; Penalty: maximum 15 years, §609.343.

State	Incest Statute	Parallel Statutory Provisions
Minnesota (cont.)		*Position of Authority:* Parent and any person acting in place of a parent, §609.341; mandatory terms for second conviction and restrictions on parole, §609.346.
Mississippi	Miss. Code Ann. §97-29-27 *Incest—Marriage Within Prohibited Degrees;* Penalty: fine of $500 and/or 10 years. Miss. Code Ann. §97-29-29 *Incest—Persons Divorced for Incest Not to Cohabit or Copulate;* Penalty: fine of $500 and/or 10 years. Miss. Code Ann. §97-29-5 *Adultery and Fornication Between Certain Persons Forbidden to Intermarry;* Penalty: maximum 10 years. *Prohibited Marriages,* §93-1-1 to 3.	*Rape—Carnal Knowledge of Female under 12 or over 12 Against Her Will;* Penalty: death or life imprisonment, or term of imprisonment as the court may determine, §97-3-65; but see *Coker v. Georgia,* 433 U.S. 584 (1977) re constitutionality of death penalty for rape. *Rape—Carnal Knowledge of Chaste Female over 12 and under 18 years of age;* Penalty: fine not exceeeding $500 or 6 months in county jail, or imprisonment up to 5 years, §97-3-67.
Missouri	Mo. Rev. Stat. §568.020 *Incest* (1979): Marries or purports to marry, or engages in sexual intercourse with a person he knows to	*Rape:* Sexual intercourse with person under 14 §566.020; Class B felony unless serious personal injury or weapon, then Class

State	Incest Statute	Parallel Statutory Provisions
Missouri (cont.)	be: an ancestor or descendant by blood or adoption; his stepchild, brother or sister, (whole or half blood), uncle, aunt or niece (whole blood); revised statute enacted 1973; Class D felony: maximum 5 years, §558.011(1).	A felony; Class A felony: minimum 10 years, maximum 30 years or life; Class B felony: minimum 5 years, maximum 15 years, §558.011(1). *Sodomy:* Deviate sexual intercourse with person under 14, §566.030; Penalty: same as for rape. *1st Degree Sexual Abuse:* Sexual contact with person under 12; Class D felony, §566.100. Also *1st* or *2nd Degree Sexual Assault, Deviate Sexual Assault, Sexual Misconduct,* or *2nd Degree Sexual Abuse,* if age restrictions apply.
Montana	Mont. Rev. Codes Ann. §45-5-613 *Incest* (1979): Knowingly marries or cohabits or has sexual intercourse with an ancestor, descendant, brother or sister (of the whole or half blood, without regard to legitimacy) and the relationships of	*Sexual Intercourse Without Consent:* Sexual intercourse if victim is under 16 and actor is 3 years older; Penalty: minimum 2 years, maximum 20 years, §45-5-503. *Sexual Assault:* Sexual contact if victim is

State	Incest Statute	Parallel Statutory Provisions
Montana (cont.)	parent and child by adoption; enacted 1947; Penalty: any term not to exceed 10 years.	under 16 and offender is 3 years older; Penalty: $500 fine, or up to 6 months in county jail, §45-5-502.
Nebraska	Neb. Rev. Stat. §28-905 *Incest; Penalty* (1975): Persons within the prohibited degrees of consanguinity who intermarry, commit adultery or fornication, or who lewdly cohabit; Penalty: minimum 5 years, maximum 15 years. Neb. Rev. Stat. §28-906 *Father Cohabiting with Daughter* (1975): Licentious cohabitation with a daughter; Penalty: minimum 20 years.	*Domestic Abuse Act* (1978): Includes civil remedies, support services to families, mandatory counseling as a condition of probation; LB 623, Laws of 1978. *1st Degree Sexual Assault:* Sexual penetration (expanded definition) when victim is under 16 and actor is over 18, §28-408.03; Class II felony: maximum 55 years, minimum one year, SL. 1977, LB 38 §5 and 6.
Nevada	Nev. Rev. Stat. §201.180 *Incest: Punishment* (1977): Person within the prohibited degrees of consanguinity who intermarry, commit fornication or adultery; Penalty: minimum one year, maximum 10 years.	*Lewdness with a Child under 14:* Any lewd or lascious act other than sexual assault, with child under 14; Penalty: minimum one year, maximum 10 years, §201.230. *Sexual Assault:* Sexual penetration (expanded definition) with child

State	Incest Statute	Parallel Statutory Provisions
Nevada (cont.)		*under* 14; Penalty: life with mandatory 5-year period of incarceration or any term of 5 years or more, §201.366.
		Statutory Sexual Seduction: Sexual intercourse, cunnilingus or fellatio by person over 18 with consenting person under 16; Penalty: if offender over 21, minimum one year, maximum 10 years and fine of up to $10,000; if offender under 21, then gross misdemeanor, §20.230(1).
New Hampshire	N.H. Rev. Stat. §639.2 *Incest* (1974): A person who marries or has sexual intercourse, or lives together with under the representation of being married, a person whom he knows to be his ancestor, descendant, brother or sister of the whole or half blood, or an uncle, aunt, or nephew or niece, provided, however, that no person under the age of 18 shall be liable under this section if the other party is at least 3 years	*Protection of Persons from Domestic Violence* (1979): Includes civil remedies, recommendation for counseling, violation a misdemeanor, Ch. 1738, L. 1979. *Aggravated Felonious Sexual Assault:* Sexual penetration (expanded definition) when victim is over 13 and under 16 and actor is a member of the same household as victim, or is related by blood or affinity to victim, or is in a posi-

State	Incest Statute	Parallel Statutory Provisions
New Hampshire (cont.)	older at the time of the act; relations include blood relations without regard to legitimacy, stepchildren, and the relationship of parent and child by adoption; Class B felony: maximum 7 yrs, §651:2 IIb. *Marriage, Degrees Prohibited, Men,* §.457:1. *Marriage, Degrees Prohibited, Women* §.457:2. *Effect of Marriage,* §.457:3.	tion of authority over victim and uses this authority to coerce victim to submit; or when victim is under 13; N.H. Rev. Stat. §532-A:2 (1974 Repl.); Class A felony: maximum 15 years, §651:2 IIa. *Sexual Assault:* Sexual contact under circumstances of aggravated felonious sexual assault, §632-A:4; Misdemeanor: maximum one year §651:2IIC.
New Jersey	Former traditional incest statute repealed in 1979, replaced by subcategory of sexual assault, which includes some forms of the prior incest.	*Aggravated Sexual Assault:* Sexual penetration when victim is under 13, or when victim is over 13 and under 16 and there is either a relationship of blood or affinity to the 3rd degree; or actor has supervisory or disciplinary power over the victim; or actor is a foster parent, guardian, or stands in loco parentis within the household; N.J. Stat. Ann. 2C:14-2a (1980); Crime of the 1st de-

State	Incest Statute	Parallel Statutory Provisions
New Jersey (cont.)		gree: 10–20 years, 2C:43-6.

Sexual Assault: Sexual contact when victim is under 13 and actor is 4 years older, or sexual penetration when victim is at least 16 and under 18 and actor is a member of the household with supervisory power; 2C:14-2b and c; 2nd degree offense: 5–10 years, 2C:43-6.

Aggravated Criminal Sexual Contact: Sexual contact when victim is over 13 and under 16 and a relationship as defined in aggravated sexual assault, 2C:14-3(a); 3rd degree offense: 3–5 years, 2C:47-6.

Criminal Sexual Contact: Sexual contact when victim is over 16 but under 18 and actor is a member of the victim's household with supervisory power, 2C:14-3(b); 4th degree offense: maximum 18 months, 2C:43-6.

State	Incest Statute	Parallel Statutory Provisions
New Mexico	N.M. Stat. Ann. §30-10-3 *Incest* (1978): Intermarrying or having sexual intercourse with persons within the following degrees of consanguinity: parents and children, grandparents and grandchildren, brothers and sisters (half and whole blood), uncles and nieces, aunts and nephews; 3rd degree felony: 3 years, §31-18-15A.	*2nd Degree Criminal Sexual Penetration:* Sexual penetration (expanded definition) on child 13 to 16 when perpetrator is in a position of authority (defined to include parent, relative, or household member) and used this authority to coerce child to submit, §30-9-11B; 2nd degree felony: 9 years imprisonment, §31-18-15A.

1st Degree Criminal Sexual Penetration: Sexual penetration (expanded definition) on child under 13, §30-9-11A; 1st degree felony: 18 years imprisonment, §31-18-15A.

Criminal Sexual Contact on a Minor: All criminal sexual contact on child under 13 or on child from 13 to 18 when perpetrator is in position of authority, §30-9-13A; 3rd degree felony: 3 years imprisonment, §31-18-15A. |
| New York | N.Y. Penal §255.25 *Incest* (1977): Marries or engages in sexual in- | *1st Degree Rape:* Sexual intercourse with female under 11, |

State	Incest Statute	Parallel Statutory Provisions
New York (cont.)	tercourse with a person known to be related, legitimately or illegitimately, as an ancestor, descendant, brother or sister of either whole or half blood, uncle, aunt, nephew or niece; Class E felony: maximum 4 years, §70(2)(3). *Statutory Corroboration Requirement,* §255.30 (added 1965). *Incestuous Marriage,* N.Y. Dom. Rel. §5.	§130.35; Class B felony: maximum 25 years, §70.00(2)(b). *2nd Degree Rape:* Male over 18 who engages in sexual intercourse with female under 14, §130.30; Class D felony: maximum 7 years, §70.00(2)(d). *3rd Degree Rape:* Sexual intercourse with female under 17, Class E felony, §130.25. *1st Degree Sexual Abuse:* Sexual contact with person under 11, Class D felony, §130.65. *2nd Degree Sexual Abuse:* Sexual contact with person under 14, §130.20; Class A misdemeanor: maximum one year, §55.05–10. *3rd Degree Sexual Abuse:* Sexual contact without consent but if age difference less than 5 years, a defense, §130.55; Class B misdemeanor: maximum 1 year, §55.05–10.
North Carolina	N.C. Gen. Stat. §14-178 *Incest Between*	*Sexual Intercourse and Sexual Offenses with*

State	Incest Statute	Parallel Statutory Provisions
North Carolina (cont.)	*Certain Near Relatives* (1969): Carnal intercourse between grandparent and grandchild; parent and child or stepchild or legally adopted child; or brother and sister of whole or half blood; Class G felony: maximum 15 years or fine, §14–1.1.	*Certain Victims:* A defendant who has assumed position of a parent, or a person having custody of a victim, having sexual intercourse or a sexual act; Penalty: minimum 2 years, maximum 15 years, §14-27.7. *1st Degree Rape:* Vaginal intercourse with child under 13, when defendant is 4 years older: Penalty: life, §14-27.2.
North Dakota	N.D. Cent. Code §12.1-20-11 *Incest* (1976 Repl.): Intermarries, cohabits or has sexual intercourse with another person related within the degrees of consanguinity within which marriages are declared incestuous and void; Class C felony: maximum 5 years, §12.1-32-01.	*Sexual Assault:* Sexual contact when person is a minor over 15 and actor is parent or guardian or otherwise responsible for general supervision of other person's welfare, §12.1-32-07; Class A misdemeanor: maximum one year, §12.1-32-01. *Gross Sexual Imposition:* Sexual act or sexual contact with victim under 15, §12.1-20-03; Class A felony: maximum 20 years, §12.1-32-01.

State	Incest Statute	Parallel Statutory Provisions
Ohio	Some categories of incest decriminalized. Former traditional incest statute repealed when comprehensive revision of the law concerning sex offenses, pornography and prostitution enacted in 1974. Former law defined separately forcible rape of a daughter, sister or child under 12.	*Domestic Violence Act* (1978): Authority of court to act, includes cohabitants and relatives, Ohio Rev. Code Ann. §2912.25. *Sexual Battery:* Sexual conduct (penetration offense) when offender is the other person's natural or adoptive parent, or stepparent, or guardian, custodian or person in loco parentis, or supervisory or disciplinary relationship, Ohio Rev. Code Ann. §2907.03A and B (Page 1975 Repl.); 3rd degree felony: minimum one year 18 months, 2 or 3 years, maximum 10 years, §2929.11b(3). Additional offenses define rape and other sex offenses in terms of age of participants.
Oklahoma	Okla. Stat. Ann. Tit. 21 §885 *Incest* (1958): Persons within prohibited degrees of consanguinity who intermarry, commit adultery or fornication, are punishable by	*1st Degree Rape:* Sexual intercourse by male over 18 when female is under 14, §1114; Penalty: death or minimum 5 years, §1115; but see *Coker* v. *Georgia*, 433 U.S. 584

State	Incest Statute	Parallel Statutory Provisions
Oklahoma (cont.)	imprisonment up to 10 years. *Prohibition Against Marriages*, Tit. 43, Marriage §2.	(1977) re constitutionality of death penalty for rape. *2nd Degree Rape:* Sexual intercourse when female is under 16 or when female is over 16 and under 18 and of previous chaste character, §1114; Penalty: minimum one year, maximum 15 years, §1116.
Oregon	Ore. Rev. Stat. §163.525 *Incest* (1977): Marries or engages in sexual intercourse or deviate sexual intercourse with a person known to be related, legitimately or illegitimately as an ancestor, descendant or brother or sister either whole or half blood; Class C felony: maximum 5 years, §161.605(3).	*Rape in the 1st Degree:* Sexual intercoure when female is under 16 and is the male's sister, of the whole or half blood, his daughter, or his wife's daughter, §163.375; Class A felony: maximum 20 years, §161.605(1). *1st Degree Sexual Abuse:* Sexual contact when victim under 12; Class C felony, §163.425. Age of consent for sexual acts is 18, §163.315; three categories of rape and two categories of sexual abuse as well as sexual misconduct are de-

State	Incest Statute	Parallel Statutory Provisions
Oregon (cont.)		fined in part by age of participants.
Pennsylvania	Pa. Stat. Ann. Tit. 18 §4302 *Incest* (1973): Knowingly marries, cohabits or has sexual intercourse with an ancestor or descendant, a brother or sister of the whole or half blood or an uncle, aunt, nephew or niece of the whole blood, including illegitimacy and adoption; 1st degree misdemeanor: maximum 5 years, §1104.	*Statutory Rape:* Sexual intercourse with person under 14 by person over 18, §3122; 2nd degree felony: maximum 10 years, §1103.
Puerto Rico	P.R. Laws Ann. Tit. 33 §4121 *Incest* (1978 Cum. Supp.): Persons who intermarry or have sexual intercourse within the prohibited degrees of consanguinity: ascendants and descendants of all degrees, collaterals by consanguinity up to the 3rd degree, including double ties and single ties and parent and child, by adoption or brother or sister by adoption; Penalty:	*Rape:* Carnal intercourse with female under 14; Penalty: minimum one year, maximum 25 years, §4061. *Lewd and Indecent Acts:* Every person who without intending to have sexual intercourse commits any indecent or lewd act with victim under 14; Penalty: minimum one year, maximum 5 years, §4067.

State	Incest Statute	Parallel Statutory Provisions
Puerto Rico (cont.)	minimum one year, maximum 10 years.	
Rhode Island	R.I. Gen. Laws Ann. §11-6-4 *Incest* (1970): Persons within prohibited degrees of consanguinity who shall intermarry, commit adultery or fornication, shall be imprisoned for not more than 10 years. *Incestuous Marriages,* §15-1-3. *Prohibited Degrees,* §15-1-1 and 2.	*1st Degree Sexual Assault:* Sexual penetration when victim is under 13, §11-37-2; Penalty: minimum 10 years, maximum life, §11-37-3. *2nd Degree Sexual Assault:* sexual contact when victim is under 13, §11-37-4; Penalty: minimum 3 years, maximum 15 years, §11-37-5. *3rd Degree Sexual Assault:* Sexual penetration by person over 18 with person over 13 and under 16, §11-37-6; Penalty: maximum 5 years, §11-37-7.
South Carolina	S.C. Code Ann. §16-15-20 *Incest* (1976): Persons who have carnal intercourse with each other within specified degrees of relationship; Penalty: fine of $500 minimum, one year in prison, or both. *Prohibited Marriages,* §20-1-10.	*1st Degree Criminal Sexual Conduct:* Sexual battery (expanded definition of sexual penetration) with victim under 11 when actor is 3 years older; Penalty: maximum 30 years, §16-3-652 and 655. *2nd Degree Criminal Sexual Conduct:* Sex-

State	Incest Statute	Parallel Statutory Provisions
South Carolina (cont.)		ual battery with victim over 11 and under 14 when actor is 3 years older or with victim over 14 but under 16 when actor is in position of familial, custodial or official authority to coerce victim to submit or is older than victim; Penalty: maximum 20 years, §16-3-653 and 655.
South Dakota	S.D. Comp. Laws Ann. §22-22-19 *Incest* (1978 Special Supp.): People who are not legally married who are within the prohibited degrees of consanguinity within which marriages are void and who have sexual intercourse; Class 4 felony: 10 years and possible fine of $10,000, §22-6-1.	*2nd Degree Rape:* Sexual penetration (expanded definition) when victim is less than 15; Class 4 felony, §22-22-1. *Sexual Contact with Child under 15:* Sexual contact with person under 15; Class 3 felony if actor over 3 years older; Class 1 misdemeanor if actor less than 3 years older, §22-22-7; Class 3 felony: 15 years or possible fine of $15,000 §22-6-1; Class 1 misdemeanor: one year in county jail, fine of $1000, or both, §22-6-2.

State	Incest Statute	Parallel Statutory Provisions
Tennessee	Tenn. Code Ann. §39-705 *Incest—Penalty* (1975 Repl.): Marriage or carnal knowledge with specified prohibited degrees of relationship; Penalty: minimum 5 years, maximum 21 years. *Prohibited Marriages,* §36-401.	*Aggravated Rape:* Unlawful sexual penetration (expanded definition) with victim under 13 or when victim is at least 13 but under 16 and actor related by blood or affinity to the 3rd degree, or actor in position of custodial or official authority over the victim; Penalty: if victim under 13, minimum 20 years; otherwise life or minimum 15 years. §39-3703. *Aggravated Sexual Battery:* Sexual contact under age circumstances of aggravated rape; Penalty: if victim under 13, minimum 15 years; otherwise minimum sentence 10 years, §39-3704.
Texas	Tex. Penal Code §25.02 *Incest* (1974): Sexual intercourse or deviate sexual intercourse with ancestor or descendant by blood or adoption; stepchild or stepparent (while marriage exists); parent's brother or sister (whole or half blood or	*Rape of a Child:* Sexual intercourse with female under 17 when actor more than 2 years older, §21-09; 2nd degree felony: minimum 2 years, maximum 20 years and possible fine of $10,-000, §12.33.

State	Incest Statute	Parallel Statutory Provisions
Texas (cont.)	by adoption); relations include illegitimate relations; 3rd degree felony: minimum 2 years, maximum 10 years, §12.34.	*Sexual Abuse of a Child:* Deviate sexual intercourse with child under 17 or exposure to child under 17; 3rd degree felony, §21.10.
	Prohibited Marriage, Family Code §2.21.	*Indecency with a Child:* Sexual contact with child under 17 or exposure to child under 17; 3rd degree felony, §21.11.
		Aggravated Sexual Abuse: Sexual abuse of child when actor causes serious bodily injury or attempts to cause death or compels submission by threat, §21.05; 1st degree felony: life or maximum 99 years, minimum 5 years, §12.321.
Utah	Utah Code Ann. §76-7-102 *Incest* (1978 Repl.): Sexual intercourse with person known to be an ancestor, descendant, brother or sister, uncle, aunt, nephew, niece, first cousin, including relations of the whole and half blood, including relations of illegitimacy and adoption	*Rape:* Sexual intercourse with victim under 14, §76-5-402; 1st degree felony: minimum 5 years, maximum life, §76-3-202.
		Sodomy: Oral genital acts with victim under 14, 1st degree felony, §76-5-403.
		Forcible Sexual Abuse: Touching of anus or

State	Incest Statute	Parallel Statutory Provisions
Utah (cont.)	and stepparent and stepchild (while marriage exists); 3rd degree felony: maximum 5 years, §76-3-203.	genitals or taking indecent liberties, 3rd degree felony, §76-5-404. *Unlawful Sexual Intercourse:* Sexual intercourse with person under 16; 3rd degree felony unless actor less than 3 years older than victim, then misdemeanor, §76-5-401.
Vermont	Vt. Stat. Ann. Tit. 13 §205: *Intermarriage or Fornication by Persons Prohibited to Marry* (1974): Persons who are prohibited to marry who intermarry or commit fornication shall be punished as for adultery; Penalty for adultery: maximum 5 years, fine of $1000, or both, §201.	*Domestic Abuse Act* (1979): Civil remedies for domestic abuse; public acts, 1979 Adj. session, No. 153. *Sexual Assault:* Sexual act with person under 16; Penalty: maximum 20 years, fine of $10,-000, or both, §3252. *Aggravated Sexual Assault:* Sexual acts with person under 16 where serious bodily injury occurs; Penalty: maximum 25 years, fine of $15,000, or both, §3253.
Virgin Islands	V.I. Code Ann. Tit. 14 §961 *Incest Defined; Punishment* (1964): Persons within the prohibited degrees of consanguinity who in-	*2nd Degree Rape:* Sexual intercourse with female under 14; Penalty: maximum 15 years, §1702.

State	Incest Statute	Parallel Statutory Provisions
Virgin Islands (cont.)	termarry commit fornication or adultery; Penalty: maximum 10 years.	*3rd Degree Rape:* Sexual intercourse with female over 14 and under 16; Penalty: $200 fine and/or maximum one year, §1703. Circumstances of forcible rape can be prosecuted under 1st degree rape (maximum 20 years, §1701) even if the age requirements of 2nd and 3rd degree are met.
Virginia	Va. Code Ann. §18.2-366 *Adultery and Fornication by Persons Forbidden to Marry; Incest* (1981): A person who commits adultery or fornication with any person whom he or she is forbidden by law to marry commits a Class 1 misdemeanor, but if with daughter or granddaughter, or son or grandson, or father or mother, then Class 5 felony, provided that if a parent commits adultery or fornication with his or her child, and such child is at least 13 but less than 15, then Class 3 felony; Class 1 misdemeanor:	*Rape:* Sexual intercourse with a female child under 13; Penalty: life or any term not less than 5 years, §18.2-61. *Carnal Knowledge of Child Between 13 and 15:* Carnal knowledge of a child over 13 and under 15; Class 4 felony if accused a minor and child more than 3 years younger; Class 6 felony if child less than 3 years younger, then accused guilty of fornication only §18.2-63; Class 4 felony: 2–10 years, 18.2-10(d); Class 6 felony: 1–5 years or one year in county jail, §18.2-10(f).

State	Incest Statute	Parallel Statutory Provisions
Virginia (cont.)	maximum 12 months and/or fine of $1000, §18.2-11(a); Class 5 felony: minimum one year, maximum 10 years or county jail for 12 months and/or fine, §18.2-10(3); Class 3 felony: minimum 5 years, maximum 20 years, §18.2-10. *Certain Marriages Prohibited* §20-38.1.	*Crimes against Nature:* If a parent commits such an act with a child at least 13 but less than 15, Class 3 felony, §18.2-361.
Washington	Wash. Rev. Code Ann. §91.64.020 *Incest* (1977): Sexual intercourse with a person known to be related either legitimately or illegitimately as an ancestor, descendant, brother, sister of either the whole or half blood, including stepchildren and adopted children under 18; Class C felony: maximum 5 years and/or fine, §9A.20.020.	*1st Degree Statutory Rape:* Person over 13 who has sexual intercourse (expanded definition) with person under 11; Penalty: minimum 20 years, without a deferred or suspended sentence, §9.79.200. *2nd Degree Statutory Rape:* Person over 16 who has sexual intercourse with person over 11 but under 14; Penalty: maximum 10 years, §9.79.210. *3rd Degree Statutory Rape:* Person over 18 who has sexual intercourse with person over 15 but under 16; Penalty: maximum 5 years, §9.79.220.

State	Incest Statute	Parallel Statutory Provisions
West Virginia	W. Va. Code Ann. §61-8-12 *Incest* (1977 Repl.): A male person who shall have sexual intercourse with his mother, sister, daughter or the daughter of a brother or sister, and a female person who shall have sexual intercourse with a father, brother or son, or with the son of a brother or sister, guilty of a felony (enacted 1882); Penalty: minimum 5 years, maximum 10 years.	*1st Degree Sexual Assault:* Sexual intercourse (expanded definition) with person under 11; Penalty: minimum 10 years, maximum 20 years, and possible fine of $10,000, §61-8B-3. *3rd Degree Sexual Assault:* Sexual intercourse by person over 16 with person under 16 and 4 years younger; Penalty: minimum one year, maximum 5 years, and possible fine of $10,000, §61-8B-5. *1st Degree Sexual Abuse:* Sexual contact with person under 11; Penalty: minimum one year, maximum 5 years, and possible fine of $10,000, §61-8B-6. *3rd Degree Sexual Abuse:* Sexual contact with victim under 16 if victim 4 years younger; Penalty: misdemeanor, §61-8B-8.
Wisconsin	Wis. Stat. Ann. §944.06 *Incest* (1979–80 Supp.): Whoever marries or has nonmarital sexual in-	*1st Degree Sexual Assault:* Sexual intercourse (expanded definition) or sexual contact with person 12

State	Incest Statute	Parallel Statutory Provisions
Wisconsin (cont.)	tercourse with a person known to be a blood relative and such relative is in fact related in a degree prohibited by marriage; Class C felony: maximum 10 years and/or fine up to $10,000, §939.50 (3)(c).	or younger, §940.225; Class B felony: maximum 20 years, §939.50(3)(b). *2nd Degree Sexual Assault:* Sexual contact or sexual intercourse with person over 12 and under 18 without consent; Class C felony. Person under 15 incapable of consent as a matter of law; person 15 to 17 is presumed incapable of consent, but the presumption may be rebutted, §940.225(4).
Wyoming	Wyo. Stat. Ann. §6-5-102 *Incest* (1977): Any stepfather who has sexual intercourse with his stepdaughter, or stepmother with stepson, or any parent and child, or brother and sister over age 16, having knowledge of their consanguinity, who has sexual intercourse, shall be imprisoned not more than 5 years or in the county jail not more than 12 months.	*2nd Degree Sexual Assault:* Sexual penetration (expanded definition) or sexual intrusion when victim is less than 12 and actor 4 years older, or when actor in position of authority (includes parent, guardian, relative and household member), §6-4-303; Penalty: minimum one year, maximum 20 years, §6-4-306. *3rd Degree Sexual Assault:* Sexual contact

State	Incest Statute	Parallel Statutory Provisions
Wyoming (cont.)		under circumstances of 2nd degree sexual assault, §6-4-304; Penalty: minimum one year, maximum 5 years; §6-4-306.
		4th Degree Sexual Assault: Sexual penetration or intrusion on victim under 16 when actor 4 years older, §6-4-305; Penalty: maximum one year, §6-4-306.

Notes

Introduction. Cinderella or Saint Dympna

1. Jakob and Wilhelm Grimm, *Grimm's Fairy Tales*, trans. Margaret Hunt, ed. James Stern (New York: Pantheon, 1944), pp. 121–128.

2. *Ibid.*, pp. 326–331. We are indebted to Julius Heuscher for calling our attention to the story of Many-Furs. For the significance of these tales in normal development, see Julius Heuscher, *A Psychiatric Study of Myths and Fairy Tales* (New York: C C Thomas, 1974).

3. Donald Attwater, *The Penguin Dictionary of Saints* (Baltimore: Penguin Books, 1965), p. 108; Herbert Thurston and Norah Leeson, eds., *The Lives of the Saints* (London: Burns Oates and Washbourne, 1936), pp. 191–193; John O'Hanlon, *The Life of Saint Dympna: Virgin, Martyr, and Patroness of Gheel* (Dublin: James Duffy, 1863).

1. A Common Occurrence

1. Sigmund Freud, "The Aetiology of Hysteria," *The Complete Psychological Works of Sigmund Freud*, trans. James Strachey, Standard Edition (London: Hogarth Press, 1962), III, 191–221; Josef Breuer and Sigmund Freud, *Studies on Hysteria, Complete Works*, vol. II.

2. Marie Bonaparte, Anna Freud, and Ernst Kris, eds. *The Origins of Psychoanalysis: Letters of Wilhelm Fliess, Drafts and Notes, 1887–1902*, trans. Eric Mosbacher and James Strachey (New York: Basic Books, 1954), pp. 179–180.

3. Sigmund Freud, *Studies on Hysteria, Complete Works*, II, 134 and 170nn.

4. For a fuller analysis of the process by which Freud came to deny the reality of his patients' reports, see Florence Rush, "Freud and the Sexual Abuse of Children," *Chrysalis* 1 (1977): 31–45.

5. Bonaparte et al., eds, *Origins of Psychoanalysis*, pp. 215–217.

6. Helene Deutsch, *Psychology of Women* (New York: Grune & Stratton, 1944).

7. D. James Henderson, "Incest," in A. M. Freedman, H. I. Kaplan and B. J. Sadock, eds., *Comprehensive Textbook of Psychiatry*, 2nd ed. (Baltimore: Williams and Wilkins, 1975), p. 1532.

8. Suzanne M. Sgroi, "Sexual Molestation of Children: The Last Frontier in Child Abuse," *Children Today* 44 (1975): 18–21.

9. John Henry Wigmore, *Evidence in Trials at Common Law*, rev. James H. Chadbourn (Boston: Little, Brown, 1970), vol. IIIA, sec. 924a, 736–747.

10. For original case histories, see William Healy and Mary T. Healy, *Pathological Lying, Accusation, and Swindling* (Boston: Little, Brown, 1915), pp. 182–187, 194–197.

11. Wigmore, *Evidence*, pp. 742–743.

12. For a critical review of the Wigmore doctrine, including documentation of the falsified cases, see Leigh Bienen, "Incest" (unpub. ms., Department of the Public Advocate, Trenton, N.J., 1980).

13. Alfred C. Kinsey, Wardell B. Pomeroy, Clyde E. Martin, and Paul H. Gebhard, *Sexual Behavior in the Human Female* (Philadelphia: Saunders, 1953).

14. John Gagnon, "Female Child Victims of Sex Offenses," *Social Problems* 13 (1965): 176–192.

15. Judson Landis, "Experiences of 500 Children with Adult Sexual Deviance," *Psychiatric Quarterly Supplement* 30 (1956): 91–109; David Finkelhor, *Sexually Victimized Children* (New York: Free Press, 1979).

16. Carney Landis, *Sex in Development* (New York: Harper & Brothers, 1940).

17. Finkelhor, *Sexually Victimized Children*, p. 88.

18. Alfred C. Kinsey, Wardell B. Pomeroy, Clyde E. Martin, and Paul H. Gebhard, *Sexual Behavior in the Human Male* (Philadelphia: Saunders, 1948), p. 167.

19. Finkelhor, *Sexually Victimized Children*, pp. 68–71.

20. J. Landis, *Experiences of 500 Children*.

21. Kinsey et al., *Female*, p. 121.

22. Kinsey saw himself as an advocate for both sexes, and he supported women's right to sexual pleasure and to birth control. But in areas where the sexual interests of men and women are in conflict, Kinsey allied himself firmly with men. For Kinsey's male bias as well as other ideological foundations of his work, see Paul Robinson, *The Modernization of Sex* (New York: Harper & Row, 1976).

23. Kinsey et al., *Female*, pp. 20–21.

24. S. Kirson Weinberg, *Incest Behavior* (New York: Citadel Press, 1955).

25. Herbert Maisch, *Incest* (New York: Stein & Day, 1972); Narcyz Lukianowicz, "Incest," *British Journal of Psychiatry* 120 (1972): 201–212; Karin Meiselman, *Incest* (San Francisco: Jossey-Bass, 1978); Blair Justice and Rita Justice, *The Broken Taboo* (New York: Human Sciences Press, 1979).

26. Maya Angelou, *I Know Why the Caged Bird Sings* (New York: Random House, 1970); Sandra Butler, *Conspiracy of Silence: The Trauma of Incest* (San Francisco: New Glide Publications, 1978); Louise Armstrong, *Kiss Daddy Goodnight: A Speak-Out on Incest* (New York: Hawthorn Books, 1978); Susan

Forward and Craig Buck, *Betrayal of Innocence: Incest and Its Devastation* (New York: Penguin Books, 1978); Katherine Brady, *Father's Days* (New York: Seaview, 1979); Charlotte Vale Allen, *Daddy's Girl: A Memoir* (New York: Simon and Schuster, 1980).

27. Setsuji Kubo, "Studies on Incest in Japan," *Hiroshima Journal of Medical Sciences* 8 (1959): 99–159, 113. The same clinical material can be interpreted very differently from a male chauvinist perspective. Another author summarizes this same case as "a domineering, overprotective widow with an only son of low cognitive status." Christopher Bagley, "Incest Behavior and Incest Taboo," *Social Problems* 16 (1969): 505–519.

28. Wenzel Brown, "Murder Rooted in Incest," in R. E. L. Masters, ed., *Patterns of Incest* (New York: Julian Press, 1963), pp. 302–330.

29. Katherine N. Dixon, Eugene Arnold, and Kenneth Calestro, "Father-Son Incest: Underreported Psychiatric Problem?" *American Journal of Psychiatry* 135 (1978): 835–838.

30. Justice and Justice, *Broken Taboo*, p. 61.

2. The Question of Harm

1. Benjamin Demott, "The Pro-Incest Lobby," *Psychology Today* 13 (March 1980): 11–16.

2. James Ramey, "Dealing with the Last Taboo," *SIECUS Report* 7 (May 1979): 1–2, 6–7.

3. Wardell Pomeroy, "Incest: A New Look," *Forum*, November 1976.

4. Philip Nobile, "Incest: The Last Taboo," *Penthouse*, December 1977, pp. 117–118, 126, 157–158.

5. Edwin J. Haeberle, "Children, Sex, and Society," *Hustler*, December 1978, p. 124.

6. Larry L. Constantine, "Effects of Early Sexual Experiences: A Review and Synthesis of Research," in L. L. Constantine and F. M. Martinson, *Children and Sex: New Findings, New Perspectives* (Boston: Little, Brown, 1980), ch. 19.

7. Judson Landis, "Experiences of 500 Children with Adult Sexual Deviants," *Psychiatric Quarterly Supplement* 30 (1956): 91–109.

8. John Gagnon, "Female Child Victims of Sex Offenses," *Social Problems* 13 (1965): 176–192.

9. Carney Landis, *Sex in Development* (New York: Harper & Brothers, 1940).

10. David Finkelhor, *Sexually Victimized Children* (New York: Free Press, 1979). In general, the testimony of boys was less negative than that of girls: only 41 percent reacted with fear, and 14 percent with shock, while 23 percent reported that they had enjoyed the experience.

11. Philip Nobile, "Incest: The Last Taboo," p. 126.

12. Interview with Joan Nelson, *Frontiers of Psychiatry*, Apr. 1, 1979, p. 6.

13. J. Landis, "Experiences of 500 Children."

14. Gagnon, "Female Child Victims," p. 189.

15. Gagnon, "Female Child Victims," p. 189.

16. David Finkelhor, "Long Term Effects of Childhood Sexual Victimization in a Non-Clinical Sample" (unpub. ms., University of New Hampshire, 1980).

17. C. Landis, *Sex in Development,* p. 34.

18. Jill Miller, Deborah Moeller, Arthur Kaufman, Peter DiVasto, Dorothy Pathak, and Joan Christy, "Recidivism among Sex Assault Victims," *American Journal of Psychiatry* 135 (1978): 1103–1104.

19. Connie Murphy, Tacoma Rape Relief, personal communication.

20. Judianne Densen-Gerber and Jean Benward, *Incest as a Causative Factor in Anti-Social Behavior: An Exploratory Study* (New York: Odyssey Institute, 1976).

21. Jennifer James and Jane Meyerding, "Early Sexual Experience and Prostitution," *American Journal of Psychiatry* 134 (1977): 1381–1385.

22. Vincent De Francis, *Protecting the Child Victim of Sex Crimes Committed by Adults* (Denver: American Humane Association, 1969).

23. Irving Kaufman, Alice Peck, and Consuelo Tagiuri, "The Family Constellation and Overt Incestuous Relations Between Father and Daughter," *American Journal of Orthopsychiatry* 24 (1954): 266–279.

24. Noel Lustig, John Dresser, Seth Spellman, and Thomas Murray, "Incest: A Family Group Survival Pattern," *Archives of General Psychiatry* 14 (1966): 31–40.

25. Paul Sloane and Eva Karpinski, "Effects of Incest on the Participants," *American Journal of Orthopsychiatry* 12 (1942): 666–673.

26. Mavis Tsai and Nathaniel Wagner, "Therapy Groups for Women Sexually Molested as Children," *Archives of Sexual Behavior* 7 (1978): 417–429.

27. Karin Meiselman, *Incest* (San Francisco: Jossey-Bass, 1978), p. 208.

28. C. W. Wahl, "Psychodynamics of Consummated Maternal Incest," *Archives of General Psychiatry* 3 (1960): 192.

29. Atalay Yorukoglu and John P. Kemph, "Children Not Severely Damaged by Incest with a Parent," *Journal of the American Academy of Child Psychiatry* 5 (1966): 111–124.

30. Lauretta Bender and Alvin Grugett, "A Follow-Up Report on Children Who Had Atypical Sexual Experiences," *American Journal of Orthopsychiatry* 22 (1952): 825–837.

31. Mavis Tsai, Shirley Feldman-Summers, and Margaret Edgar, "Childhood Molestation: Variables Related to Differential Impacts on Psychological Functioning in Adult Women," *Journal of Abnormal Psychology* 88 (1979): 407–417.

32. Louise Armstrong, *Kiss Daddy Goodnight* (New York: Pocket Books, 1979), pp. 259–260.

3. The Question of Blame

1. Gen. 19:30–36.

2. Vladimir Nabokov, *Lolita* (New York: Berkley Medallion Edition, 1966), pp. 122–123.

3. Editorial, "Ball in the Family," *Chic*, October 1978.

4. Lauretta Bender and Abram Blau, "The Reaction of Children to Sexual Relations with Adults," *American Journal of Orthopsychiatry* 7 (1937): 514.

5. D. James Henderson, "Incest," in A. M. Freedman, H. I. Kaplan, and B. J. Sadock, eds., *Comprehensive Textbook of Psychiatry*, 2nd ed. (Baltimore: Williams and Wilkins, 1975), p. 1536.

6. Maya Angelou, *I Know Why the Caged Bird Sings* (New York: Bantam Books, 1971), pp. 62–63.

7. Katherine Brady, *Father's Days* (New York: Seaview, 1979), pp. 29–30.

8. Philip Nobile, "Incest, the Last Taboo," *Penthouse*, December 1977, p. 157.

9. Bruno Cormier, Miriam Kennedy, and Jadwiga Sangowicz, "Psychodynamics of Father-Daughter Incest," *Canadian Psychiatric Association Journal* 7 (1962): 207.

10. David Walters, *Physical and Sexual Abuse of Children: Causes and Treatment* (Bloomington: Indiana University Press, 1975), p. 124.

11. David Raphling, Bob Carpenter, and Allan Davis, "Incest: A Genealogical Study," *Archives of General Psychiatry* 16 (1967): 505–511.

12. Blair Justice and Rita Justice, *The Broken Taboo* (New York: Human Sciences Press, 1979), pp. 97–98.

13. Herbert Maisch, *Incest* (New York: Stein and Day, 1972), p. 139.

14. A. Nicholas Groth and H. Jean Birnbaum, *Men Who Rape: The Psychology of the Offender* (New York: Plenum, 1979), p. 140.

15. Charlotte Vale Allen, *Daddy's Girl: A Memoir* (New York: Simon and Schuster, 1980), pp. 56–57.

16. Allen, *Daddy's Girl*, p. 49.

17. Justice and Justice, *Broken Taboo*, p. 97.

18. Lora Heims and Irving Kaufman, "Variations on a Theme of Incest," *American Journal of Orthopsychiatry* 33 (1963): 311–312.

19. Ruth Kempe and C. Henry Kempe, *Child Abuse* (Cambridge: Harvard University Press, 1978), p. 48.

20. For a particularly vulgar vignette, see Pax Quigley, "Incest," *Chic* (October 1978).

21. Narcyz Lukianowicz, "Incest," *British Journal of Psychiatry* 120 (1972): 201–212.

22. S. Kirson Weinberg, *Incest Behavior* (New York: Citadel Press, 1955), p. 190.

23. Yvonne Tormes, *Child Victims of Incest* (Denver: American Humane Association, 1968), pp. 11–12.

24. David Finkelhor, "Risk Factors in the Sexual Victimization of Children" (unpub. ms., University of New Hampshire, 1979).

25. Herbert Maisch, *Incest* (New York: Stein and Day, 1972).

26. Diane Browning and Bonny Boatman, "Incest: Children at Risk," *American Journal of Psychiatry* 134 (1977): 69–72.

27. Richard Sarles, "Incest," *Pediatric Clinics of North America* 22 (1975): 637.

28. Finkelhor, "Risk Factors."

29. Tormes, *Child Victims*, pp. 34–35.

4. The Rule of the Father

1. Thomas Murdock, *Social Structure* (New York: Macmillan, 1949), ch. 10.

2. David Schneider, "The Meaning of Incest," *Journal of Ploynesian Society* 85 (1976): 149–169.

3. Claude Levi-Strauss, "The Family," in *Man, Culture and Society,* ed. Harry Shapiro (New York: Oxford University Press, 1956), p. 278.

4. David Aberle, Urie Bronfenbrenner, E. H. Hess, David Schneider, and J. N. Spahler, "The Incest Taboo and the Mating Patterns of Animals," *American Anthropologist* 65 (1963): 253–265.

5. Morton Adams and James Neel, "Children of Incest," *Pediatrics* 40 (1967): 55–62; E. Seemanova, "A Study of Children of Incestuous Matings," *Human Heredity* 21 (1971): 108–128; W. J. Schull and J. V. Neel, *The Effects of Inbreeding on Japanese Children* (New York: Harper & Row, 1965).

6. Aberle et al., "Incest Taboo and Mating Patterns of Animals."

7. Leslie Segner and A. Collins, "A Cross-Cultural Study of Incest Myths" (unpub. ms., University of Texas, 1967), cited in Gardner Lindzey, "Some Remarks Concerning Incest, the Incest Taboo, and Psychoanalytic Theory," *American Psychologist* 22 (1967): 1051–1059.

8. Florence Rush, *The Best Kept Secret: Sexual Abuse of Children* (Englewood Cliffs, N.J.: Prentice-Hall, 1980).

9. Vera Frances and Allen Frances, "The Incest Taboo and Family Structure," *Family Process* 15 (1976): 235–244.

10. Norbert Bischof, "The Biological Foundations of the Incest Taboo," *Social Science Information* 11 (1968): 7–36.

11. Sigmund Freud, *Totem and Taboo, Complete Works,* vol. XIII.

12. Brenda Seligman, "The Problem of Incest and Exogamy: A Restatement," *American Anthropologist* 52 (1950): 305–316.

13. Talcott Parsons, "The Incest Taboo in Relation to Social Structure and the Socialization of the Child," *British Journal of Sociology* 5 (1954): 57–77.

14. John Schwartzman, "The Individual, Incest, and Exogamy," *Psychiatry* 37 (1974): 171–180; Jerome Neu, "What Is Wrong with Incest?" *Inquiry* 19 (1976): 27U39.

15. Naphtali Lewis, "Aphairesis (Reclaiming a Daughter) in Athenian Law

and Custom," in J. Modrzejewski and D. Liebs, eds., *Symposion 1977: Vorträge zur griechischen und hellenistischen Rechtsgeschichte* (Cologne, 1981).

16. Juliet Mitchell, *Psychoanalysis and Feminism* (New York: Pantheon, 1974); Helen Block Lewis, *Psychic War in Men and Women* (New York: New York University Press, 1976); Nancy Chodorow, *The Reproduction of Mothering* (Berkeley: University of California Press, 1978).

17. Ruth Brunswick, "The Preoedipal Phase of the Libido Development," in Robert Fliess, ed., *The Psychoanalytic Reader: An Anthology of Essential Papers with Critical Introductions* (New York: International Universities Press, 1940), pp. 231–253.

18. Sigmund Freud, "Some Psychical Consequences of the Anatomical Distinction between the Sexes," *Complete Works*, XIX, 243–258.

19. Chodorow, *Reproduction of Mothering*, esp. pp. 191–209.

20. For the male monopoly on perversions and sex crimes, see Lewis, *Psychic War*.

21. Chodorow, *Reproduction of Mothering*.

22. Mitchell, *Psychoanalysis and Feminism*, chs. 8–9; Chodorow, *Reproduction of Mothering*, ch. 7–8.

23. Sigmund Freud, "The Dissolution of the Oedipus Complex," *Complete Works*, XIX, 172–179.

24. Phyllis Chesler, "Rape and Psychotherapy," in Noreen Connell and Cassandra Wilson, eds., *Rape: The First Sourcebook for Women* (New York: New American Library, 1974), p. 76.

25. Helene Deutsch, *Psychology of Women*, vol. I (New York: Grune & Stratton, 1944), pp. 251–253.

26. Claude Levi-Strauss, *The Elementary Structures of Kinship* (Boston: Beacon Press, 1949/1969). See also Leslie White, "The Definition and Prohibition of Incest," *American Anthropologist* 50 (1948): 416–435.

27. Levi-Strauss, *Elementary Structures of Kinship*, p. 481. See also Marshall Sahlins, *Stone Age Economics* (Chicago: Aldine-Atherton, 1972).

28. Yehudi Cohen, "The Disappearance of the Incest Taboo," *Human Nature*, July 1978, pp. 72–78.

29. Levi-Strauss, *Elementary Structures of Kinship*, p. 115.

30. Gayle Rubin, "The Traffic in Women: Notes on the Political Economy of Sex," in Rayna Reiter, ed., *Toward an Anthropology of Women* (New York: Monthly Review Press, 1975), p. 174.

31. Lev. 18: 6–18.

5. Incestuous Fathers and Their Families

1. Class backgrounds were determined in accordance with criteria in Harry Braverman, *Labor and Monopoly Capital* (New York: Monthly Review Press, 1974). "Middle class" is shorthand for the combined categories of "middle layers of employment" and "self-employed."

2. Maya Angelou, *I Know Why the Caged Bird Sings* (New York: Random

House, 1970); Anne Moody, *Coming of Age in Mississippi* (New York: Dial Press, 1968); Toni Morrison, *The Bluest Eye* (New York: Holt, Rinehart & Winston, 1970); Gayl Jones, *Corregidora* (New York: Random House, 1975).

3. I. B. Weiner, "Father-Daughter Incest: A Clinical Report," *Psychiatric Quarterly* 36 (1962): 607–632.

4. Herbert Maisch, *Incest* (New York: Stein & Day, 1972).

5. Weiner, "Father-Daughter Incest"; Hector Cavallin, "Incestuous Fathers: A Clinical Report," *American Journal of Psychiatry* 122 (1966): 1132–1138.

6. Noel Lustig, John Dresser, Seth Spellman and Thomas Murray, "Incest: A Family Group Survival Pattern," *Archives of General Psychiatry* 14 (1966): 31–40.

7. S. Kirson Weinberg, *Incest Behavior* (New York: Citadel, 1955), p. 63.

8. Bruno Cormier, Miriam Kennedy, and Jadwiga Sangowicz, "Psychodynamics of Father-Daughter Incest," *Canadian Psychiatric Association Journal* 7 (1962): 206.

9. Maisch, *Incest*, p. 139.

10. David Raphling, Bob Carpenter, and Allan Davis, "Incest: A Genealogical Study," *Archives of General Psychiatry* 16 (1967): 505–511; Lukianowicz, "Incest," p. 304; Werner Tuteur, "Further Observations on Incestuous Fathers," *Psychiatric Annals* 2 (1972): 77.

11. Joseph Peters, "Children Who Are Victims of Sexual Assault and the Psychology of Offenders," *American Journal of Psychotherapy* 30 (1976): 411.

12. David Walters, *Physical and Sexual Abuse of Children* (Bloomington: Indiana University Press, 1975), p. 122.

13. Richard Rada, Robert Kellner, D. R. Laws, and Walter Winslow, "Drinking, Alcoholism, and the Mentally Disordered Sex Offender," *Bulletin of the American Academy of Psychiatry and Law* 6 (1978): 296–300.

14. Maisch, *Incest*.

15. Yvonne Tormes, *Child Victims of Incest* (Denver: American Humane Association, 1968).

16. Cavallin, "Incestuous Fathers."

17. Narcyz Lukianowicz, "Incest," *British Journal of Psychiatry* 120 (1972): 301–313.

18. Tormes, *Child Victims of Incest*, p. 26.

19. Several other authors have commented on the oldest daughter's particular vulnerability to incestuous abuse. See e.g. Tormes, *Child Victims of Incest;* Browning and Boatman, "Children at Risk"; Weinberg, *Incest Behavior;* Karin Meiselman, *Incest* (San Francisco: Jossey-Bass, 1978).

20. Maisch, *Incest*.

21. Maisch, *Incest*.

22. Lukianowicz, "Incest"; Irving Kaufman, Alice Peck, and Consuelo Tagiuri, "The Family Constellation and Overt Incestuous Relations Between Father and Daughter," *American Journal of Orthopsychiatry* 24 (1954): 266–277.

23. Anonymous letter, May 1979, in *Reaching Out*, newsletter of RESPOND,

an organization working with women and domestic violence in Somerville, Mass.

24. Weinberg, *Incest Behavior;* Maisch, *Incest;* Kaufman et al., "Family Constellation"; Lukianowicz, "Incest"; Tormes, *Child Victims of Incest.*

25. Cormier et al., "Psychodynamics"; Lustig et al., "Family Group Survival Pattern."

26. Cavallin, "Incestuous Fathers."

27. Christine Adams-Tucker, "Sex-Abused Children: Pathology and Clinical Traits," paper presented at Annual Meeting of the American Psychiatric Association, May 1980; Vincent De Francis, *Protecting the Child Victim of Sex Crimes Committed by Adults* (Denver: American Humane Association, 1969), pp. 152–180.

28. Virginia Abernethy and her colleagues describe a family constellation which they associate with a high risk for unwanted pregnancy in young women. Though overt incest is not mentioned, the family dynamics that these authors describe are similar to those observed in incestuous families. They note the presence of a powerful father, a devalued mother, an exclusive relationship between father and daughter, and the reassignment of some maternal functions to the daughter. They interpret the pregnancy as a flight from the "threateningly incestuous" situation. Virginia Abernethy, Donna Robbins, George Abernethy, Henry Grunebaum, and Justin Weiss, "Identification of Women at Risk for Unwanted Pregnancy," *American Journal of Psychiatry* 132 (1975): 1027–1031.

29. Cavallin, "Incestuous Fathers"; Lukianowicz, "Incest"; Paul Sloane and Eva Karpinski, "Effects of Incest on the Participants," *American Journal of Orthopsychiatry* 12 (1942): 666–673; A. M. Gligor, "Incest and Sexual Delinquency: A Comparative Analysis of Two Forms of Sexual Behavior in Minor Females" (Ph.D. diss., Case Western Reserve University, 1966).

6. The Daughter's Inheritance

1. We are indebted to A. Nicholas Groth for this term. Personal communication.

2. Center for Women Policy Studies, *Reponse to Violence and Sexual Abuse in the Family* 2, no. 3 (January 1979): 3.

3. David Finkelhor, "Long-Term Effects of Childhood Sexual Victimization in a Non-Clinical Sample" (unpub. ms., University of New Hampshire, 1980).

4. Karin Meiselman, *Incest* (San Francisco: Jossey-Bass, 1978), pp. 245–261.

5. Ralph Grundlach, "Sexual Molestation and Rape Reported by Homosexual and Heterosexual Women," *Journal of Homosexuality* 2 (1977): 367–384. Grundlach's data are somewhat puzzling, because the heterosexual women reported a very *low* rate of sexual molestation or rape by relatives.

6. For other individual accounts of the development of a lesbian identity in response to prolonged incestuous abuse, see Katherine Brady, *Father's Days*

(New York: Seaview, 1979); Angela Romagnoli, "Our Sexuality," *The Leaping Lesbian* 3 (1979): 17–19.

7. Seductive Fathers and Their Families

1. Ann Burgess and Lynda Holmstrom, "Adaptive Strategies and Recovery from Rape," *American Journal of Psychiatry* 136 (1979): 1278–1282.
2. Karen Horney, "The Overvaluation of Love," reprinted in *Feminine Psychology* (New York: Norton, 1967), p. 185.
3. Horney, "Overvaluation of Love," pp. 194–195.
4. Horney, "Overvaluation of Love," p. 201.

8. The Crisis of Disclosure

1. Roy Moe and Millicent Moe, "Incest in a Rural Community" (unpub. ms., Child Protective Service, Bonner County, Idaho, 1977), pp. 13–14.
2. Data from Harborview Sexual Assault Center, Seattle, Washington, 1977.
3. Clara Johnson, *Child Sexual Abuse Case Handling in Florida* (Athens, Ga.: Regional Institute of Social Welfare Research, 1979).
4. Idaho Code, Title 16, Chapter 16 (Child Protective Act of 1976).
5. Massachusetts General Laws, Chapter 119, Section 51A.
6. American Humane Association, *Child Protective Services: A National Survey* (Denver, Colo., 1967).
7. *National Analysis of Official Child Abuse and Neglect Reporting, 1977*, U.S. Department of Health, Education, and Welfare Publication No. (OHDS) 79-30232 (Washington, D.C., 1979), pp. 19–21.
8. In Massachusetts, for example, a survey by the Office for Children found that as of May 1978, 65 percent of protective service workers had less than one year of protective service experience. Only one third had master's degrees. *Survey of the Implementation of the New Protective Services Model of the Massachusetts Department of Public Welfare* (Boston: Massachusetts Office for Children, 1978).
9. Quoted by Connie Paige in *The Real Paper* (Cambridge, Mass.), Jan. 19, 1980, p. 13.
10. *National Analysis*, p. 59.
11. Sharon Rosen, Susan Newsom, and Carol Boneh, *Protective Service Reports in May, 1978: A Preliminary Analysis* (Boston: Commonwealth of Massachusetts, Department of Public Welfare, 1979), p. 34.
12. Lisa Lerman, "Civil Protection Orders: Obtaining Access to Court," *Response to Violence in the Family* 3 (April 1980): 1–2.
13. Moe and Moe, "Incest in a Rural Community."

9. Restoring Families

1. Henry Giarretto, personal communication, 1977.

2. Peter Coleman, personal communication, 1977.

3. Florence Rush, "The Sexual Abuse of Children: A Feminist Point of View," in Noreen Connell and Cassandra Wilson, eds., *Rape: The First Sourcebook for Women* (New York: New American Library, 1974), p. 71.

4. Robert Langs, *The Technique of Psychoanalytic Psychotherapy*, vol. I (New York: Jason Aronson, 1973), p. 82.

5. Murray Bowen, "Theory in the Practice of Psychotherapy," in Philip Guerin, Jr., ed., *Family Therapy: Theory and Practice* (New York: Gardner Press, 1976), pp. 42–90; Salvador Minuchin, *Families and Family Therapy* (Cambridge: Harvard University Press, 1974).

6. Henry Giarretto, Anna Giarretto, and Suzanne Sgroi, "Coordinated Community Treatment of Incest," in Ann Burgess, A. Nicholas Groth, Lynda Holmstrom, and Suzanne Sgroi, eds., *Sexual Assault of Children and Adolescents* (Lexington, Mass.: D. C. Heath, 1978), p. 234.

7. Peter Coleman, "Incest: Family Treatment Model" (unpub. ms., Child Protective Service, Tacoma, Washington, 1978).

8. Joseph Peters and Robert Sadoff, "Psychiatric Services for Sex Offenders on Probation," *Federal Probation*, September 1971, p. 35.

9. A. Nicholas Groth, personal communication, 1979.

10. Henry Giarretto, personal communication, 1977.

11. Steven Silver, "Outpatient Treatment for Sexual Offenders," *Social Work*, March 1976, pp. 134–140.

12. See e.g. Berkeley Planning Associates and Urban and Rural Systems Associates, "Evaluation of the Clinical Demonstration of the Treatment of Child Abuse and Neglect" (Report submitted to U.S. Department of Health, Education, and Welfare under contract #105-78-1108, 1979); Edward Brecher, *Treatment Programs for Sex Offenders* (Washington, D.C.: U.S. Government Printing Office, 1978), pp. 13–21.

13. Chuck Wright, Presentence Diagnostic Unit, Seattle, Washington, personal communication, 1977.

14. Lucy Berliner, Harborview Sexual Assault Center, Seattle, Washington, personal communication, 1980. For a detailed typology of incest offenders and appropriate treatment setting for each type, see Roland Summit and JoAnn Kryso, "Sexual Abuse of Children: A Clinical Spectrum," *American Journal of Orthopsychiatry* 48 (1978): 237–245.

15. Jerome Kroth, *Evaluation of the Child Sexual Abuse Demonstration and Treatment Project* (Sacramento: Office of Child Abuse Prevention, California Department of Health, 1978), pp. 121–210.

16. Lucy Berliner, personal communication, 1977.

17. Peter Coleman, personal communication, 1977.

18. Kroth, "Evaluation," p. 158.

10. Criminal Justice

1. Mary Katherine Daugherty, "The Crime of Incest Against the Minor Child and the States' Statutory Responses," *Journal of Family Law* 17 (1978–79): 93–115.

2. See Leigh Bienen, *Chart of the Incest Statutes*, Appendix to this volume, for information on incest statutes cited throughout this chapter.

3. Karin Meiselman, *Incest* (San Francisco: Jossey-Bass, 1978), p. 177.

4. John Gagnon, "Female Child Victims of Sex Offenses," *Social Problems* 13 (1965): 176–192.

5. Teri Talan, "The Child Advocate Association: Project Narrative," (unpub. ms., Child Advocate Association, Chicago, Illinois, 1978).

6. *Sex Problems Court Digest* 6 (1975): 6.

7. Henry Giarretto, Anna Giarretto, Suzanne Sgroi, "Coordinated Community Treatment of Incest," in Ann Burgess, A. Nicholas Groth, Lynda Holmstrom, and Suzanne Sgroi, eds., *Sexual Assault of Children and Adolescents* (Lexington, Mass.: D. C. Heath, 1978), p. 233.

8. Jean Goodwin, Doris Sahd, and Richard Rada, "Incest Hoax: False Accusations, False Denials," *Bulletin of the American Academy of Psychiatry and the Law* 6 (1978): 269–276.

9. Vincent De Francis, *Protecting the Child Victim of Sex Crimes Committed by Adults* (Denver: American Humane Association, 1968), pp. 181–194.

10. See e.g. David Walters, *Physical and Sexual Abuse of Children* (Bloomington: Indiana University Press, 1975), ch. 9.

11. De Francis, *Protecting the Child Victim*, pp. 10–11.

12. Lucy Berliner, personal communication, 1977.

13. Diane Hamlin, "Harborview's Sexual Assault Center: Two Years Later," *Response to Violence in the Family* 3 (March 1980): 3.

14. Lucy Berliner, personal communication, 1977.

15. Lucy Berliner and Doris Stevens, "Guidelines for Criminal Justice Personnel" (Harborview Sexual Assault Center, Seattle, Washington, 1977). For the use of play therapy, drawings, and other special techniques in interviewing young children, see Ann Burgess and Lynda Holmstrom, "Interviewing Young Victims," in Burgess et al., *Sexual Assault of Children and Adolescents*, pp. 171–180.

16. Charles Bahn and Michael Daly, "Criminal Justice Reform in Handling Child Sex Abuse," in *Child Abuse: Where Do We Go from Here?* (Conference Proceedings, Children's Hospital National Medical Center, Washington, D.C., 1977), pp. 143–146.

17. David Libai, "Protection of the Child Victim of a Sexual Offense in the Criminal Justice System," *Wayne Law Review* 15 (1969): 955–1036.

18. Talan, "Child Advocate Association."

19. Libai, "Protection of the Child Victim."

20. Libai, "Protection of the Child Victim." For possible constitutional objections to these reforms and alternative legal options for handling sexual

abuse cases, see Howard Davidson and Josephine Bulkley, *Child Sexual Abuse: Legal Issues and Approaches* (Washington, D.C.: American Bar Association, 1980).

21. Florence Rush documented in *The Best Kept Secret: Sexual Abuse of Children* (Englewood Cliffs, N.J.: Prentice-Hall, 1980), that the legal age of consent has been the focus of an historic struggle between child welfare reformers and feminists, on the one hand, who attempt to raise it, and the forces of organized vice (pimps, "white-slavers," and pornographers), on the other hand, who attempt to lower it. The laws as written often fail to distinguish between sexual exploitation of children by adults and consenting sexual relations between adolescent peers. Hence the recent attempts of some reformers to define a range of sexual offenses based on the age difference between the offender and victim. See e.g. the New Jersey statute as outlined in the Appendix.

22. Ohio Revised Code, par. 2907.03 (1974).

23. Leigh Bienen, "Rape III: National Developments in Rape Reform Legislation," *Women's Rights Law Reporter* 6, no. 3 (Rutgers-Newark School of Law, 1981), n. 204.

11. Remedies for Victims

1. Narcyz Lukianowicz, "Incest," *British Journal of Psychiatry* 120 (1972): 201–212.

2. Alvin Rosenfeld, "Incidence of a History of Incest among 18 Female Psychiatric Patients," *American Journal of Psychiatry* 136 (1979): 791–796.

3. Angela Romagnoli, "Incest," *The Leaping Lesbian* 3 (1978): 29–30.

4. Bernard Glueck, "Early Sexual Experiences and Schizophrenia," in Hugo Beigel, eds., *Advances in Sex Research* (New York: Harper & Row, 1963), p. 248.

5. Robert Stein, *Incest and Human Love: The Betrayal of the Soul in Psychotherapy* (New York: Third Press, 1973), pp. 45–46.

6. Quoted in Sandra Butler, *Conspiracy of Silence: The Trauma of Incest* (San Francisco: New Glide Publications, 1978), p. 170.

7. J. C. Holroyd and A. M. Brodsky, "Physical Contact with Patients," *American Psychologist* 32 (1977): 843–847.

8. S. H. Kardener, M. Fuller, and I. N. Mensh, "A Survey of Physicians' Attitudes and Practices Regarding Erotic and Nonerotic Contact with Patients," *American Journal of Psychiatry* 130 (1973): 1077–1081.

9. Herbert Freudenberger, "The Male Therapist as a Returning Patient" (Paper presented at American Psychological Association, September 1978), reported in *Psychiatric News*, Oct. 20, 1978, p. 40.

10. Susan Forward and Craig Buck, *Betrayal of Innocence: Incest and Its Devastation* (New York: Penguin Books, 1979), p. 166.

11. Forward and Buck, *Betrayal*, p. 163.

12. Mavis Tsai and Nathaniel Wagner, "Therapy Groups for Women Sexually Molested as Children," *Archives of Sexual Behavior* 7 (1978): 417–427.

13. Hollis Wheeler, "Peer Support Grouping as a Self-Help Technique" (unpub. ms., Everywoman Center, University of Massachusetts, Amherst, Mass., 1979), pp. 5–6.

14. Wheeler, "Peer Support Grouping," pp. 8–9.

15. Hollis Wheeler, "The Self-Help Model for Victims of Incest," in Ann Burgess and Bruce Baldwin, eds., *Crisis Intervention Theory: A Clinical Handbook* (Englewood Cliffs, N.J.: Prentice-Hall, 1981).

16. Barbara Myers, personal communication, 1979.

12. Preventing Sexual Abuse

1. Quoted in *Incest: The Victim Nobody Believes* (San Francisco: Mitchell Gebhardt Film Co., 1977).

2. Deborah Anderson, "Child Sexual Abuse Prevention" (unpub. ms., County Attorney's Office, Minneapolis, Minn., 1978).

3. Sandra Butler, *Conspiracy of Silence: The Trauma of Incest* (San Francisco: New Glide Publications, 1978), p. 189.

4. See Grace Abbott, *The Child and the State*, vol. I (Chicago: University of Chicago Press, 1938).

5. Connie Murphy, Pierce County Rape Relief, personal communication, 1977.

6. Linda Sanford, *The Silent Children: A Parent's Guide to the Prevention of Child Sexual Abuse* (New York: Doubleday Anchor Press, 1980), pp. 233–234.

7. See Shulamith Firestone, *The Dialectic of Sex: The Case for Feminist Revolution* (New York: Morrow, 1970).

8. Abbott, *The Child and the State*, vol. I.

9. See Nancy Chodorow, *The Reproduction of Mothering: Psychoanalysis and the Sociology of Gender* (Berkeley: University of California Press, 1978), pp. 217–219.

10. Christopher Lasch, *Haven in a Heartless World: The Family Besieged* (New York: Basic Books, 1977), p. 169.

11. U.S. Department of Commerce, Bureau of the Census, *Current Population Reports*, 1979, reported in *The New York Times*, Aug. 17, 1980, p. 29.

12. Milton Kotelchuck, "The Infant's Relationship to the Father: Experimental Evidence," in Michael Lamb, ed., *The Role of the Father in Child Development* (New York: John Wiley & Sons, 1978), ch. 10.

13. Peggy Ban and Michael Lewis, "Mothers and Fathers, Girls and Boys: Attachment Behaviors in the One-Year-Old," *Merrill-Palmer Quarterly* 20 (1974): 195–204.

14. Frieda Rebelsky and C. Hanks, "Fathers' Verbal Interaction with Infants in the First Three Months of Life," *Child Development* 42 (1971): 63–88.

15. F. A. Pedersen and K. S. Robson, "Father Participation in Infancy," *American Journal of Orthopsychiatry* 39 (1969): 466–472. See also Kotelchuck, "Infant's Relationship to the Father."

16. See Michael Lewis and Marsha Weinraum, "The Father's Role in the Child's Social Network," in Lamb, ed., *Role of the Father* ch. 4.

17. Henry Biller and Dennis Meredith, *Father Power* (New York: David McKay, 1974).

18. Henry Biller, "The Father and Personality Development: Paternal Deprivation and Sex Role Development," in Lamb, ed., *Role of the Father*, ch. 3.

19. John Munder Ross, "Fathers in Development" (Paper presented at 133rd Annual Meeting of the American Psychiatric Association, May 1980).

20. See Redstockings, *Feminist Revolution*, ed. Kathie Sarachild (New York: Random House, 1978); Sara Evans, *Personal Politics* (New York: Random House, 1979).

21. See e.g. Eli Zaretsky, "Capitalism, the Family, and Personal Life," *Social Revolution* 13-14 (1973): 69-126; 15 (1973): 19-70.

22. Benjamin Spock, *Baby and Child Care*, 4th ed. (New York: Pocket Books, 1976), pp. 47-48.

23. Biller and Meredith, *Father Power*, p. 282.

24. Nora Harlow, *Sharing the Children: Village Child Rearing Within the City* (New York: Harper & Row, 1975), pp. 129-130.

25. Harlow, *Sharing the Children*, p. 142.

Index

Abandonment. *See* Separation
Abel, Gene, 229
Abortion, 197, 208
Academic achievement, 118–119
Adultery, 111–112
Adults, consenting, 4
Aetiology of Hysteria (Freud), 9
Al-Anon, 208, 210
Alaska, incest laws in, 163
Albuquerque, N.M.: rape crisis center, 29–30; child protective agency, 166–167
Alcoholics Anonymous, 155
Alcoholism, 8, 76, 77, 78, 111, 119, 157, 207–209; incest victims and, 99, 108, 178; seductive fathers and, 111, 119; self-help groups and, 198, 199
Alimony, 216
Allen, Charlotte Vale, 44–45
American Humane Association, 135
American Journal of Psychiatry, 224
American Medical Association, 239
American Psychiatric Association, 225, 239

American Psychological Association, 239
Angelou, Maya, 40–41, 44, 162
Animals: incest among, 51–53; rescue of, 213
Armstrong, Louise, 34–35
Aversion therapy, 154

Baby and Child Care (Spock), 215–216
Barbaree, Howard, 230, 231
Battered women, 8, 18, 73–74, 81: incest and, 30, 101, 178, 197; shelters for, 196, 199, 208, 210
Beauvoir, Simone de, 202
Bender, Lauretta, 33, 39
Berliner, Lucy, 159, 170–171
Bestiality, 50
Betrayal of Innocence (Forward), 177
Bible, incest in, 36–37, 44, 60–61
Biller, Henry, 216
Biological theory of incest, 51–53, 70
Birth control, 207, 210
Bisexuality, 25
Boatman, Bonny, 48

Boston, study of fathers in, 213
Bowen, Murray, 152
Boys as incest victims, 14
Brady, Katherine, 41–42
Broken Taboo, The (Justice and Justice), 20–21, 43, 46
Brother-sister incest, 17, 29, 60, 94
Brown, Wenzel, 20
Browning, Diane, 48
Burnout, 136
Butler, Sandra, 204

California, incest laws in, 164
Cannibalism, 50
Capitalism, 214
Castration complex, 56
Center for Rape Concern (Philadelphia), 130–131
Chesler, Phyllis, 57–58
Chic magazine, 39
Child abuse, 24
Child Abuse Prevention and Treatment Act, 222
Child Advocate Association (Chicago), 164, 174
Child beating, 74
Child care, fathers and, 212–218
Child labor, 4
Child molestation, 56
Child Protective Service (Tacoma), 29, 131, 146, 148, 159
Children: dependency of, 3; sexual abuse of, 18; sexuality of, 25, 26–27, 42; socialization of, 53; unwanted, 142–143
"Children Not Severely Damaged by Incest with a Parent" (Yorukoglu and Kemph), 33
"Children, Sex, and Society" (Haeberle), 25
Children's rights, 16, 25–27
Child Sexual Abuse Treatment Program (San Jose), 130, 140, 146, 147, 154–155, 158, 159, 166
Child slavery, 24
Child Victims of Incest (Tormes), 48
Chodorow, Nancy, 55
Christopher Street Self-Help Program (Minneapolis), 198–201
Cinderella story, 1–2, 44
Class as incest factor, 12, 14, 67
"Clothesline Project, The," 221
"Cognitive interference," 154
Coleman, Peter, 148, 159

Complete Introductory Lectures of Psychoanalysis (Freud), 7
Confidentiality in therapy, 152
Consciousness raising, 202–203, 215, 220
Conspiracy of Silence (Butler), 204, 205
Constantine, Larry, 26–27
Cormier, Bruno, 43
Courage to Heal, The, 221
Cousins, sexual assaults by, 7
Crews, Frederick, 236
Criminal justice. *See* Laws
Cultures, primitive, 50
Cure, 158–159
Custody, 204, 216
Cutting, Linda, 227, 231

Daddy's Girl: A Memoir (Allen), 44–45
Day care centers, 217–218
"Dealing with the Last Taboo" (Ramey), 23–25
DeFrancis, Vincent, 30
DeMott, Benjamin, 23
Denial of incest, 3, 11, 18–19, 22, 130
Denmark, incest treatment in, 172
Dependency of children, 3
Depression, 77, 119
Desertion, 144–145. *See also* Separation
Deutsch, Helene, 10–11, 58, 109
Divorce, 29, 80, 88, 132
Drug addiction, 8, 99, 108, 178; seductive fathers and, 119; treatment of, 154; self-help and, 198, 199
DSM-IV, 225, 239
Dympna, Saint, 2–3

Economics, 211
"Effects of Early Sexual Experiences" (Constantine), 26–27
"Effects of Incest on the Participants" (Sloane and Karpinski), 31
Elementary Structures of Kinship, The (Levi-Strauss), 50, 59–60
Evidence in Trials at Common Law (Wigmore), 11
Exhibitionism, 8, 12, 13, 17
Exogamy, law of, 59

False Memory Syndrome Foundation (FMSF), 234–241
Families, 110; effects of incest taboo on, 24–25; kinship relations among, 59; size of, 77–78; female-headed, 213, 214. *See also* Fathers; Mothers

Families and Family Therapy (Minuchin), 152
Families Reunited (Tacoma), 146, 159
"Family Constellation and Overt Incestuous Relations Between Father and Daughter, The" (Kaufman et al.), 30–31
Family therapy, 152
Fantasy in incest, 157
Farrell, Warren, 25, 28
Father-daughter incest, 219
"Father-Daughter Incest" (Weiner), 72
Father Power (Biller and Meredith), 216
Fathers, victims' attitude toward, 41–42, 71–72, 81–84, 184
Father's Days (Brady), 41–42
Father-son incest, 14, 20
Feminism, 3, 103, 169–170, 210, 215, 216–217; incest treatment and, 198–201; child welfare and, 206–207; radical, 215. *See also* Women's liberation movement
Feminist psychology, 53–57
Finkelhor, David, 12–14, 28, 29, 47–48
Flex-time concept, 215
Fliess, Wilhelm, 10
Florida, incest laws in, 163
"Follow-up Report on Children Who Had Atypical Sexual Experiences, A" (Bender and Grugett), 33
Force, use of, 14
Forum magazine, 25
Forward, Susan, 177
Foster care, 138, 204
France, incest in, 18
Fraser, Sylvia, 232
Freud, Sigmund, 7, 9–11, 55; on incest taboo, 53; castration complex theory of, 56
Freyd, Pamela, 235, 241
Friendship, 121

Gagnon, John, 12, 28–29
Gereberus, 2
Germany, incest in, 18, 23–24
Gestalt therapy, 199
Gheel (Belgium), hospital in, 2
Giarretto, Henry, 166
Goldfarb, Sally, 234
Grandfathers, 17
Greece, ancient, 54
Groth, Nicholas, 43

Group therapy, 194–195
Grugett, Alvin, 33
Guilt 97, 189, 237

Haeberle, Edwin J., 25
Harborview Sexual Assault Center (Seattle), 130–131, 132, 159, 172
Harlow, Nora, 216–218
Heims, Lora, 46
Henderson, D. James, 40
Hennepin County (Minn.) education program on sexual assault, 203
Homosexuality, 14, 16, 20, 25
Homey, Karen, 123
Hustler magazine, 25, 39
Hysteria theory, 9

Idaho (Bonner County), 140
I Know Why the Caged Bird Sings (Angelou), 40–41, 44, 162
Illinois, incest laws and, 164, 165
Inbreeding, incest and, 51–53
Incest: girls as major victims of, 3; men as major perpetrators, 3, 10, 14; as crime, 4; repetition of, 14, 94, 158; as "positive" experience, 23–25; self-image and, 29, 30–32, 97–103, 119, 187, 189, 194; possessiveness and, 31–32, 73, 91–92, 116–117; inbreeding and, 51–53; among non-blood relatives, 52, 54; respectability and, 71; perpetrators' characteristics, 72; length of relationship and, 86; as addiction, 87; illness from, 88, 91; later relationships and, 99–101, 192; careers and, 105–106; covert, 109; invisibility of, 219; survivors of, 224, 225, 226, 229, 232, 237, 239; overlooked in mental health profession, 228; accountability for, 233, 234
"Incest" (Henderson), 40
"Incest" (Lukianowicz), 46
Incest (Maisch), 43, 48, 67, 72, 78, 82, 85
Incest (Mieselman), 32
"Incest" (Sarles), 48
"Incest: A Family Group Survival Pattern" (Lustig et al.), 72
"Incest: A New Look" (Pomeroy), 25
"Incest: Children at Risk" (Browning and Boatman), 48
"Incest: The Last Taboo" (Nobile), 25, 28
Incest Behavior (Weinberg), 18, 46–47

Incest perpetrators, 229–233, 234, 239;
  threatened by psychotherapy, 240
Incest taboo, 23–25, 50–63, 245; Freud
  on, 53; Parsons on, 53; socialization
  and, 53; boys and, 55–56; girls and,
  57–58; law of exogamy and, 59; gift-
  giving and, 59–60; concepts of, 70
"Incest Taboo in Relation to Social
  Structure and the Socialization of the
  Child" (Parsons), 53
"Informed consent" concept, 26–27
Institute for Sex Research, 3, 18, 23
Institutionalization, 29
Intercourse, 8, 26, 70, 83–85, 131; non-,
  8, 51–52, 53, 54, 83–85
International Tribunal, 238
Intervention, social, 23–25, 133–135
Intimacy, nonsexual, 24, 155, 205
Ireland, incest in, 18
Isolation, 97–98, 99
Israel, incest treatment in, 172–173

Japan, incest in, 18, 19–20
Justice, Blair and Rita, 20–21, 43,
  46

Karpinski, Eva, 31
Kaufman, Irving, 30–31, 46
Kemph, John, 33
Kentucky, incest laws in, 163
Kinsey, Alfred, 12, 16–17, 25
Kinsey Report, 12, 16–17, 23
Kinship relations, 59
Kiss Daddy Goodnight (Armstrong),
  34–35
Kroth, Jerome, 158

Labor, sexual division of, 55, 62, 72
Landis, Carney, 28, 29
Landis, Judson, 12–14, 28–29
Langs, Robert, 152
LaRoche, County Sheriff Dan, 240
Laws: incest and, 11, 25, 153–154, 162–
  172; sexual restrictions of, 16–17; en-
  forcement of, 129; state, 133, 139–
  141, 163–165, 167, 175, 176; trial of
  abuser and, 173–174. See also Appen-
  dix
League of Women Voters, 206
Legal profession, 11
Lesbianism, 104–105
Levi-Strauss, Claude, 50, 59–60
Lewis, Helen Block, 55
Loftus, Elizabeth, 238, 239
Lolita (Nabokov), 36–38, 45, 223

Lot, biblical story of, 36–37, 44
Lukianowicz, Narcyz, 46
Lustig, Noel, 72

Maisch, Herbert, 43, 48, 67, 72, 78, 82,
  85
Male supremacy, 3, 22, 62, 72–73, 124–
  125, 152, 163, 203; legal system and,
  163. See also Patriarchal family
Many-Furs fairy tale, 2
Marriage, 99–101, 102; forced, 3; as es-
  cape from incest, 94, 118
Marshall, William, 230, 231
Masochism, 58, 125
Massachusetts: incest laws in, 133; in-
  cest study in, 137; rape speakout in
  Northampton, 196; study of fathers
  in, 213
Masturbation, 16, 23
Maternity leaves, 215
Mathilda (Shelley), 96
Meiselman, Karin, 32
Memories: traumatic, 227; disturbances
  of, 228
Men's magazines, 3, 23, 25–26, 38–39,
  42–49, 45
Men Who Rape (Groth and Birnbaum),
  43
Mental illness, 12, 77, 91
Meredith, Dennis, 216
Minnesota, treatment programs in,
  198–201, 203
Minorities, 12
Minuchin, Salvador, 152
Mississippi, incest laws in, 163
Mitchell, Juliet, 55
Mother-daughter relationship, 31, 44–
  46, 83, 88, 99–100, 184, 190–191,
  200; illness and, 77–81, 88–91; seductive fathers and, 110–111, 112, 124;
  rivalry in, 113, 114, 115–116, 123;
  restoration of, 131, 145–149, 160,
  206–207
Mothers: role in incest, 36, 42–49, 132,
  133, 137–138, 150; awareness of incest, 46–48, 88; powerlessness of, 47–
  49; as nurturers, 55, 79; role functioning, 77–81; victims' attitude toward, 81–84, 89–91; incest victims as,
  106–107; effects of incest on, 137–
  138; sentimentalizing of, 142–143;
  family reuniting and, 160; support of
  incestuous fathers by, 165; economic
  condition of, 211; working, 214. See
  also Surrogate mother

Mother-son incest, 18–20, 21, 31, 47, 52, 55–56, 60
"Murder Rooted in Incest" (Brown), 20
Murillo, Zoilamerica Narvaez, 231

Nabokov, Vladimir, 36–38
National Advisory Board on Child Abuse and Neglect, 222
National Association of Manufacturers, 206
National Incidence Survey, 223
National Institute of Mental Health, 227
National Organization of Women: Legal Defense and Education Fund of, 234
National Organization of Victim Assistance, 221
National Study of Child Abuse and Neglect Reporting, 136
Neighbors, sexual assaults by, 7
Nelson, Joan, 28
New Jersey, incest laws in, 176
New York: child protective agency in, 30; incest laws in, 167
New York Review of Books, 236
New York Times Book Review, 236
Nobile, Philip, 25
Nurturance, 55, 79

Oedipus complex: in women, 7, 57; in men, 55
Offender: concept of, 4; treatment centers for, 149–161
Ohio, incest laws in, 175, 176
Oklahoma, incest laws in, 163
Open marriage, 25
Ortega, Daniel, 231
"Overvaluation of Love, The" (Horney), 123

Parents: power and needs of, 3–4; incest victim's attitude toward, 41–42, 71–72, 81–84, 89–91, 184; relationship between, 143–144; confrontation of, 195, 200
Parents United, 147, 155, 156, 159, 161; creed, 144
Parent support groups, 146–147
Parsons, Talcott, 53
Paternity leaves, 214
Patriarchal family, 9, 110, 202–203, 204, 211, 218; incest in, 9, 24–25, 54, 55–58, 61, 124–125; boys in, 55–56; girls in, 56–58; seductive fathers and, 124–125. See also Male supremacy

Penthouse magazine, 25, 39, 42–43
People v. Willmore (Illinois), 165
Physical and Sexual Abuse of Children (Walters), 43
Pierce County Rape Relief Center (Tacoma), 204
Playboy magazine, 39
Pomeroy, Wardell, 25
Pornography, 46, 154; child, 24, 25
Poverty, 12
Power, 27, 73–76, 206
Pregnancy, 77–78, 94, 118, 207
"Progress of Nations, The" (UNICEF), 220
"Pro-Incest Lobby, The" (DeMott), 23
Promiscuity, 100
Prostitution, 4, 17, 29, 30, 92, 98–99, 168
Protective custody, 141–142
Protective agencies, 131, 133–143
Psychic War in Men and Women (Lewis), 55
Psychoanalysis, 39–40
Psychoanalysis and Feminism (Mitchell), 55
Psychodrama, 193, 199
"Psychodynamics of Consummated Maternal Incest" (Wahl), 32–33
"Psychodynamics of Father-Daughter Incest" (Cormier et at.), 43
Psychological theory of incest, 51, 53–58, 70
Psychology, 18–19, 211; feminist, 53–57
Psychology of Women (Deutsch), 10–11, 58, 109
Psychosis, 33
Psychotherapist: denial of incest by, 8–9; female, 182–185; male, 185–189; sexual relations with patients, 187–188
Psychotherapy, 8, 9, 177–197
Putnam, Frank, 227

Race as incest factor, 12, 14, 67
Rainbow Retreat (Arizona shelter), 101
Ramey, James, 23–25
Rape, 3, 18, 56, 197; incest and, 24, 27, 101–102, 119, 178, 200; in marriage, 54, 100
"Rape and Psychotherapy" (Chesler), 57–58
Rape crisis centers, 170, 196
Rape Relief Program (Tacoma), 148

"Reaction of Children to Sexual Relations with Adults, The" (Bender and Blau), 39
Recidivism, 158
Reproduction of Mothering (Chodorow), 55
Reproductive freedom, 206
"Risk Factors in the Sexual Victimization of Children" (Finkelhor), 47–48
Role playing, 193
"Rule of the gift" concept, 59
Runaways, 92, 118; shelters for, 196
Rural areas, 12
Rush, Florence, 149
Russell, Diana, 223, 224

Sadomasochism, 25
Salter, Anna, 240
Sanford, Linda, 205
Sarles, Richard, 48
Schatzow, Emily, 227
Schizophrenia, 33
Seattle, treatment programs in, 157
Second Sex, The (de Beauvoir), 202
Secrecy, 22, 88, 129–135, 163–164, 177, 196–197
Self-help groups, 198–201
Separation, fear of, 80, 88, 111. See also Divorce
Sex, extramarital, 16
Sex education, 110, 203
Sex offenders, 149–161
Sex roles, 46, 54–55, 62, 72–73, 110–111
Sexual abuse: by father or stepfather, 223; by relative, 223
"Sexual Abuse of Children, The: A Feminist Point of View" (Rush), 149
Sexual Behavior in the Human Female (Kinsey), 18
Sexual division of labor, 72
Sexual harassment, 8
Sexuality, 29, 31, 33, 98–100, 105, 120, 122, 123, 187–188, 197
Sexual liberation, 16, 23, 25–27
Sexually Victimized Children (Finkelhor), 12–14, 28, 29
Sexual Trauma Treatment Program (Hartford), 131
Shame. See Guilt
Sharing the Children (Harlow), 216–218
Shelley, Mary Wollstonecraft, 96
Shelters, women's, 145, 199

Siblings, 73, 94, 106, 115, 132, 182, 192, 205
SIECUS newsletter, 23–25
Silverman, Sue William, 232
Single-parent families, 213, 214
Slavery, 24, 27
Sloane, Paul, 31
Socialism, 213
Social scientists, 11, 12, 23
Social theory of incest, 51, 58–62, 70
Society for the Prevention of Cruelty to Children (Brooklyn, N.Y.), 169
Spock, Benjamin, 215–216
Sponsorship concept, 146–147
Stepfathers, sexual assaults by, 7
Sterilization, 208, 210
Studies on Hysteria (Freud), 9
Suicide, 7–8, 77, 99, 108, 119, 178; fathers and, 144, 145; self-help groups and, 198, 199
Sunshine Girls (Tacoma), 148
Surrogate mother: for victim, 31, 90, 191; victim as, 45–46, 49, 79–80, 83
Sweden, incest treatment in, 172

Treatment of Psychoanalytic Psychotherapy, The (Langs), 152
Temperance movement, 213
"Theory in the Practice of Psychotherapy" (Bowen), 152
"Therapy Groups for Women Sexually Molested as Children" (Tsai and Wagner), 31, 33
Tormes, Yvonne, 48
"To Tell the Truth," 221
Treatise on Evidence (Wigmore), 11
Treatment programs, 130, 172–173, 203
Tsai, Mavis, 31, 33

Uncles, sexual assaults by, 7, 9, 17, 29
Underwager, Ralph, 235, 240
Utopian experiments, 213

"Variations on a Theme of Incest" (Heims and Kaufman), 46
Venereal disease, 11
Vice suppression movement, 213
Victim: concept of, 4; blamed for, 36; attitude of, 86–87, 96–97; social life, 91–92; as outcast, 96–98, 99; view of men, 102–103, 107; view of women, 103–104; advocate for, 170–172, 173; admission of incest, 196–197
Victimization: patterns of, 29–30, 32; psychology of, 55